W9-AHT-121

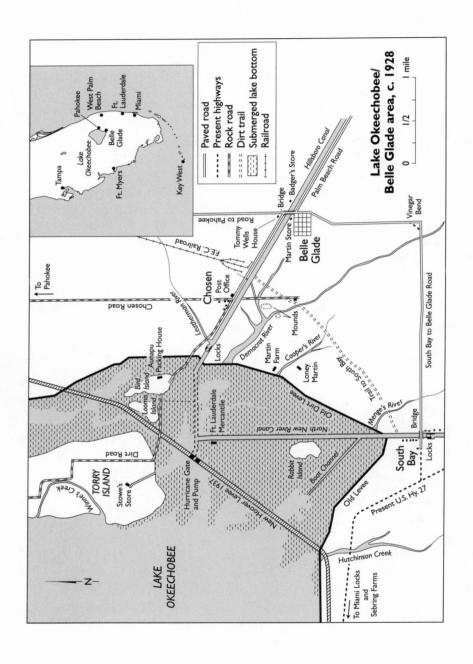

Lake Okeechobee/ Belle Glade area, c. 1928

Legend:
- Paved road
- Present highways
- Rock road
- Dirt trail
- Submerged lake bottom
- Railroad

Scale: 0 — 1/2 — 1 mile

Inset map locations: Tampa, Pahokee, West Palm Beach, Belle Glade, Ft. Lauderdale, Miami, Lake Okeechobee, Ft. Myers, Key West

Map labels:
LAKE OKEECHOBEE
N
TORRY ISLAND
Stowe's Store
Winne's Creek
Dirt Road
Hurricane Gate and Pump
New Hoover Levee 1937
Ft. Lauderdale Mercantile
Rabbit Island
Boat Channel
North New River Canal
Old Dirt Levee
Loomis' Island
Bird Island
Aunapu Packing House
Locks
Leatherman River
Chosen Road
To Pahokee
Chosen
Post Office
F.E.C. Railroad
Tommy Wells House
Martin Store
Badger's Store
Road to Pahokee
Bridge
Belle Glade
Hillsboro Canal
Palm Beach Road
Vinegar Bend
Martin Farm
Democrat River
Cooper's River
Mounds
Loney Martin
Trail to South Bay
Menge's River
South Bay to Belle Glade Road
Old Levee
South Bay
Locks
Bridge
Present U.S. Hwy 27
Hutchinson Creek
To Miami Locks and Sebring Farms

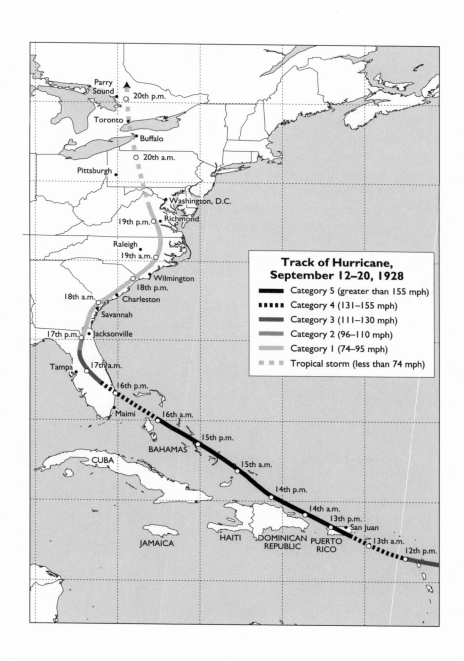

Parry
Sound
Toronto
Buffalo
Pittsburgh

○ 20th p.m.

○ 20th a.m.

● Washington, D.C.
19th p.m. ○ ● Richmond

Raleigh
19th a.m. ○

Wilmington
18th p.m. ○
18th a.m. ○ ● Charleston
Savannah
17th p.m. ○ ● Jacksonville

Tampa ○ 17th a.m.

16th p.m.

Miami ○ 16th a.m.

15th p.m. ○

BAHAMAS

15th a.m. ○

CUBA

14th p.m. ○

14th a.m. ○

13th p.m. ○ ● San Juan

JAMAICA   HAITI   DOMINICAN   PUERTO   13th a.m.
                          REPUBLIC   RICO   12th p.m.

**Track of Hurricane,
September 12–20, 1928**

━━━ Category 5 (greater than 155 mph)
▪▪▪▪ Category 4 (131–155 mph)
━━━ Category 3 (111–130 mph)
━━━ Category 2 (96–110 mph)
━━━ Category 1 (74–95 mph)
▪ ▪ ▪ Tropical storm (less than 74 mph)

KILLER cane

KILLER 'cane

THE DEADLY HURRICANE OF 1928

ROBERT MYKLE

Cooper Square Press
NEW YORK

First Cooper Square Press edition 2002

This Cooper Square Press hardcover edition of
Killer 'Cane is an original publication.
It is published by arrangement with the author.

All photos courtesy of the author, unless otherwise noted.

Maps by Bill Nelson. Map of Lake Okeechobee (Belle Glade Area, c. 1928,
adapted from Lawrence Will, *Swamp to Sugar Bowl* (Belle Glade, Fla.: Glades
Historical Society, 1984). Used by permission of the Glades Historical Society.

Published by Cooper Square Press,
A member of the Rowman & Littlefield Publishing Group, Inc.
200 Park Avenue South, Suite 1109
New York, NY 10003

Distributed by National Book Network

Library of Congress Cataloging-in-Publication Data

Mykle, Robert, 1948–
    Killer 'cane : the deadly hurricane of 1928 / Robert Mykle.— 1st
Cooper Square Press ed.
        p. cm.
Includes bibliographical references and index.
    ISBN 0-8154-1207-X (hardcover : alk. paper)
    1. Everglades (Fla.)—History—20th century. 2. Hurricanes—
Florida—Everglades—History—20th century. 3. Everglades (Fla.)—
Biography. I. Title.
    F317.E9 M95 2002
    975.9'39—dc21   2002001286

Printed in the United States of America

♾™ The paper used in this publication meets the minimum requirements of
American National Standard for Information Sciences—Permanence of Paper
for Printed Library Materials, ANSI/NISO Z39.48-1992.

In memory of the victims of the '28 storm
and for the survivors and my family.

CONTENTS

DRAMATIS PERSONAE

BELLE GLADE

The Henry Martin Family

Henry
Bessie Mae
Annie Mae
Nancy Rachel
Raymond
Thelma Irene
Henry Jurden "Sonny"
Ernestine
Minnie Lucy
Robert
Loney Martin

The Wells Family

Thomas Jefferson
Willie Emma
Edward

Arlin Woodham
Aaron Martin
Lawrence Will
Walter Greer

George Tedder
Charles Riedel
Ardie Peterson
Sheriff Clarence Everett
Richard "Dickey" J. Bolles
Dr. William Buck

PAHOKEE

The Shive Family

Calvin
Ruth
Lillian
Paul

Noble Padgett
Duncan Padgett

SOUTH BAY

Ed Forbes
Felix Forbes
Charles Forbes

Bill Rawle
Ivan Van Horn
Lee Rawls
Maribell Rawls

MIAMI LOCKS
The Boots Family
Bill
Mattie Mae
Roy
Virgil
Vernie Adrian
William "Willie"
The Thomas Family
Charles
Susan
Charles "Mutt"
Victor Thirsk

TORRY & KREAMER ISLANDS
Aunapu Family
Frede
Albert
Elizabeth BeaDer
The Lee Family
Clarence
Hilda
Jesse
Fitzhugh
Cliff Councilman

CHOSEN
Isaac West
Hans Stein
Jacob Porter

MIAMI
Juanita Wilson

PROLOGUE
OUT OF AFRICA

I t was hot. Hot like each summer in the Sahara Desert. A relentless sun burned in a cloudless sky, baking sand and rocks, driving temperatures in the shade to over 130 degrees Fahrenheit. There was no vegetation; nothing grew because of the heat. Scorched sands, barren mountain ranges, and lifeless plains a continent wide stretched three thousand miles from the Nile River in Egypt to the Atlantic coast of Mauritania. It was the Earth's largest expanse of hot desert.

Rising from superheated sands, the atmosphere lost its transparency. Shimmering columns of air danced across sand dunes and rock-strewn plains, rising higher and higher, churning inward, upon itself. The air gathered form until it was large enough and until inertia was overcome. Then it began to move. A wall of heat one thousand miles long, eighty miles wide, three miles high and growing, it snaked its way westward, undulating like a python, a living, breathing entity that was parched and desired moisture. Since the Sahara has no water, only mirages, the undulating mass sought to quench its insatiable thirst in the waters of the north Atlantic Ocean.

From the warm waters off the African coast, it drank its fill, and then it moved south and westward before colliding with the substantially cooler airs along the Gulf of Guinea. Cooled, the supersaturated air condensed into clouds—large, elegantly shaped anvil clouds—a few at first, then a dozen, then a dozen dozen, until a massive wall of thunderstorms formed. Forced by the spin of the earth, it curved around in endless circles until it created a funnel. Then, spinning in a deliberate counterclockwise direction, it grew, gained momentum and spun faster. The agitated air sucked up more energizing, warm water from the ocean surface, feeding its thunder, giving it strength to spin faster and faster still, until it had formed an eye. Now, it could see. It was big but not yet mature. In fact, it was entering adolescence; and like an errant teen, it was doomed and determined to test its limits. Spawned in the heat of Africa, a perfect killer was in the making that would leave six thousand dead in its wake, many of them children of its native sons.

CHAPTER ONE
GENESIS, THE FIRST BOOK

And God said, "Let the waters under the heavens be gathered together into one place, and let the dry land appear." And it was so. God called the dry land Earth, and the waters that were gathered together Seas. And God saw that it was good.

—*Genesis, the first book of Moses*

BELLE GLADE, SEPTEMBER 12, 1928

It was raining. Actually, it was thundering, and the rain came down in sheets between the lightning. Gale-force winds threw torrents of rain across flat land, bending trees, rattling windows. The already-saturated earth, crisscrossed with straight canals, refused to absorb more water, causing canals to rapidly overflow. Pools of water formed like quicksilver over the coal-black earth of freshly plowed fields.

Farm animals, as silent as forlorn statues, faced away from the wind and lowered their heads. Water rolled off their backs and heads in streams, as they waited patiently, knowing it would pass. Men taking shelter where the storm caught them—under eaves, on porches, and in stores—were also patient through no choice of their own. Step out and you'd be drenched in thirty seconds. Walk and you'd sink up to your knees in muck. Drive a truck or car and, if you didn't get stuck in mud, the engine would get wet and stall. So they waited, some envying the lucky ones who gathered in groups where they could talk shop, where conversations touched on planting, the heat, the dry spell, the rain. As farmers, weather was foremost on their minds.

At least the heat had broken; the rains had cooled the air, and for a moment after the downpour the land became fresh, sweet smelling. A rainbow

1

blessed the southeast sky. With the sun came the humidity; the air thickened until it became an oppressive mush. People moved in suspended animation because the slightest exertion brought on a sweat. Clothing stuck to their bodies. There were no air conditioning, no fans, and no electricity. There was no relief from the humid heat.

Off in the distance, the reassuring hum of one of the massive irrigation pumps could be heard straining to empty the fields. They sucked up black mucky water from the canals and spit it over a five-foot-high mud dike that separated Lake Okeechobee from the flat plains of reclaimed south Florida farmland. Lately, due to the rain, the pumps had been running constantly. Late August was the rainy season in Florida, and summer rain was not only expected but also necessary to balance the long, dry winter season. This was the Everglades, where muckland abounded, said to be the richest, most fertile land in the world. This was the Everglades, America's winter breadbasket.

Slicing across this fertile plain was the forty-foot-wide Hillsboro Canal. Beginning at Lake Okeechobee in Chosen or Stein Locks, as the locals called them after the lockkeeper Hans Stein, the canal ran fifty-seven miles in a nearly straight line to Deerfield, where it emptied into the Intercoastal Waterway. The canal had long been the economic heart of the Everglades. A crosscut canal connected the Hillsboro Canal to Palm Beach Canal and facilitated boat traffic between Belle Glade and West Palm Beach. The waters of the Hillsboro Canal had carried many early pioneers from the East Coast to their new homes. Boats still plied the canal, but the new hard-surfaced road to West Palm Beach would soon condemn it to being an oversized drainage ditch.

The town of Belle Glade began as a trading post on the Hillsboro Canal. Paralleling the canal along its banks were two roads. Both were named West Canal Street. On the south side of the canal, West Canal Street had been the commercial center of the area even before Belle Glade was founded. Along the canal banks were stores, actually homes with a front room converted into a shop. They had docks where supply boats would drop off merchandise and at harvest time pick up produce for West Palm Beach and northern markets. As Belle Glade grew, so did Canal Street commerce. Automobiles and the new road soon replaced boats and the canal. And Main Street, lined with automobiles, was poised to replace West Canal Street as the commercial thoroughfare of Belle Glade.

Two blocks west of Main Street along West Canal Street and facing the Hillsboro Canal stood a one-story grocery store, outside of which stood a phlegmatic sign proclaiming that groceries, dry goods, and other sundry merchandise were sold within. Two storefront windows displayed the more coveted goods to draw in customers. Henry Wilson Martin, the owner, was slim but strongly built, with a full head of dark hair and serious eyes. He was tall, over six feet, and able to reach the dry goods, hardware, and kitchen utensils on the top shelves without standing on a stepladder. His tanned, deeply lined faced indicated the many hours he had labored in fields under the bright Florida sun, and he spoke in the slow southern drawl indigenous to central Florida.

Aside from dry goods, Henry Martin sold fresh vegetables, grown on his farm a mile south of Belle Glade on the banks of the now dried Cooper's River. Bessie Mae Martin, Henry's wife, supplied eggs from her flock of chickens. There was some cheese, butter, and at times milk from one of the cows the couple had pastured at Loney Martin's farm. Belle Glade was a farming town, and most people grew their own vegetables, though they liked to treat themselves to bananas, apples, or peaches when affordable.

The bulk of Henry Martin's business was in dry goods and hardware. In the front, to the left of the entrance, stood half a dozen chairs where the locals, mostly men, would sit and gossip. It was good for business. They bought soft drinks and occasionally sticks of chewing tobacco. No one noticed if someone pulled out a little flask and took a discrete swig of home-brewed whiskey. Prohibition, the noble experiment, was in full swing.

The Martin family had been early settlers along Lake Okeechobee's southeastern shore. In 1917, Henry's brother, Loney Martin, and Jimmy Griffith, a brother-in-law, had been among the first to farm along the banks of two "dead rivers" between what was to become Belle Glade and South Bay. They owned the farms on each side of Henry that fronted Lake Okeechobee. Among the three families, the Martin clan owned one of the largest combined tracts of prime bottom lake land—the best of the best. With the new dike to control high lake waters and keep his fields dry, Henry Martin could plant three crops a year, most of which were sold to buyers who shipped the fresh produce north at high prices. Henry was doing so well that he had recently opened another store in South Bay. With the new crop in the ground and all the "new people" coming into town, Henry Martin and most of the other old-timers felt very good about the future of Belle Glade and the Everglades.

ON Wednesday, September 12, 1928, Henry quickly glanced at the headlines of the *Palm Beach Post*. The top story concerned President Calvin Coolidge and his consideration of the budget and the Antiwar Treaty. No one in the Everglades really cared much about that, not from a lame duck president, especially when this was an election year and most people were interested in the race between Herbert Hoover and Al Smith. Democrats complained that "Hoover Democrats" were not supporting Al Smith. Henry Martin was a lifelong Democrat who had never voted Republican in his life. Yet he would find it very hard to vote for a Roman Catholic. One column in particular in the *Palm Beach Post* exposed the fabricated story that Democratic presidential candidate Al Smith had been seen drunk in public, which was part of the anti-Catholic and pro-Prohibition campaign that plagued Al Smith, the first Catholic to run for president. The story amused Henry. True or not, if the man could handle a drink once in a while, then maybe Henry Martin could vote for him.

At the very bottom of the front page was the weather column. It predicted partly cloudy skies with local thunderstorms. Further down, at the bottom of the weather column, was a more ominous notice. In bold letters was a storm warning issued the day before yesterday from Washington, D.C., by the National Weather Bureau:

```
Tropical disturbance of considerable intensity central
near 18 North, 56 West, moving west or west-northwestward.
Its center will likely pass near Lesser Antilles North
of Martinique, Wednesday.
```

Henry paid it no mind. Storms were always forming in the Atlantic, and this was a typical southern Florida summer afternoon with its inevitable thunderstorms. No one needed a weatherman to predict that; it happened every afternoon.

If he listened to each and every warning, he would still be living in central Florida struggling to grow crops in sandy, harsh soil. He would never have risked everything he had—his family, his fortune, his life— to begin anew in the wilds of the Everglades if he did not have a gambler's heart—and Henry Martin had a true gambler's heart. Whether with the turn of a card at a high-stakes game or planting a crop before the rains began, Henry enjoyed risk. So far the gods of chance had been good to him.

He looked at his watch and put the newspaper down. He'd finish it later. First he had to check the mail because he was expecting a letter from his cousins in West Frostproof. He walked along the plank sidewalk raised above the street down to the Main Street Bridge. He crossed the one-lane steel structure spanning the Hillsboro Canal. The bridge, with its high steel cross beam and cables, would swing around to let boat traffic pass. As he crossed the bridge, Henry looked over at the old bridge tender's house. The new Buick that was usually parked on the north side under the large rubber tree was gone. His brother-in-law, Tommy Wells, must be working across town. Tommy's wife, Willie Emma, would be inside tending to Edward, their two-week-old baby who had been born with a broken arm. Henry had to pay her a visit, but he'd wait until Sunday when Bessie Mae, who hadn't seen the baby, would come to town. Taking a right east down Canal Street, he walked the half block to Badger's store. Frank Badger was the postmaster, and, even though Henry liked Badger, it irked him that he had to visit his competition for his mail. But there was no time to dwell on commercial rivalries; Henry Martin was too busy. Prosperity had arrived in the Everglades, and Henry Martin, along with most of the old-timers, was flourishing.

Belle Glade's streets were crowded. Its two hotels were nearly full, mostly with "new people" from outside the Lake Okeechobee area. In the restaurants, patrons waited in lines for orders of southern-fried catfish and alligator tail. Along Main Street and Avenue A, a profusion of Model T's and a few of the recently introduced Model A Fords vied for scarce parking spaces. There was a profusion of real estate offices that seemed to have popped up like mushrooms overnight in every storefront and living room, with plenty of buyers for all. Land sales were up; prices rose daily.

New construction was at an all time high. Lucky Charles Riedel, the founder of Belle Glade, had barely finished a new addition to his Belle Glade Hotel when he was given a price he couldn't refuse. "You sold too cheap, Charlie," he was told. But, within a week's time, Charlie Riedel's luck would prove to be holding. His competitor, George Tedder, was putting the final touches on his new Glades Hotel located across the street. A large sign proclaimed it the Glades Hotel and Café while a smaller sign below enticed clients with "hot and cold baths." Using salvaged materials from the demolished wing of Henry Morrison Flagler's famous Royal Poinciana Hotel in Palm Beach, he built (overbuilt, some said) a sturdy, comfortable hotel. All too soon, Tedder's choice of materials would prove to be auspicious.

A half block down Main Street, Lawrence Will was constructing his new Pioneer Service Building. He could be seen at any time of the day or night pumping gasoline, cleaning windshields, changing oil, or checking air pressure for his customers. Tall and lanky with a receding hairline, the gregarious Will knew everyone in town, and for those new people he didn't know, he made every effort to remember their names. All of them were potential customers. "I just like people," he would say. Will was a jack-of-all-trades—his occupations as boat captain, dredge operator, farmer, and pioneer had taken him across the entire state of Florida. However, like many of the early settlers who had left the area, he had returned to the Everglades, attracted by the new prosperity. The real reason for his return was he had "muck in his shoes," as the saying went for those who could not stay away from the rich Everglades' mucklands.

Across from Will's new service station were rows of new Model A's and older Model T Fords in the recently built Ford Garage, lodged under a half-acre roof. The dealership's owner, Clarence Everett, moonlighted as Belle Glade's sheriff. Ford was still the most prominent automobile, as a glance down any street would attest. Though a few Dodges were making their appearance, the highly popular Model T had very nearly become America's car, a full decade before Hitler's Volkswagen. The cost of a new automobile had dropped to $290 by 1926, and at that price, all but the very poor could afford a Model T car or truck.

Belle Glade was unaccustomed to so much activity. The spring before, the *Everglades News*, a local newspaper, noted that the town had only two stores, a gas station, and one hotel, and was still unincorporated. One year later, Belle Glade was still a small town with an immediate area population over two thousand, and growing. Belle Glade, the belle of the Everglades, was experiencing a miniboom.

Since the end of World War I, all of Florida had undergone a spectacular real estate boom. Land prices doubled, even tripled, every few months. Then the East Coast real estate market, fueled by rank speculation, Ponzi-type land deals and astonishing greed, finally collapsed under the burden of its own weight. Fortunes were lost overnight, banks failed like falling dominos, and desperate, unemployed people tried to feed their families. It was an ominous portent for the Roaring Twenties bull market that had one more year to run.

In 1926, the fate of the doomed Florida real estate market was sealed by an act of nature. A powerful category 4 Cape Verde Island hurricane, packing 130-mile-an-hour winds, struck Miami head-on, killing 373 people and leveling three-fourths of the city—a crippling blow from which it would take the city twenty-five years to recover. All of South Florida was thrown into a deep depression—except the Everglades. Unemployed people flocked to the modest settlements around Lake Okeechobee. In Belle Glade, Pahokee, Clewiston, and Moore Haven, they could buy a farm and live off the land. At least they would not starve. Houses and farms were sold and resold. Belle Glade was changing so fast that it incorporated in April 1928—making it a scant five months old this September day.

Still, Belle Glade was a farming town. Its motto would declare, "Her Soil Is Her Future." In mid-September 1928, many of the farmers had their fields plowed and planted. A good year was anticipated because the price of vegetables was predicted to be high that winter—just in time for the harvest, if there was not a hard, long freeze like the one that had struck last New Year's Eve.

Not everyone, however, shared in the good times. Along with the farmers, the townspeople, the new people, and the speculators, the area was populated with black migrant farmworkers. Some four thousand strong, they had come to help prepare the soil, plant, and then pick the crops.

Many would stay through the harvest, living in shacks and shanties supplied by the farmers on the land they worked. In the spring, a few would migrate north to follow the fruit and vegetable harvests. A few would travel as far as the apple orchards in upper New York state, a round-trip journey of three thousand miles. The majority were American born, but many were from the Bahamas, joined by a few Jamaican and other Caribbean islanders. In general, they stayed out of the way, unseen, uncounted, unwanted, except at planting and harvest time. No one thought very much about them, though it was their labor that brought most of the prosperity to Belle Glade.

Nor did anyone really think about hurricanes. True, the great 1926 Miami hurricane had been a wake-up call. People had more respect for the big storms—some even made cursory preparations in case of another hurricane—but most felt that the Miami hurricane had been a fluke, an aberration of nature. It had been the only major hurricane to hit the area since the great storm of 1910—a hiatus of sixteen years. Belle Glade had come through the Miami hurricane, which had passed it to the south with little damage. Whereas Moore Haven had lost 150 lives when that town's muck dike collapsed, the Belle Glade dike held, and the state had reinforced the dike's obvious weak spots with more muck. Except for a few old-timers, most people in Belle Glade had never felt the wrath of a major hurricane. Plus, everyone knew that, like lightning, another hurricane would not strike the same spot a second time. Or so the popular thinking went.

When the 1910 hurricane struck, barely a half dozen people were living on the southern shore of Lake Okeechobee; maybe another dozen farmed the rises on Ritta, Kreamer, and Torrey Islands. One lone hunter camped near present-day Clewiston had his lean-to, rifles, and skins blown away as he scrambled up a tree and rode out the storm. On the lake islands, farmers were flooded out, their crops lost. Some houses and makeshift barns were blown away, but loss of life was minimal. Most of the island people had retreated to higher ground. As if a presage of the summer of 1928, the rains were exceptionally heavy the weeks before and during the storm. Even though the hurricane had passed to the west of the lake and quickly degenerated into a tropical storm, the lake waters quickly rose five feet. The winds sloshed the lake waters to one side, then the other. The dike on the lake had not yet been built, and the water overflowed the low custard apple tree ridges surrounding the southern edge of Lake Okeechobee and spilled evenly into the Everglades—the way Mother Nature had intended.

The 1910 hurricane was the first documented "loop hurricane." The U.S. Weather Bureau at first thought it was following two storms when two days later its weather watchers in Cuba reported another hurricane striking the Cuban coast. The storm had actually drifted off and then looped back and struck Cuba again. The storm's erratic path added to the lore of the fickleness of a hurricane.

Nobody was scared away by the 1910 hurricane. In fact, serious real estate development only began immediately after it. That year land developer Richard "Dickey" J. Bolles finished his hotel on the lakeshore where the Miami Canal enters Lake Okeechobee via a series of locks. The small settlement was called Ritta, soon to be changed to Miami Locks; today it's Lake Harbor. The Bolles Hotel was a palace in the jungle, a tropical Garden of Eden, a developer's come-on. Dickey Bolles's hotel was his best-selling tool. The well-built inn had screened porches, a large social lobby on the first floor, and a small but well-appointed kitchen. Special attention was given to the outside landscaping. The area around the hotel was planted with flowering plants and citrus trees, and, taking a cue from Palm Beach, four straight-trunk royal palm trees were planted on the lake side of the hotel, and they became an alluring beacon for miles around.

While the 1910 hurricane should have been taken as a warning, it was generally ignored. Floridians were used to storms—lots of storms—and Florida is a state of storms. It's their magnitude that was relative. When the storm years returned in 1926, few people were thinking about hurricanes. Hurricanes were a distant, ominous threat churning in the Atlantic and killing hundreds of people in foreign countries where they didn't even speak English. Surely we Americans were safe, they thought.

Hurricanes were not the only gun Belle Glade was living under. There was the Lake Okeechobee dike—a wall fifty-plus miles long built of muck dredged up from the lake bottom. In the summer rainy season, the dike held back tens of millions of gallons of water. During the rains when the lake was full, most of Belle Glade, Chosen, South Bay, and Moore Haven were below water level. The major concern was that if there were a large break in the dike, the lake would send a five-foot wall of water to reclaim its lost lands. While a hurricane's vicious winds can do enormous damage, the truly big killer in a storm is water, the solvent of life. Belle Glade had plenty of water, and it was getting more than its fair share of rain now, with more on the way.

Looking down Main Street, at the automobiles parked at the curbs, the new buildings, the bustling hotels, beyond the town to the neatly plowed fields and quaint houses sheltered under large shade trees, it would be hard to imagine that a decade and a half ago this was all under water and that the shore of Lake Okeechobee reached another mile to the east. The

Belle Glade area was a stark, pristine watery wilderness. It was the last American frontier.

1916, RITTA ISLAND—THE BOTTSES

A baby's cry in the wilderness echoed from a small two-room clapboard house with one minute window facing east across the swampy shores of Ritta Island and Lake Okeechobee. Inside, covered in amniotic fluid and blood up to his elbows, William "Bill" Boots wiped dark mucous from the baby's face. With his large, powerful hands, he examined it, turned it over, and smiled. There were no visible defects, no curved spine, no enlarged head or limp legs; it was a healthy, stocky boy. A son. Bill Boots cut the umbilical cord and quickly tied it. Then he gently washed the baby before giving him to Mattie Mae Boots, the baby's exhausted but elated mother.

Outside the sun was setting a brilliant red, sending rosy reflections over the watery horizon of Lake Okeechobee—a good sign. Flocks of birds—ibises, egrets, and herons, a thousand strong—winged their way across the sky to roost in distant trees, while big bull alligator bellows echoed across the water. It was 1916, and Ritta Island had just witnessed the birth of William "Willie" Boots, the first Caucasian child born in the northern Everglades.

The child's father, Bill Boots, was a big man. He stood six foot tall with muscular arms, a broad back, brown hair, and brown eyes. His long face was tanned and lined. He was a powerful man who, when unloading a truckload of fuel, could take a fifty-five-gallon drum of oil and lift it alone. He prided himself on his strength. However, in the Boots family, he was considered small; his brother Adrian was 6' 3". The Boots family had strong genes.

Mattie Mae Boots contrasted well with her large husband. She was 5' 6", a slim size 6 with dark eyes that would sparkle at her husband's jokes. She kept her brown hair—which had never known a pair of scissors—tied in a bun off her slender neck, for keeping in style and for combating the heat.

She was an excellent seamstress known for her sewing, making all her own clothes and most of the clothes worn by her family. An artistic strain showed in the elaborate bed covers and tablecloths she made, though most of her needle time was taken up with mundane clothes mending. She tended house with no conveniences, but including a wood stove with a fire that, despite the heat, rarely went out, and water collected in a bucket at the lake bank. There was no ice, and food spoiled rapidly in the heat of summer. Sugar, or "squeezings," was brown flaky molasses crushed from the cane grown on the south side of the house. It sweetened the family's food and also was fed to the mules for quick energy. She cooked with few herbs except those grown in her little house garden. There was no meat except what hunters would bring. Deer, raccoons, and otter were plentiful in the forests on the mainland; ducks in large flocks, or rafts, covered the lake waters. Mostly, however, they ate fish caught in front of the house or bartered for with fishermen.

Like all pioneer women, Mattie Mae had experienced a hard life. Luckily her pregnancy had not been difficult. She was a strong woman, and after the second birth, the rest came rather easily. An hour after Willie was born, she was up cooking. But, like all women, she still feared pregnancy because it was the greatest killer of young healthy women. To be pregnant in the primitive conditions of the Everglades, far from any medical help, was even more dangerous. And Mattie Mae was no longer young—she was nearing forty. Willie had been her fifth of children by two husbands. Her first husband—a mailman in Pierce, Arizona—had died from an infection that started as a small boil. (Penicillin was still twenty years away.)

Mattie Mae had four sons by Bill Boots. Her oldest, Roy, was now approaching six, and having lost his baby fat had retained a cuteness that would make him a hit with the girls. Vernie Adrian was four and a half years old, a very inquisitive child who was always getting into things; Virgil was almost two and still in diapers. And now there was Willie, the baby.

Most pioneer marriages in those days were partnerships built on mutual trust, forged out of necessity. In adverse conditions, neither partner could survive without the other. When a man reached deep inside his wife and extracted a son or daughter, a bond was created that would last "until death do them part."

Not all women suffered in stoic resignation. In 1909 at Sulfur Springs Valley, near Pierce, Arizona, Bill Boots's first wife, unhappy with the hard life of a farmer's wife, divorced him and took his two daughters, Joyce and Gladys, for the greener pastures and glamour of California. He never saw them again. Soon after that, he met the widow, Mattie Mae Rawle.

After Mattie Mae Rawle married Bill Boots, her sixteen-year-old son Bill Rawle, anxious to strike out on his own, left soon after the harvest for Florida. Looking for adventure and opportunity, he ended up in one of the fishing camps on Lake Okeechobee catfishing. Catfishing was the only industry on the lake, and aside from an occasional professional hunter, only catfishermen populated it. It was hard, messy, smelly work, but Bill Rawle had an open personality that made him a favorite among the hard-living catfishermen. They had well-deserved reputations of being hard drinkers. Many found the lake's isolation to be a perfect sanctuary from the law. The fishermen skinned and cleaned, then stored the catfish in barrels of ice. A buyer boat gathered up the catches and quickly shipped the fish to the town of Okeechobee, Fort Lauderdale, and down the Caloosahatchee River to Fort Myers.

Felix Forbes, who had just founded the Pioneer Boat Line, quickly befriended Bill Rawle. Forbes needed someone he could trust and who knew the lake, the area, and the fishermen. Bill Rawle became Captain Forbes's trusted employee. Forbes settled Ritta Island and built a hotel to house his passengers.

At first, as an ex-policeman Forbes was looked on with suspicion by many of the fishermen. There were draft dodgers and criminals, petty and otherwise. Some were wanted for crimes committed in Florida or wanted by authorities in other states. A couple took on Billy the Kid–size legends. Ex-cowboys, like Mart Manning near the Pahokee Ridge and Edgar Watson on the Chatham River in Ten Thousand Islands, were reputed to have killed more than their share of men and, in Watson's case, a couple of women, too.

A boat captain had to know not only the canals, the lake, and the tricky shifting shoals but also how to handle sudden storms that would rise up on a minute's notice, sending the lake into a frenzy of chopping waves and strong winds that could strand a boat on a hidden shoal. He needed a boat captain that could also negotiate and bargain with the fishermen—not always an easy task. More than one catfish buyer had had a shot fired at him if one of his clients thought he had been cheated. To break into the catfish business, Forbes needed someone both he and the fishermen could trust.

Captain Forbes had an alternative motive for taking Bill Rawle under his wing. The hardworking young man was courting his brother's oldest daughter, Louise. He hoped that Bill would do the sensible thing and marry into the Forbes family.

Indeed, the following year, Bill Rawle married Louise Forbes and was taken into the family business. He captained a number of the Pioneer Line's boats. When Felix Forbes told Rawle he needed people to help him farm and manage the farmlands, Bill Rawle knew just the person—his stepfather, Bill Boots.

In 1916, Bill Boots, lured by stories of the incredible rich lands in the Everglades with its frost-free free land, and more water than you knew what to do with, packed up Mattie Mae and their three baby boys and made the long, hard trip across the southern United States to Fort Lauderdale, which was barely a stopping-off place at that time. They continued up the recently finished North New River Canal, across the sawgrass sea, through the locks at South Bay, and out onto Lake Okeechobee and to Ritta Island.

The lake was changing. The professional hunters had all but disappeared. There were still a lot of catfishermen on the lake, but unlike the catfishermen, the newcomers were a more stable people—farmers who brought their families and were settling the land. Most of the hunters and the catfishermen were Crackers, native Floridians accustomed to living off the land. The farmers, on the other hand, were mainly immigrants from Georgia, the Carolinas, the Midwest, and the Northeast. Though they had to put up with the hard living, alligators, snakes, and mosquitoes along with the Bootses, the settlers were determined to make a good life for themselves and their families.

OKEELANTA—LAWRENCE WILL

A hot afternoon sun was finally lowering itself in the western sky as the mail boat from Fort Lauderdale churned slowly up the North New River Canal. From the steer house of the two-story, eighty-foot-long vessel, Captain Felix A. Forbes kept a sharp eye out for floating logs, caved in banks, and oversized alligators, anything that might impede their progress. For the last two hours the boat had plied past the great waterlogged sawgrass plain—the plain that had given the Everglades its name. Except for a few treed hummocks, as far as the eye could see there was nothing but flat land covered in six-foot-high, jagged-leaf sawgrass. In what seemed the middle of nowhere, the boat stopped. "This is it," the passengers were told. Captain Forbes unceremoniously deposited his four young passengers and their supplies onto the canal bank before chugging off to South Bay and Lake Okeechobee four miles away. It was late and Captain Forbes had a schedule to keep, but he assured the four men that he would check on them upon his return.

For young Lawrence Will and his three companions, this was the end of a long odyssey that had begun in Washington, D.C., a year before. As they glanced around at the utter isolation of their new home, they wondered why they had been in a rush to arrive there. The land salesmen in Washington and Fort Lauderdale had told them that there was a land rush in the Everglades and that they had better purchase their land before there was nothing more to buy at the incredibly low prices being offered.

Will wondered, "Where was everybody?"

There was nothing around them except miles and miles of unending sawgrass prairie. There were no roads, no facilities, and the only communication with the rest of the world was the newly dug canal literally on the settlers' front doorstep. But they had no boat. However, what they lacked in material comforts they made up in enthusiasm. They quickly erected their tents, set up their stoves, and stacked burlap bags filled with small seed potatoes. The soil was black and rich, and they surely would reap a fantastic crop of potatoes in a short time.

As darkness descended, Lawrence Will and his three companions prepared to spend their first night in the Everglades. They watched as large flocks of herons, egrets, and ducks winged their way to an evening roost. A chorus of frogs rose to a deafening crescendo. Their worries of ferocious wild cats and panthers venturing into their camp while they slept were soon replaced by a more immediate danger—mosquitoes. They were relentlessly attacked by an array of flying, biting, sucking insects. They had come prepared to build a hut, plant potatoes, and clear land, but they had not purchased a single mosquito net.

"They came in swarms; they zinged and bored; they even brought in droves of fireflies to light up the massacre," Will said.

Then he remembered with irony a line from the land company's literature: "Mosquitoes are almost unknown in the Everglades."

Lawrence Will and his companions were not the first, nor would they be the last, to be enticed by blatant false advertising in Florida land sales. Within twenty years, Florida land deals, especially those in the Everglades, would become synonymous with rip-off artists, low tides, and underwater lots.

Lawrence Will was raised in Washington, D.C., where his father, Dr. Thomas Will, was an administrator in the Department of Agriculture. Enticed by the reports that crossed his desk on the fertility of the Everglades sawgrass lands, Dr. Will was eager to try out new farming methods being developed by the department. Like thousands of others, he purchased sight unseen a section of land in the upper Everglades. He had it surveyed and then platted into five- and ten-acre lots for resale with the idea of forming the town of Okeelanta. Depending on your point of view, the Wills were like hundreds of other early land buyers—either developers or land speculators.

Fresh out of high school and anxious for adventure, Lawrence Will set out for Jacksonville by ship, took a train to Fort Lauderdale, and then boarded a boat for a fifty-seven-mile all-day journey to his plot. The only trails were those cut by the surveyors. Okeelanta was isolated, and even at four miles, it was situated too far from Lake Okeechobee, the center of commercial activity. Still, against the odds, the enthusiastic Will worked hard preparing the soil, digging canals, raising dikes, laying out dike roads, and encouraging new settlement. Thanks in great part to his efforts, Okeelanta became the largest settlement on the Okeechobee south shore, if only for a short time.

OKEECHOBEE is the Seminole word for "the big water." Though still impressively big at 730 square miles, the lake was about a third larger before drainage and reclamation began. Lake Okeechobee is a shallow, bowl-shaped depression in the middle of Florida. In its prime, the lake at its deepest point was never more than twenty feet deep, actually at sea level. On average it was nine feet deep. Catfishermen, hand seining out of sight of land in all directions, could stand on the bottom with water up to their armpits.

The lake is principally fed by water from the Kissimmee River to the north, with a drainage basin that extends north to Orlando. Smaller rivers, such as Fisheating Creek and Taylor Creek, supplied minor amounts of water. In the summer, or rainy season, the lake would fill and overflow like a water-filled plate gently tilted forward. Since Lake Okeechobee has no direct outlet, the Caloosahatchee River rising out of Lake Hicpochee near Moore Haven and emptying into the Gulf of Mexico was the lake's principal outlet. Pushing through the custard apple ridge were scores of elongated inlets called dead rivers. These dead rivers began at the lake edge as wide outlets, but further downstream they became progressively smaller until they vanished. Early explorers, coming upon what looked like rivers, followed them until they petered out or dead-ended, and so they called them dead rivers.

The dead rivers as seen by the first explorers appeared to be slow, if not stagnant, bodies of water; however, they were anything but dead. Along their banks in the shallows were the major fish hatcheries for the lake. During the rainy season, the dead rivers were outlets—safety valves allowing the overflow of the lake to build up gradually—but they could, after a vigorous thunderstorm, turn into raging torrents.

Except for the ridge around the southern edge, Lake Okeechobee had no boundaries, and its shores constantly fluctuated. The water's edge was fluid and seasonal, shrinking in the dry season and expanding in the wet. Waving seas of sawgrass were not unlike sea grass. The Everglades is comparable to a vast tidal marsh, which it probably was and more than likely will be again.

Dotting the lake were half a dozen islands, mostly at the southern end of the sandy ridge that skirted the eastern side of the lake before diving under the lake waters at Bacom Point just south of Pahokee. Being higher and dry for most of the year, the islands comprised the first settlements on the southern section of the lake. They had two added advantages over the mainland: they rarely suffered from frost damage, and they suffered less from insects since comfortable evening breezes blew the pesky biters across the lake.

The lake was dominated by three big islands—Kreamer, Torry, and Ritta—just off shore from Chosen and Miami Locks. Observation Island, another large but low-lying island, was further west, close to Moore Haven. Separating Torry Island from the mainland were a series of shallows and two smaller islands, Bird and Loomis, over which a causeway was built with the dredging spoils from the Hillsboro Canal.

Surrounded by forests until the 1900s, the north side of the lake was covered in pine tree, cypress forests and sprinkled with some live oaks. These were the sandlands composed of a sandy and well-drained soil. Less desirable for farming, the sandlands were coveted for the stands of cypress and pines for lumber that, when cleared, offered passable cattle grasslands.

The south side from Moore Haven to Pahokee was the muck side of the lake. It was covered by expansive custard apple forests draped in massive moonvine blankets, creating a leafy tent that stretched in a semicircle for forty miles. The custard apple, like the ocean mangroves, had knotty branching roots that retained some of the soil and debris from the lake overflow. At their base a low-rising natural dike formed around the lake, just enough to keep a few more feet of water in the lake, but not enough to prevent the movement of water over its banks during the rains.

Though the bottom soil of the lake was mostly muck, the water was transparent and would remain clear if unmolested.

"When we kids swam in the lake, you could see every ripple on the bottom," Lillian Padgett, an early resident of Pahokee, related.

In the early years, one of the lake's greatest mysteries could be seen through the clear waters. The lake bottom, just off the north end of Kreamer Island and between Observation Island and the town of Clewiston, was littered with nearly a hundred bleached skeletons.

"Their skulls looked like pumpkins in a field," said Mrs. Hovencamp, the first Caucasian woman to live on Ritta Island.

How these remains of Indians got on the lake bottom, why they were never buried, and what, or who, killed them has never been satisfactorily answered. In 1919, Connally Nall, a surveyor farming on a recently dried island in the lake, dug up fifty additional skeletons. He noted that the bones were unusually large. Unfortunately, they were lost in the hurricane of 1926.

Serving as the storage basin for the Everglades, Lake Okeechobee held water, doling it out in times of plenty and scrounging it during droughts. It made sure that the Everglades had water. If a drought baked the sawgrass plains, the lake helped retain a high enough water table to feed the roots of the great sawgrass plains to the south. For animals and birds, it was a last-ditch refuge for water in emergencies when their watering holes dried up. From the beginning, Lake Okeechobee was the heart of the Everglades, pumping life-giving water.

For thousands of years, immediately after the great ice ages and before the formation of Everglades, South Florida, except around the lake, was dry—a hard bedrock kind of place that was unfriendly to the lush vegetation so common today. Men were there, hunters and gatherers migrating from the North who were attracted by the profusion of animals that gathered around and on the lake. These men were the first mound builders. At Chosen they constructed the first of many levels at the great mound on the edge of Lake Okeechobee at the head of the Democrat River, a large dead river. The first level was built on the foundation of muck covered with oölite limestone brought in from miles away.

As the climate warmed and the freshwater table rose, sawgrass began to grow. It spread until it was a sea of grass stretching from Lake Okeechobee south to Florida Bay. As the sawgrass died and decomposed, it formed a rich organic peat.

While the mammoths and saber-toothed tigers had disappeared, the warmer climate encouraged a population explosion of smaller mammals, birds, and fish. It was a hunter and gatherer's paradise. The mound builders stayed, and as the water table rose, they built their mounds higher, using the readily available mud and sand. Each year the sawgrass grew, flowered, and then died back before decomposing into a massive expansive peat bog that eventually reached twelve feet deep in places. Three thousand years later, different men would migrate from the North and discover that this peat, once broken up and tilled, became fertile muck—the black gold of the Everglades.

THE first Euro-Americans to settle around Lake Okeechobee were hunters. They built lean-tos, hunting shacks, and an occasional cabin. They were, for the most part, seasonal residents who hunted during the winter and avian breeding seasons and then sought the more hospitable climes of the Gulf coast or Georgia during the rainy summers when mosquitoes were at their worst. These were solitary men who, carrying a rifle, a blanket, and enough cartridges, salt, sugar, coffee, and tobacco to last the season, would venture up the Caloosahatchee or down the Kissimmee to hunt and trap.

Commercial hunters followed the seasonal residents, trapped otters, raccoons, and muskrats, skinned rattlesnakes, and nailed their hides to trees to dry. Everything that moved had value to the hunters. Most hunters had a good eye and a sense of nature. While none were getting rich, none would have done anything else. By 1900, a few had brought their wives.

Early access to Lake Okeechobee was from the Gulf coast. Tampa and Fort Myers were the major population centers, while the East Coast was sparsely populated. Mosquito County covered one-fourth of the state from just south of Jacksonville to the Florida Keys. A contemporary PR person must have realized that Mosquito County was never going to attract settlers, and the name was changed to Dade in honor of the U.S. Army lieutenant massacred by Seminoles. Stretching from Stuart in the north to the Keys in the south, a total of 7,200 square miles, Dade County boasted a total of 726 residents by 1888. They were white residents, mostly, though there were a few black settlers and Indians who were not counted.

At the turn of the century, the United States, flush with the success of the building of the Panama Canal, was canal-crazy. The construction of the lock-laden interoceanic Panama Canal was a crowning achievement of American engineering know-how and persistence. After draining the great malarial swamps in the mountainous jungles of Panama, Florida looked easy, since it was flat—perhaps the flattest area in the world. The land under that swamp was extraordinarily fertile, crying out to be drained. Plus, it was in the United States of America, near railroads, supply lines, and tens of thousands of land-hungry pioneers ready to clear, settle, farm, and, of course, purchase the newly reclaimed land. If anything, the drying of the Everglades was a business proposition, a monumental land sale, and the number one hawker was the state of Florida.

Named after the Corsican general-turned-emperor, Napoleon Bonaparte Broward could be excused for having a Napoleonic complex. Nothing he did was small-scale. As a young man he worked to free an entire country—that helped precipitate an international war. In the late 1890s, Broward ran guns to poet-turned-revolutionary Jose Marti's *insurectos* in Cuba before the Spanish American War. His activities posed a diplomatic problem, as the United States and Spain were friends. On more than one occasion, the young freebooter was almost apprehended by Spanish and American authorities. With the sinking of the USS *Maine* in Havana harbor, war was declared, and the gunrunner became a hero.

When he grew older, he dreamed of being governor of Florida. Broward campaigned on the promise that the state would drain the Everglades. He was opposed by the large developers and the railroad concerns that wanted to develop the Everglades themselves. Broward was a popular grassroots politician. Lacking the big money the railroads and developers put into the war chests of his opponents, he campaigned through the back-country, literally stumping: many times, his pulpit was a pine tree stump. He talked the language of the people, and in 1904 he won the governorship in a landslide.

Aside from the railroad barons and their allies, others opposed to his plans declared that it was impossible to drain the Everglades. Governor Broward knew that Lake Okeechobee was twenty feet above sea level and declared the obvious: "Water will run downhill."

The state bought four large dredges, and workers began to dig out canals, starting from Fort Lauderdale and Miami. Broward personally attended the July 4, 1906, opening ceremonies in Fort Lauderdale when the first dipper-full of earth was dredged out of the North New River Canal. The new canal brought many well-paying jobs to Fort Lauderdale, as the first lands drained were just west of that village. Almost immediately after the dredging, development began and has continued up to the present. As the population grew and Dade County was divided up, a grateful populace named their new county Broward, for the man who put Fort Lauderdale on the map.

Broward's big dredges hoped to finish the work begun thirty years before by Hamilton Disston, heir to the Keystone Saw, Tool and File works of Philadelphia, makers of the famous Disston hand saws. In 1881, for twenty-five cents an acre, Disston purchased four million acres of south Florida land. Florida was a desperately poor state, bordering on bankruptcy, and needed the income. The Disston purchase ranged from Orlando south near Sable Island and ran east to within a few miles of Fort Lauderdale. With one stroke of the pen, the thirty-seven-year-old Hamilton Disston was transformed into the largest private landholder in the United States, and he formed the Disston Land Company. Disston's development plans called not only for agricultural land development and sales but also for industry. Disston and his partner, Rose, formed the St. Cloud Sugar Plantation, planted sugar cane, and constructed a processing plant that handled two hundred tons per day.

Disston also began a large-scale canal-building program. He connected a number of lakes and rivers in the Kissimmee. Another Disston company, the Okeechobee Land Company, started a canal to Miami and dug canals to Lake Hicpochee near Moore Haven. He envisioned a waterway from the Gulf of Mexico to Jacksonville that would run up the Caloosahatchee River, across Lake Okeechobee, up the Kissimmee River, and then down the St. Johns River. Another canal to Shark River from Lake Okeechobee was planned, but neither project was finished. Hamilton Disston died, and his family, lacking vision, refused to invest more money in swampland projects. Disston's dream of an empire in the sun died with him. His great dredges lay rusting and many

of his canals began to silt up and revert back to everglades. Nature began to reclaim its own.

THREE thousand years before the first white hunters or pioneer farmers arrived in the Everglades, the Calusa Indians dominated southern Florida. A
tall race, from Spanish accounts and the bones recovered from burial
mound excavations, the Calusas were basically hunters and gatherers. They
had a complex social and political organization, kept slaves, and extracted
tribute from the Tequesta, Jagua, and other tribes on the East Coast. Their
hegemony ranged from the Caribbean islands of Cuba and Hispaniola,
north to Cape Canaveral and Tampa. The tribute, for the most part, was
food, animal skins, and wreckage from Spanish treasure fleets. Such was the
treasure gathered off Florida's coast and taken to Carlos, one of the great
Calusa chiefs, that the legend of King Carlos's treasure originated.

Drawing on the abundance of fish and game, the Calusas had enough
leisure to construct large living, ceremonial, and burial mounds. They
also carved intricate lifelike wooden statues similar to the totems built by
the Indian cultures in the Pacific Northwest. Along the coasts, the
mounds were built with seashells discarded over hundreds of years. Lacking a steady supply of shellfish, the Indians constructed the mounds
around Lake Okeechobee mostly of muck and sand.

Some mounds were simply refuge heaps or middens, while others covered up to one hundred fifty acres. There were mounds and thirty-foot-
high hill complexes at Indian Mound in Martin County. Some of the
shell mounds were so large that many of Florida's early road-paving
programs used material excavated from them for fill.

In the 1930s, the Smithsonian Institute excavated the Chosen mound.
On one distinct level of the Chosen mound, the graves of small-boned,
short people with elongated heads were found, reminiscent of the Maya
and very different from the tall, large-boned Calusas. The Maya, a trading
society, had trade routes that ran from Venezuela and Bacatá (Bogotá) to
the Bahamas. Emeralds that could only come from the Chivor mines in
Colombia were found in Mexico. On an expedition to conquer the Incas,
Francisco Pizzaro intercepted an oceanic raft from Peru heading north to
Costa Rica. A trade link or influence connecting Lake Okeechobee and
the Meso-American Mayas was a real and intriguing possibility.

One canoe dredged up in the Boca Raton area in 1957—made out of a
cypress tree trunk—was forty-six feet long. It was an ocean canoe, one
that would take thirty people and trade goods to the Bahamas or Cuba.
During the Spanish colonial period, it was not unusual for Calusa traders
to make the two-day canoe trip across the Florida Straits to barter with

their brethren in Cuba. When the Americans assumed control over Florida, the last of the Calusas packed their belongings in their sea canoes and fled to Cuba, preferring a life in exile under the Spanish.

While not fearing the ocean, like the Polynesians of the Pacific, the Calusas respected their seas. Their dread was reserved for their god of evil, Huracan, named after the storms that wreaked such havoc on their exposed villages. They understood the power of hurricanes and built their mounds with tropical storms in mind. On the night of September 16, 1928, thirty-one people attested to the foresight and engineering skills of the Calusa Indians as they weathered the storm on top of a two-thousand-year-old mound, in the savage winds, torrential rains, and tidal flood that killed over two thousand people.

THE Calusas and northern Florida tribes were decimated through attrition, disease, and slave raids by Creek Indians. North Florida became a no-man's land. Into this void the Indians that came to be known as Seminoles migrated. They were Southern Creek tribes including the Miccosukees, who were being forced out of the Carolinas and northern Georgia by British colonists. Settling in Spanish Florida, they prospered by raising cattle and farming. The Spanish allowed the Seminoles to remain in the backwaters of Florida as long as they did not interfere with the Spanish administration. The Seminoles actually helped the local economy by selling their crops and cattle to the Spanish outposts at St. Augustine and elsewhere.

From the beginning, Florida was an irritant, first to the English and then to the Americans. It was Spanish, it was Catholic, and its Indians and blacks had unprecedented freedom. The Spanish had colonized Florida only to protect its treasure fleets. The Spanish Main passed directly through the narrow straits between Florida and the Bahamas. From protected inlets, coves, and cayos, pirates and freebooters sallied to raid the treasure-laden galleons. A strong Spanish presence discouraged these assaults. Spanish Florida also deprived Protestant England of further southern expansion. The Spanish had little interest in developing or settling Florida, which was, in comparison to their gold- and silver-rich colonies in Mexico, Peru, and Colombia, a wasteland.

While the Seminoles occasionally raided across the border into Georgia and the Carolinas, the major concern of the Americans was that Florida was being used as a safe haven for escaped slaves. Florida was the terminus of the first Underground Railroad. For slaves from Georgia, the Carolinas, and up to Virginia, Florida meant freedom. Many of these former slaves settled with the Seminoles, took on their customs, intermarried, and in all essence became Seminoles—black Seminoles.

In 1819, Spain agreed to sell Florida to the United States for a face-saving $4 million. Almost immediately, the United States began a military campaign against the Seminoles and their black allies.

The fate of the Seminoles was sealed with the election of President Andrew Jackson. The seventh president of the United States was the first "western" president—the first president born and raised west of the Appalachian Mountains in a state other than one of the original thirteen colonies. As a child of a settler family during the French and Indian War, he shared the fears of Indian attacks. A frontiersman, he had often fought the Indians and had the pioneer's hatred of Native Americans. Joining the army and rising to general, he defeated the Creek Indians in 1813 and never completely stopped defeating them at every opportunity. To Andrew Jackson and most of his frontier constituents, Indians were the United States' greatest impediment to progress. They had to go.

The first Seminole War forced the Indians to retreat from North Florida. After a number of skirmishes, the Treaty of Payne's Landing was signed in 1832, requiring all Indians to be relocated west by 1835. The Second Seminole War began in 1835, when many of the Seminoles resisted efforts to relocate. As president, Jackson was determined to enforce the Indian Relocation Act, forcing all the Indians east of the Appalachians to migrate west. The forced and brutal ejection of the Europeanized Christian Cherokees out of Northern Georgia and western Carolina is one of the blackest pages in American history. Hundreds of Indians—men, women, and children—died in the long march to Oklahoma along the trail of tears—an act that today would be declared officially sanctioned genocide.

It is hard to understand the determination of the U.S. government to rid the Everglades of Indians at this date, considering the cost in lives and money—fifteen hundred dead and $20 million—out of the coffers of a young, cash-strapped country. There was no move to open the Everglades to white settlement. After the Indians were expelled, no one ventured into the Everglades for another forty years. Maps of Florida showed a blank in the middle of the state. In reality, except for the Indians, nobody wanted it.

Retreating farther and farther into the impenetrable Everglades, small bands of Indians held out against the white men. They were known as the wild Seminoles. Insular and wary of all contact with whites, they were still living in the Everglades as late as 1950. The Florida Miccosukee Indians are the only known Native Americans to have never signed a treaty with the United States because they never surrendered.

IN 1916, the state run Everglades Drainage District made its first attempt to regulate water levels in Lake Okeechobee. It built concrete locks at the lake end of each canal to retain water and control the flow into the canals. Thus began the attempts to regulate the water level of Lake Okeechobee that continues today. From the start, the water managers made no one happy. The boat transporters and the fishermen argued for a high water level, while farmers wanted it lowered. Actually, the farmers would have been happy if the entire lake were drained.

Water from Lake Okeechobee was drained by six canals, the first being Three Mile Canal, dug by Hamilton Disston, that connected Lake Okeechobee to Lake Hicpochee, the source of the Caloosahatchee River. After the Caloosahatchee was dredged, boats could navigate from Kissimmee to Fort Myers. On the eastern coast, a canal was dug from Port Mayaca to the St. Lucie River, draining waters to the Atlantic. The Miami Canal carried water from Miami Locks to Biscayne Bay, the North New River Canal cut through the Everglades from South Bay to Davie and Fort Lauderdale. The Hillsboro Canal began at Chosen, passed through Belle Glade, then emptied at Deerfield; the Palm Beach Canal started at Canal Point and ended at the turning basin in West Palm Beach, just west of the railroad across Okeechobee Boulevard from today's Kravis Center. Of these, only the Caloosahatchee River, the North New River, and the Palm Beach Canal were used for regular transportation. A side canal was dug to connect the Hillsboro Canal with the Palm Beach Canal, giving direct water access between Belle Glade and West Palm Beach. To help drain his company's property, developer Dickey Bolles dug a parallel canal from the Miami Canal to the Hillsboro Canal that still bears his name. A series of lateral canals were dug to drain the fields. Farmers dug smaller drainage canals until the entire agricultural area was a maze of crisscrossing canals and dikes.

Some farmers experimented with pumps, but for the great part, people depended on gravity to drain the Everglades—a system that soon proved to be woefully inefficient.

Though the Miami Canal was the first canal completed from the populous Miami area, it wasn't until the deeper North New River Canal was finished that people began to flock into the Everglades.

The old Miami Canal was too shallow for year-round traffic. Boats would catch on a ledge of marl and be left high and dry by the dropping water level until the next rains. The New River Canal was to be dug deep enough to allow all-season transportation.

Huge dredges worked through the week like earth-eating monsters digging, scooping, and piling sand and muck. Menacing dark smoke billowing from the wood-burning boilers of the ponderous dredges could be seen on the horizon from any direction. More than anything else these behemoths, and the canals they dug, were the real signs of progress to the glades farmers. When the canals were finished, Lake Okeechobee would fall six feet.

On December 29, 1911, while digging the southern end of the New River Canal, a dredge crew unearthed a corpse. Still clothed in Seminole dress, the body was identified as DeSoto Tiger, the lost son of Seminole Indian leader Tom Tiger. The discovery of DeSoto Tiger's body began a bloody saga that would end thirteen years later with a toll of twelve people dead.

THE MARTINS

In 1851, the U.S. Army dispatched a young engineering lieutenant named George Meade to scout a site for a fort seventy miles north of Lake Okeechobee. The strategically placed fort overlooking the Peace River ford sat along the middle of the military trail that was to connect Fort Pierce on the Atlantic to Fort Brooke at the head of Tampa Bay. Fort Meade, as it was later known, was one of a dozen forts built across the girdle of Florida during the Seminole Indian wars. Their object was to keep the Seminoles penned in to the south.

After the United States declared victory in the last Seminole War, George Meade left Florida for Massachusetts. Later, he fought in the Mexican War. During the height of the Civil War, he replaced General Joseph Hooker as commander of the Army of the Potomac three days before the Army of Northern Virginia, led by Robert E. Lee, crossed the Potomac River into Maryland.

Meade's military apogee was to be short-lived. Lee's objective was the capture of Harrisburg, the capital of Pennsylvania, but a skirmish forced him to confront Meade's army at a small town called Gettysburg. The Confederates were defeated and withdrew from Union soil. But the victorious Meade, instead of being celebrated, was berated by an angry President Abraham Lincoln for not pursuing Lee's retreating army and destroying it. Lincoln replaced Meade with Ulysses S. Grant, who then hounded Lee all the way to Appomattox and a Union victory.

After the Civil War, thousands of displaced farmers, mostly demobilized Confederate soldiers, settled in central Florida. A pent-up demand for land by millions of young men returning from war flooded the western United States and Florida, America's two frontiers. The West would be conquered by the 1890s, South Florida not until 1916.

Aaron Henry Martin, originally from Alabama had moved to North Florida four years before the outbreak of the Civil War. When word of the attack on Fort Sumter reached Florida, he enlisted in the Confederate cause. His unit fought in Tennessee and saw action at the battle of Chickamauga and Murfreesboro. Returning to Florida after the war, a disenfranchised Aaron Martin found a state occupied by Yankee troops, run by carpetbaggers and former slaves in positions of power. Disgusted, he packed his family and possessions into a wagon and left their home in North Florida—searching for a place far from the carpet-bagging Yankees.

The Martins continued south as far as they could go, finally settling near the small town that had formed around the old Fort Meade. It was the frontier where some of the old-timers still remembered "forting up" during the Indian wars and the vigilante Regulators. Cow hunters, Florida cowboys, still scoured the scrub brush for free-roaming cattle. About this time even the native-born Floridians began to call themselves "Crackers," a term taken, according to one account, from the cracking of the bullwhip used by the cow-hunters.

This isolated frontier had one major attraction: land was cheap. For Aaron Martin, this was the end of the road. He acquired a small farm, built a wood plank house, and had five children: Robert, Loney, William, Bernice, and Henry Wilson, who was born October 18, 1885.

The Martin children, like 70 percent of all Americans in the 1880s, grew up on a farm. America was rural: the west was still wild, and in Florida civilization ended a scant fifty miles south of the Martin family farm. Children around Fort Meade were brought up on frontier tales of Indian wars, cattle thieves, damn Yankees, and killer frosts.

Henry Martin grew tall. At six foot, he was thin but solidly built with brown eyes and closely cropped dark hair. Even as a youth, he had an assumed serious demeanor. Like all children, he worked hard at backbreaking jobs around the farm. In his midtwenties, he began to court a fifteen-year-old local girl named Shelly Barber. They were married a year later.

Polk County was rural, and a man never left town without his rifle or shotgun, not only for protection but in case he spotted any game. The chance to bring home free meat was not to be missed. An avid hunter, Henry spent many mornings and weekends hunting ducks and wild boar. Shelly liked being on the water, and she had Henry take her out in his small skiff whenever he could. Two months after they were married, Shelly insisted on going with Henry for an early-morning row. As usual, Henry took along his shotgun in case he spotted some ducks. As he stepped into the bow, he tripped and the shotgun roared. Shelly gave out a soft groan and keeled over. Two hours later she was dead. Henry Martin, lost in grief, fled Fort Meade and the haunting memories of his bride for northern Florida.

A year later while working in Mayo, Florida, he met Bessie Mae Wells, who was visiting relatives. A smitten Henry Martin carried on a whirl-wind courtship, and two months later they were married.

Like Henry Martin, Bessie Mae Wells was a true blue "cracker"—born and raised on the Wells's family farm near Jasper, Florida, just south of the Georgia state line. She was a short woman, just five feet. When she walked with Henry, she fit snugly under his arm. With long dark brown hair and large blue eyes, she was a bit on the heavy side. Later her children would jokingly call her "five-by-five," an appellation she took in stride. She had a heart like a child and would join the children as they skipped rope, played hide-and-seek, and swam in the lake. Henry affectionately called her "Kid." To Henry, Bessie Mae was an overgrown kid. To Bessie Mae, Henry was always Mister Martin.

Bessie Mae sadly bid good-bye to her family. She would be especially missed by her younger brother Tommy. Their mother had died when Tommy was barely three years old, and Bessie Mae had raised him like a mother. Their father had never recovered from his wife's death, and he spent long periods of time away from the house. Tommy had started to show a rebellious streak, and Bessie Mae worried what he might do without proper supervision. Trying to reassure him, Bessie told Tommy he was always welcome in her home. The newlyweds settled at Fish Bone near Cedar Key, where Henry hoped to earn some money fishing before moving back to Polk County

Annie Mae Martin, Henry and Bessie's first child, was born in 1912 at Cedar Key. Henry had another mouth to feed, and Gulf fishing was on the wane. Enticing letters arrived from home with news about the opportunities at the new phosphorous mines operating in Polk County. After a few months, a discouraged Henry took Bessie and Annie Mae and returned to Polk County. He landed a job at the Tiger Bay phosphate mine in central Florida. Tiger Bay was a large strip mine where tracked wheeled bulldozers cleared off topsoil to mine the exposed rich phosphorous rock. Bone Valley in Polk County had the richest deposit of phosphorous in North America.

Henry was a hard worker and a good provider. But on Fridays he would linger with the other men at a bar, or backroom, where they would play cards. Stakes were never high, but a poor player could quickly lose his paycheck. Bessie Mae never begrudged him his Friday night card games and never knew if he won or lost. Gambling, though prevalent, was strongly frowned upon and not discussed in polite company. She only knew the family never lacked for anything, and for Bessie Mae, that was sufficient.

A year later, Nancy Rachel was born, followed two years later by their first son, Raymond. In 1916, Bessie Mae gave birth to Thelma Irene. Their second son, Henry Jurden, was born in 1919. Called "Sonny" by everyone, he was born two months early, weighing only two and a half pounds. The doctor who delivered him doubted he would live. Using a handkerchief as a diaper, Bessie Mae and the rest of the family lovingly nursed the tiny infant who was placed in a shoe box lined with cotton to keep him warm. With tender care, Sonny eventually grew into a husky young boy.

Secure as he was in life, Henry dreamed of being his own man. He knew working for others was not the way to get ahead and yearned to open his own store. He and Bessie Mae saved a much as they could on his salary and her egg money.

After six years, the Tiger Bay deposit ran out, and the Martins returned to Fort Meade. Henry staked out a homesteaded of one hundred sixty acres ten miles east of Fort Meade, at West Frostproof, where he planted vegetables and worked during the season on the neighboring orange plantations. Once he had enough money saved, he planted his own orange grove—fifteen acres—of dark-leafed Valencia orange trees. He also finally opened up a store of his own, a butcher shop where he also sold vegetables and dry goods. Henry had the store he always wanted, but Frostproof was a small town with little prospect of growth.

The Martins had one persistent visitor. Tommy Wells regularly ran away from home to seek out Bessie Mae, his surrogate mother. Henry saw a lot of himself in the young Tommy, who was a hard worker, loved adventure, and, in spite of his small stature, never slacked off on the heaviest jobs. Bessie and Henry would let Tommy stay with them until he had to go back to school, but in Tommy's eyes the spare country around Fort Meade was his true home.

Even as Henry planted his orange groves, change was in the air. To the east, a sign of progress was working its way south. Through Polk County, the Atlantic Coast Line Railroad was constructing a spur line from Haines City to Moore Haven on Lake Okeechobee.

While his farm was doing well, persistent stories filtered north to West Frostproof that around Lake Okeechobee a new more fertile land was opening up. The sandy soil around Frostproof was more suited to citrus than produce. Henry Martin was tired of just etching out a living while other dirt farmers brought in bumper crops and were flush with cash for years. The fast cash was in produce, not citrus. A gamble, yes; but the return was so much greater, and there were two things that Henry Martin had learned to respect: a good gamble and fast cash.

A wind of opportunity wafted inexorably from the south. The Everglades called, the same as it had beckoned Ponce de León in his search for King Carlos's gold. There was still treasure in the Everglades, though it was not gold, or an El Dorado, or a fountain of youth. The true treasure of the Everglades was the rich earthy blackness called muck.

CHAPTER TWO
THE EVERGLADES

America's Last Frontier

Instances of astonishing results had lent a halo of romance around the magic world "Everglades" and many who failed to investigate and who had no previous experience thought they had a rainbow with its proverbial pot of gold and of course suffered disillusionment.

—*Nathan Mayo, "Possibilities of the Everglades," Florida Quarterly Bulletin of the Department of Agriculture*

Weather-wise Florida is a state of superlatives. More lightning strikes Florida than any other state; more thunderstorms form on and off its coasts; more hurricanes make landfall in Florida than in any other part of the United States. Forty percent of all U.S. hurricanes strike the Sunshine State. During the last one hundred years, eighteen intense hurricanes, with sustained winds of 111 miles per hour or higher—categories 3 to 5—made landfall in South Florida.

While hurricanes are the meteorological headline grabbers, it is seasonal thunderstorms that rule South Florida's ecosystem. During the summer, fed by tropical southeast "trade" winds blowing from the West Indies, billowing afternoon thunderstorms form along frontlike convergence lines. They move like great warships of the line, bullying their way across the flat peninsula, at times displaying frightful exhibitions of sheer force. These thunderstorms are the lifeblood of Florida, for without them the state would be an arid, dry peninsula—an oversized Aruba.

Weather is, simply, a response to unequal rates of radiational heating and cooling within the Earth's atmosphere. Areas exposed to the direct rays of the sun are warm; those that are not are cold. The warmed land and water in turn heat the air. As every elementary school child is taught, warm air rises; cold air falls. This simple tenet is the keystone to all weather.

As warm air rises, it expands, lowering density and creating a lower-pressure area. Nature abhors a vacuum—or, in this case, low pressure, which acts like a vacuum. Wind, moving air, is the great equalizer—it loathes differences in pressure and rushes to correct any variances in air pressure. Thus, wind speed is a function of air pressure. On a meteorological map, air pressure is denoted by a series of lines drawn in amoeba-like circles called *isobars*. Like a topographical map with mountains and valleys, it shows high- and low-pressure areas. The closer together these lines are, the greater the pressure difference is over a given area and the greater the wind velocity. Pressure is directly related to the change in air temperature, or the rising or falling of air—warm air rises; cold air falls.

A hurricane is a massive warm-air machine. Heat and the transfer of heat comprise the engine—in reality, a steam engine—that energizes a hurricane. Heated air, when exposed to water, absorbs water in the form of vapor through evaporation. Water vapor retains more heat than dry air. The unique ability to force warm, moisture-laden air high into the atmosphere, creating powerful high-altitude thunderstorms, fuels a hurricane and gives it energy. It is this energy that generates the extreme winds and rains that make a hurricane such a destructive force, again based on the simple principle that warm air rises; cold air falls.

When viewed from above, the Earth is like a child's colorful marble—an array of blues and whites with shades of continental brown. Around the equator, like a fluffy white girdle, a band of persistent clouds encircles the Earth. Here the direct rays of the sun strike the planet, warming the water and the air above it. The warm, humid air rises. The water vapor, when it reaches certain heights, cools, condenses, and forms clouds, creating the equatorial band. Air rising along the equator creates a low-pressure area known as the *intertropical convergence zone*—the birthplace of tropical storms.

Into this low-pressure area flow the trade winds, those dependable air currents, blowing from the northeast, that sailboat captains know they can rely on. The angle of the trade winds is created by the spin of the Earth—a phenomenon recognized in the early 1800s by French scientist Gaspard de Coriolis and thus called the Coriolis effect.

Steady trade winds are constantly under attack by outside anomalies trying to disrupt their patterns. Many of these anomalies are super-heated low-pressure winds called *easterly waves* wafting off the Sahara Desert. When an easterly wave enters into the trade winds, it bends the trade winds counterclockwise into their centers. If there is enough air pressure difference, a complete circle will form and spin will begin. Warm ocean water is evaporated into the air, energizing the system. With sufficient energy, the hot moisture-laden air will be driven high into the upper atmosphere, developing massive thunderstorms. Thus is born the seeding condition for a hurricane. But not all seeds germinate. Scores of seeding events form each year, but only a select few develop into full-scale hurricanes.

Hurricanes are unique weather phenomena. In any given year only an average of ten tropical storms form in the Atlantic; of these, only six become hurricanes. Of all the hurricanes that have made landfall in the United States during the last hundred years, sixty-three were category 3 or 4, and only two reached category 5 strength. A severe or catastrophic hurricane is a very rare event. Meteorologically, hurricanes are extremely complex. Given the number of variables a hurricane needs, it is surprising they ever form. Some years they don't. Other years they line in queues, one after the other, rolling across the Atlantic like an automobile assembly plant. But those are abnormal years.

The birth of a hurricane does not take place in isolation. A hurricane has many midwives. First, in order to develop, a hurricane needs warm ocean waters. The sea surface temperature, or SST, must be at least 80 degrees Fahrenheit to a depth of approximately of 150 feet. This is the source of warm water that supplies the heat for a hurricane's engine. Officially, hurricane season starts June 1, when the sun's rays directly strike the ocean surface near the equator, raising the SST. Since liquids retain heat better than solids, the ocean will remain warm enough for hurricane formation through the shortened days of November. Already warm, the water is readily evaporated by hot air blowing off Africa. Large amounts of moisture-laden air billow high into the atmosphere, actually increasing the air temperature. Again: warm air rises, cold air falls.

To understand the importance of heat transfer in a tropical storm, the unique properties of water must be examined. A cubic centimeter of water in a liquid state weighing one gram needs 580 calories of energy to evaporate, or vaporize. All water vapor carries 580 calories of heat. The cooling effect of water evaporating off skin is heat transfer from the body to water vapor. This heat transfer is called *latent heat*. As the hot air carries the vaporized water higher into the atmosphere, it cools. The dew point falls until the air is saturated, or reaches 100 percent humidity. The water then condenses into liquid, and the 580 calories of heat it had as a vapor are transferred into the air around it. Multiply the hundreds of millions of gallons of water evaporated from the warm oceans and carried tens of thousands of feet into the atmosphere, then dropped as rain, and the enormous amount of energy released by heat transference in a hurricane becomes apparent. Less than 1 percent of that heat is used to spin up the hurricane's winds. Most of the heat released bounces away from the hurricane as gravity waves in the upper tropospheric outflow.

Aside from warm sea surface temperature, the atmosphere must be able to cool the rising moisture—and cool it fast enough to form thunderstorms. A hurricane needs lots of thunderstorms, or what the meteorologists call Mesoscale Convection Complexes (MCCs). It is the thunderstorms that allow the heat stored in the ocean waters to be released, developing the hurricane. Once the thunderstorms unite in a tight circle, they begin to spin madly like white-robed dervishes.

Along with warm SST and thunderstorms, a relatively moist layer of air about three miles high must be present. A relationship with a high rate of rainfall in equatorial Africa along the Gulf of Guinea has been established with active hurricane seasons. These rains supply a large part of a hurricane's high-altitude moisture.

The storm must form at least three hundred miles from the equator for *cyclogenesis*—cyclone formation—to occur. As the Earth spins, it affects both air and water—the Coriolis effect, which is stronger as you get farther away from the equator. The Coriolis effect maintains the low pressure of the storm.

There should be little vertical wind shear between the surface and the upper troposphere to cut off circulation from the ocean to the troposphere—no jet stream to decapitate its thunderheads or, let's say, "to steal its thunder."

This complex list of weather events must be present for a hurricane to develop. Even with all these necessary prerequisites, there is no guarantee that a hurricane will form. However, when atmospheric conditions are optimal for hurricane formation, the Cape Verde corridor will spit out tropical storms in rapid succession. In one satellite photograph taken at the height of hurricane season, two tropical depressions and four full-blown hurricanes were storming their way across the North Atlantic Ocean—a very productive week.

While a tropical cyclone does need a series of complicated prerequisites to form, once that initial inertia is overcome, the storm becomes self-perpetuating. The faster winds pick up, the more vitalizing warm water arises, which in turn energizes the thunderstorms. Water and air rise faster, lowering the eye's atmospheric pressure, creating more wind and faster spins, evaporating more water. Once the winds reach 75 miles per hour, the storm officially becomes a hurricane. When those winds reach above 120 miles per hour, it becomes a deadly effective combination of gas and liquid. Above 150 miles per hour, the difference between the two becomes blurred.

FLORIDA'S history has been shaped by hurricanes. On July 16, 1495, during his second voyage to the new world, Christopher Columbus was battered by a hurricane. Forewarned by native Caribe Indians that the god Huracan was about to strike, Columbus found safe harbor in Hispaniola and rode out the storm but lost two of his ships. Only the diminutive *La Niña* survived. In 1565, the Spanish settlement of San Augustine, then a collection of huts and a wooden stockade, was saved when a French Huguenot fleet from Fort Caroline, near present-day Jacksonville, bent on destroying the Spanish settlement, was struck by a hurricane. The French fleet was sunk, Fort Caroline destroyed, and Florida secured for Spain.

Ponce de León sailed out of Havana with a dozen ships and hundreds of settlers set to colonize the Tampa Bay area. The fleet was caught by a hurricane on the Gulf of Mexico coast, and all but a score died, setting back Spanish settlement of the Tampa Bay area one hundred years. On the east coast of Florida, the aptly named Treasure Coast is littered with the remains of Spanish ships and the treasure lost in hurricanes.

From 1910 to 1926, it would not be hurricanes that affected Florida's well-being but rather the lack of them. During this God-sent reprieve, events thousands of miles from the marshlands of the Everglades were set in motion that would directly affect southern Florida, and the rest of the nation.

ON June 28, 1914, Gavrilo Princip, a young tuberculer Serb Nationalist unwittingly became a major force in the development of the Everglades. No one in the Everglades knew him. No one in South Florida had ever heard of him, either. In fact, no one in the United States even knew he existed. Few Americans had even heard of his home state, Serbia; fewer still even knew there existed an obscure Austria-Hungarian Empire province named Bosnia-Herzegovina or its capital Sarajevo. But all that changed when Gavrilo Princip emptied his revolver into Archduke Franz Ferdinand and his wife, killing the heir to the Austria-Hungarian throne and precipitating the world into its first world war.

By October, with winter rapidly approaching on all fronts, the Axis and Allied powers realized they were not engaged in a quick decisive conflict. As front lines were drawn and three and a half million men dug trenches, the combatants knew they were in for a long war. They also realized they had to feed their troops. Most of the soldiers manning the trenches were European farm boys who would not be planting crops that year. With little available refrigeration, vegetables—especially vegetables that traveled well, such as green beans—were in high demand.

While many Americans sympathized with the Allies after Germany's attack through neutral Belgium, most Americans favored a strong isolationist foreign policy. The United States was home to many recent immigrants who had fled poverty and war in Europe. They were not anxious for their children to return to the Old World in uniform. America, as its leaders well knew, would have to be dragged protesting into the war.

To meet the new demand for vegetables, the U.S. government encouraged its farmers to plant. More Everglades land was drained, plowed, and planted. With expectations of good crop prices and cheap land, more and more people migrated to the Everglades. British buyers and American middlemen blanketed America's agricultural areas with promises of purchasing entire crops at high prices.

Then in May 1915, a German U-boat sank the British ocean liner *Lusitania*. With continued unfettered submarine warfare and the anti-German hysteria generated by the yellow press, an apathetic public was finally roused in favor of war in 1917, and President Woodrow Wilson asked Congress for a Declaration of War. By the time America entered the war, cultivated land in the Everglades had doubled. Farmers searched further for new land. Custard apple forests were cut down and tough sawgrass was plowed under—any apparently dry spot was a potential vegetable field. At this rate, in a few years there would be no undrained or unplanted land in the Everglades. As the air of Europe turned green and yellow with the pale of chlorine and mustard gas, the Everglades farmers thrived.

RITTA ISLAND: THE 1917 FREEZE

As he did every morning, Bill Boots woke early and stepped out onto his front porch. He gazed contentedly across his fields at the bushy bean shoots draped with the first small white flowers. Seventy rows of beans stood at attention in orderly files, across flat fields. Light green shoots tall and strong glowing against the coal black soil were a beautiful sight to a farmer.

The previous fall he had brought in a good crop. With the war in Europe raging, the price for produce was high, the highest it had been in twenty years. Though the United States was just two months away from declaring war on the Axis powers, the country was still at peace. Washington bureaucrats were pushing farmers to plant as part of the effort to feed Europeans who were too busy killing each other to plant. There were buyers for all beans that could be grown. Even the seconds and thirds that in other years would be plowed under had a price. With the sale of the fall crop, Bill Boots had added a small room to the house. He hoped to build Mattie Mae a new house either on Ritta Island or on the mainland where there was more land to be had at cheaper prices. But first he needed another bumper crop, so he invested his entire savings in the second crop, planting twice as many beans.

On the evening of February 3, 1917, a bright red sun set quickly in a cloudless sky and there was a coolness in the air. Farmers who were working outside wore jackets and hats, while their women hovered in stove-warmed kitchens. That night Bill awoke and discovered that something was different: he was cold. Even with two blankets on his bed he shivered. He got up, lit a lamp, put on a sweater, and went out to the front porch, his breath billowing before him like hoary fog. The night was quiet: no insects chirped, no frogs croaked, no alligators groaned. It was still as death.

Dawn's first light sparkled on a crystalline landscape. A thin sheet of ice covered the water barrow. Puddles of water had become ice-hard, glassy mirrors reflecting red morning light. The ground crunched under each step as Bill Boots walked slowly through his green beans. The stalks and leaves glistened like tiny diamonds in the morning light. Within an hour the ice melted, and the plants drooped sadly to the ground. By noon they withered up and turned black. Helplessly, Bill Boots watched his future waste away. The entire crop, three months of backbreaking work, was a total loss. Standing in the middle of his fields, he felt the perverse optimism that carries a farmer through good and bad drain from his soul like from an open spigot. He stood in complete defeat. The promises of the promoters and settlers rang like a false bell: *It never freezes on the islands. Never.* Yet, that winter, like Bill Boots, nearly every farmer in the Everglades had lost their winter crop. Florida had suffered a massive freeze that killed vegetables, crops, and citrus trees from the Georgia border to Key West. The temperature in Miami hit a low of 27 degrees.

The frost ended the Boots's tenure in the Everglades. With their savings gone and no prospects left in the Everglades, Bill and Mattie Mae Boots once again packed up their children and belongings and crossed the country back to Pierce, Arizona.

Mud-caked Allied soldiers in the front lines trenches of Le Main would be a little bit hungrier that winter.

THE great freeze of 1917 devastated the Everglades, but it did not strike everyone equally. Running halfway down the eastern side of Lake Okeechobee was a sand ridge called East Beach, later renamed Pahokee. For centuries it had been a stopping place for migrating Seminoles on their way to summer camping grounds around Kissimmee. Rising six feet above the surrounding Everglades, it offered a dry repose from wind tides and floods.

Hunters were the first white Americans to call the ridge home. They camped on the lake side of the ridge and watched egrets and herons flock to roost. During mating season, the egrets' elegant white plumes would grow up to three feet long—perfect for fashionable ladies' hats. Once the plume-bird flocks were depleted, the hunters left or turned to fishing.

Fish-buying boats came down the Kissimmee River and bought all the catfish available. Scaled fish like bass, or crappies, were considered trash fish and discarded.

Hoping to make money fishing, Noble Padgett arrived in 1914 and set up his fish camp near the sandy ridge. Like everyone in the Everglades, when fishing or hunting slowed, he planted enough for food to see him through the slow season. He first farmed on what became known as Padgett's Island, which is located about a mile to the east of the ridge where the Pelican River forked before it emptied into Pelican Lake and Pelican Bay. With the war demand, he planted more vegetables but never considered himself a farmer.

But fate's gentle hand touched Noble Padgett's shoulder. The only area not affected by the February freeze was the land along the East Beach. His small crop had survived. He watched as his produce quadrupled in price. With his newfound wealth in hand, Padgett bought more land, and the fisherman was on his way to becoming one of the largest landholders in the Pahokee area.

FURTHER north, belying its namesake, Frostproof froze. The February freeze had destroyed much of the citrus crop in Polk County, sending the county into a serious economic depression. Henry Martin, though, saved most of his young trees by using smudge pots and wood fires. They were alive and, after a judicious pruning, would sprout new branches. He had lost maybe one year on their growth—a serious but not fatal setback for his farm.

Henry was two years into his homestead. The law required that he farm the land for another three years, after which time it would be "'proved up," and Henry would gain clear title to the land. He was disappointed with the pace at which the new trees were maturing, but he was a patient. He had too much time and money invested in his homestead, and now he had a family.

His older brother Loney wanted land of his own. After hearing stories of the fabulously fertile land open to homesteading south around Lake Okeechobee, nothing could keep Loney in Polk County.

Moore Haven was, in 1917, the gateway to the Everglades. A bustling town, its prosperity was based on farming and land speculation. The "free" land Loney was seeking, he was told, was on the opposite eastern shore, the far shore of the lake, which for the people in Moore Haven might as well have been across the Atlantic Ocean.

While Moore Haven was a recognizable town with organization and had grown and progressed, the eastern shore of Lake Okeechobee was bogged down in a swamp of legal entanglement and remained undeveloped and wild. Dickey Bolles's visionary empire in the swamp was reduced to a few cleared areas and a luxury hotel squat in the middle of nowhere. Most of the land buyers had long ago forfeited on their lots, leaving their property in the hands of a litany of lawyers, litigators, and liquidators. At the town dock Loney took the mail boat to Torry Island where he rented a small dinghy and bought a half roll of black tarpaper and some fresh food. Then he loaded his suitcase and tools into the boat and, standing upright, carefully poled his way across the lake. He rounded Ritta Island, where cultivated fields planted in green beans reached to its banks. He crossed the shallow channel behind the island to the eastern shore and finished the dangerous lake journey as dusk settled. He poled up Cooper's River, a shallow dead river between the Hillsboro and Miami canals, and spent his first night sleeping under a cluster of custard apple trees wrapped in a bedroll, with a blanket tossed over his head to ward off mosquitoes.

The attraction this isolated, mosquito-infested marsh held for Loney was that it was new land that had not been included in the 1913 government survey, because it was then part of the lake—underwater. Since then, thanks to Broward's canals and the exceptionally dry summers, the level of Lake Okeechobee had fallen, exposing thousands of acres of former lake bottom. It was land that Loney, and a few other adventurous souls who followed him, hoped they could homestead and eventually acquire clear title for. As land went, it was the very best of the best: fine organic silt, free from heavy overgrowth, easily cleared and plowed— a farmer's dream.

Arriving in April, Loney had missed the big freeze that had driven most of the farmers away. Few people were willing to risk clearing new land and planting so close to Ritta Island. Freezes did not, however, worry Loney. Free land was too strong of a draw. He found that a small area that had been cleared was marked with two broken posts jutting out of the earth. It was all that remained of a house, another farmer's former dream.

The next morning Loney Martin built a tarpaper and brush lean-to with a palmetto-leaf roof. With an axe and hand saw, he hacked out lumber from local trees and, in two days, had built a tarpaper shack to last him through the first planting season. Laboring with only an axe and a hand plow, it took him a month to cut, burn, and plow an acre of land. Into the black soil he placed wrinkled green bean seeds. Even with the additional cost of ferrying his crop across the lake and then onto a train, his crop would sell at a handsome profit. Demand was high.

Alone in his shack, far from civilization, Loney thrived. He was a quiet man who kept to himself; therefore, the solitude of the Everglades appealed to him. Loney Martin silently harbored a secret. A curse, he thought. A curse he tried to fight and hide his entire life, for Loney Martin's real name was Bologna Dinkins Martin, a name he hated.

As long as the heavy rains were kept at bay, life was bright for Loney. The lake remained low, allowing Loney to bring in his first crop and thereby earn enough money to build a real house.

Loney's closest neighbors were settlers across the strait on Ritta Island. To purchase supplies he went either to one of the general stores at the head of the North New River Canal at South Bay or to the Hillsboro Canal community of Chosen. By land, the way was blocked by soggy terrain and impassible tangles of moonvine-covered apple custard forests. Loney had to pole his way from the dead river to the open lake. Then he traveled along the shore and down either the North New River or Hillsboro Canal. Any trip was a day's journey by boat.

Loney wrote home extolling the unbelievable productivity of the Everglades. Enticed by his letters, the following year his sister Bernie and her husband Henry Griffith settled a half-mile north of Loney's claim. At the shore of the lake they built a large, one-room house that sat four feet above the ground on stilts pounded five feet into the muck. But the best news was that the lake had retreated another hundred feet, giving Loney another two acres of easily cleared land to farm.

Loney Martin, like many settlers, believed the Everglades had been tamed. They believed Lake Okeechobee was in full retreat. It took just one look at the array of canals, locks, and the modern technology, the hundreds of acres of new land being cleared and planted, to know the Everglades had been beaten. Napoleon Bonaparte Broward's drainage program was declared a great success.

But the old-timers knew better.

MOORE HAVEN

While people slowly filtered into Pahokee and the Belle Glade area, across Lake Okeechobee, at Moore Haven, progress was more apparent. Within a few years of its founding, Moore Haven was the largest town in the Everglades. Hundreds of people arrived monthly seeking new opportunity. Moore Haven's driving engine was the energy and promotional skills of its founder, James Moore. He understood the value of advertising and spared no expense in getting out the word. Specially built powerboats were sent to Miami to bring back prospects in speed and style. A power plant was built, the First Bank of Moore Haven was incorporated, and a schoolhouse opened. The apogee of Moore Haven's importance was the arrival in 1918 of an Atlantic Coast Line Railway spur from Haines City in Polk County. With the first train came even more people eager to begin anew in the Everglades.

Though Loney Martin's unbounded exuberance for the Everglades was infectious, it was a full year later before Henry Martin made his first trip to the Everglades. First, he had to tend to his obligations. There was the farm—he had to keep his homestead claim active—the citrus trees that were recovering nicely from the big freeze, and, most important, his family. The Martins now had four children.

Once the crops were harvested and his trees pruned, Henry Martin finally had time to visit Loney. He took the train to Moore Haven, where he found a bustling town, streets lined with new construction, and populated with salesmen and binder boys who greeted each arriving train. The unwary would be shanghaied by promoters and worn down by relentless sales pitches until they bought a lot sight unseen in the Everglades. But Henry Martin was not to stay in Moore Haven. Instead of succumbing to promotion pressure, he took the mail boat to Torry Island where Loney met him in his small flat-bottomed skiff. With a large grin, Loney smiled and said, "Welcome to the Everglades, little brother."

Loney's new stilt house was built four feet above the ground. "When it rains, the lake rises," he explained to Henry but then assured him it had fallen back within a few days. Behind his house grew an impassable tangle of custard apple forest that stretched from Pahokee to Moore Haven. In front were three acres planted in cabbage, romaine lettuce, potatoes, and green beans. Beyond was the lake, quiet now, flat like a mirror spreading out to the horizon. But what most caught Henry's eye was the soil— the unfathomably black soil, that incredibly rich dirt that shamed the tan-colored sandy loam of Frostproof.

Standing at the edge of Lake Okeechobee, Loney Martin showed Henry where the lake was retreating. "We've gained two acres in a couple of months," he said, all but taking credit for what they'd both consider an act of God.

New land for a farmer was like finding gold. As Mark Twain advised, "Buy land; they've stopped making it." The great American author had never seen the Everglades where they *were* making land—lots of land, free land. Just a couple of stakes in the ground and a cabin could give a man thousands of dollars of rich, fertile land. It was a siren call too strong for a farmer like Henry Martin to ignore. The seed had been planted. Like the first sweet taste of a narcotic, the idea of owning a piece of that black soil planted itself and smoldered in Henry Martin's brain.

As the sun set over the lake and the air filled with flocking birds returning to their roosts, the sheer natural beauty of the Everglades and Lake Okeechobee exhibited itself. It was still a wild land, as nature had intended. But man's heavy hand was falling ponderously upon the Everglades, anxious to mold and sculpture it in his own image as if he could do a better job than the Creator. It was an arrogance that sooner or later would have to be paid for.

Night fell with a stark reminder that their presence was barely tolerated: a cloud of punishing, blood-sucking insects forced them indoors.

THE Everglades was an amphibious land, dry part of the year and wet the other. It was neither land nor water in its natural state but, depending on the season, a netherworld swaying between the two. Lake Okeechobee was in a constant state of flux, its shoreline oscillating with the rains. Pioneers had to deal with high water and took the summer rains and the rising lake in stride. Many took the opportunity to make summer pilgrimages back to their ancestral homes in northern Florida and Georgia. In the fall the rains slacked off and their fields dried out, allowing them to prepare the land, repair fences, and plant.

The years between the opening up of the canals and the high demand for fresh produce during World War I had been exceptionally dry years—perfect years for bringing in record crops. While dry years are the bane of most farmers, in the Everglades they were a blessing. Even during the dry years, a heavy summer rain would raise the lake a foot in a few hours. In the Everglades with water never more than three feet from any farmer's hoe, too little was seldom a problem, whereas too much created havoc.

Lake-bottom farming carried a high risk. A farmer could be wiped out overnight by frost, floods, or rabbits. There were rabbits everywhere, lobbing across fields, hiding behind every elderbush and under the custard apple forests.

"Our bean rows weren't very long," Dick LeFils, an early pioneer lamented. "They had water at one end, rabbits at the other, and frost in the middle."

But it was the flooding that discouraged farmers. Every rainy season, at the arrival of the first storms, the shoreline that had retreated a hundred yards or two would creep back. It covered recently planted fields, crawled under houses and over pastures. It was a cycle, part of nature's grand design. Farmers in those parts soon learned what farmers have learned the world over: plant with the cycle. The Everglades farmers would pray for dry spells, while they'd curse the politicians for not completely draining the Everglades. Most recognized that draining alone would not protect their fields. A barrier was needed to protect them from high lake waters and wind tides. A dike. What the Everglades needed was a dike to tame Lake Okeechobee.

For now dry year followed dry year, and the banks of Lake Okeechobee continued to retreat. Squatters still rushed in and staked the new land at the edge of the lake. The poorest had the best land: the fertile silt lake bottom. Though the Everglades was not a forgiving land, given good weather a farmer could actually watch his crops grow before his eyes. As the shoreline of Lake Okeechobee shrunk, farmer and promoter alike assumed that the draining of the Everglades, the great experiment, had succeeded. Within three years, they would be proven wrong.

Rain was not the only cause of flooding. Shallow lake waters were exceptionally susceptible to wind action. The basin of Lake Okeechobee was like a water-filled saucer. Sustained winds pushed water across the lake, up and over the banks, leaving hundreds of acres under a foot or two of water. During the rainy season, wind-driven water covered the fields for days, if not weeks at a time. The farmers along the southern and eastern shores knew when the wind blew out of the west their fields would flood.

Though on higher ground than the eastern and southern shores, the lake islands were vulnerable to wind tides. Among the first island settlers, the Aunapu family had a general store on the Hillsboro Canal on Bird Island that as often as not was flooded by wind tides. The Lee, the Braddock, and the BeaDer families had built field dikes around their Torry Island farms.

"We had a saying: 'A west wind blows no good,'" said Elizabeth BeaDer.

In time Torry Island was entirely surrounded by a three-foot-high dike and was crisscrossed by field canals and dikes. People walked along paths like sidewalks on top of the dikes. Shallow draft boats plied the ditches. Wind tides are short-lived phenomena, and the waters would rapidly retreat as the wind died down. During the dry season, wind tides were actually welcomed. Farmers regarded these periodic wind tide floods as a cheap form of God-sent irrigation. However, they would have preferred their weather to be more predictable.

Rain, wind, and wind tides dominated Everglades life. For the next six years, the weather would play the Everglades farmer like an accordion. And while a west wind off Lake Okeechobee might not blow any good, it was winds blowing off the coast of Africa that would change life on the islands and in the Everglades forever.

CHAPTER THREE
NOAH'S CURSE

The Flood Years

Water, the universal solvent, the very building block of life sure can be a pain in the ass sometimes.

—Carl Monet

WEST PALM BEACH

On the other side of the county, a scant forty miles but one universe away from Belle Glade, was storied Palm Beach. The slug-shaped island nestled up against the Atlantic Ocean was the winter residence of many of America's wealthiest people. Names like Stotesbury, Phipps, and Singer, the cream of Philadelphia, Baltimore, and New York society—or at least the most moneyed—flocked each winter to their newfound paradise. Few remembered that just forty years before Palm Beach was a jungle-covered spit of land, a sandy barrier island, home to a half dozen farmers and ten thousand coconut palm trees.

This idyllic Eden was changed literally overnight by a visit from industrialist Henry Morrison Flagler. Flagler had made his millions as a partner in Standard Oil. He was John D. Rockefeller's right-hand man and owned, aside from a large position in Standard Oil, a number of luxury hotels and the Florida East Coast Railroad. He was very familiar with Florida. His San Augustine hotel was Florida's most luxurious hotel, but he was looking for something else: a place he could call his own, where he could reign and rule as in his own duchy. As he walked through the coconut groves of Palm Beach, kicking sand out of his shoes, he knew exactly what this island paradise needed—a first-class hotel to house the rich and a railroad to transport them.

"It occurred to me very strongly, " Flagler said, "that someone with sufficient means ought to provide accommodations for that class of people who are not sick, but who come here to enjoy the climate, have plenty of money, but could find no satisfactory way of spending it."

Florida up to that time was a haven for the infirm no longer able to cope with the cold northern winters. Many of the people who would change Florida came for the curative powers, realized or imagined, that the "Fountain of Youth" state offered. But Flagler was not sick. He was rich. With an iron will and a disposable income of millions of dollars, Flagler built both his railroad and his hotel in record time. The Royal Poinciana Hotel was, arguably, the world's most magnificent hotel. Reaching eight stories high, it was touted as the planet's largest wood structure. Built on Lake Worth, it faced west, and the spectacular sunsets over the water drew wealthy people who, in turn, were followed by the superrich to whom even Flagler's magnificent hotel was not up to their elevated standards. They built hundred-room cottages along the ocean, competing with each other in grandeur and exclusivity. To the world, Palm Beach meant money, big money; money so big that not only did it not have to work, it did not have to think.

It was the dawn of the Roaring Twenties, and even staid Palm Beach was changing. Old money was being replaced by new money. A road made its way through the north-end jungle of the island. Tourists traveled in two-seat carts pedaled by "Negroes" called "Afro-mobiles" that would soon be replaced by automobiles. A beach censor still roamed the beaches checking the decency of women's bathing suits and stockings. Within a year he'd be out of a job. Even the majestic Royal Poinciana had been supplanted. People preferred the newer Breakers Hotel and its oceanfront beaches. But the changes in Palm Beach paled in comparison to the hustle and bustle in West Palm Beach directly across the wide, formerly freshwater Lake Worth.

Designed by Flagler to house "the help" for Palm Beach, West Palm Beach was always a working person's town. There lived the maids and butlers for the hotel and the cottages, the day laborers, gardeners, train porters, construction workers, police and firemen, those necessary people who were expected to keep out of sight except when needed. However, in 1921 the help was getting uppity. Some of them were actually getting rich. West Palm Beach was in the beginning throes of the Florida real estate boom, with Clematis Street as its center.

On and off of Clematis Street, dozens of real estate offices with hundreds of salesmen peddled lots like monopoly properties. Inside each office there were vague maps hanging on the walls with hurriedly drawn lines delineating lots in subdivisions with melodious sounding names. The more sophisticated operations had models of little towns on tables with painted black paved streets and tiny automobiles, a veritable utopia with one minor defect: much of the land was still underwater. Prospective buyers were given free trips to visit their lots. But these excursions usually ended in a luxury hotel where the buyer was wined and dined until darkness necessitated their rapid return to West Palm Beach, many times without seeing their lot. Still they came and they bought.

Often the salesmen had no offices. They were "binder boys," mostly northerners, who scurried from office to office, waving signed contracts and the 10 percent "binder." Most of these contracts would be sold and resold again to people who never saw, and would never see, their purchase. West Palm Beach was in a real estate feeding frenzy.

Some of the speculators and con men stayed in the Royal Poinciana, but most bedded near the action. People buying swamp land lots were not living in Palm Beach. Quite a few buyers knew land, or at least earth. These were the farmers and would-be farmers who flocked from the Midwest, Georgia, and the Carolinas along with a few city folk from New England and New York. While some bought land in the Everglades for the climate, most were attracted by its rich black soil affectionately called muck. People who had never turned over a spade of earth were eager to plunk down a handful of money for the right to dig a plow into that incredibly fertile Everglades muck. Normally sensible, stalwart people threw all caution and common sense to the wind. The rules no longer applied. Into this caldron of money worship and rampant speculation came a man of God.

CALVIN SHIVE

Like his lifelong inspiration Jesus Christ, Calvin H. Shive was a carpenter. He was one of nine brothers, all of whom became carpenters. He excelled at woodwork, framing, and design. Notwithstanding the satisfaction he reaped from his trade, his first real love was preaching. At twenty-two he was ordained into the Christian Church, a fundamentalist Protestant sect much like the Methodist, except they practiced total-immersion baptisms. As a country minister, he had spent many of his days journeying to small towns and isolated communities throughout the Midwest and South to bring the good people the word of God. Many communities had no churches, and he would preach in a neighbor's house or a small country church that had no sitting minister. With his brown hair and bright blue eyes, he was considered good-looking. He was of medium height, but people swore he grew another two feet while preaching.

In 1898, Calvin married Rhoda Jane Lovesce. The newlyweds, fresh with the optimism of the young, traveled to the Indian Territories— today's Oklahoma—as missionaries hoping to convert the natives. Sincere Calvin Shive accompanied by Rhoda on the piano made an attractive couple and a refreshing curiosity for the Native Americans and the recent wave of American settlers.

Oklahoma was already home to thousands of former Floridians who were not tourists nor homesteaders nor oilmen. They were the remnants of the Seminole Indians who had been captured, kidnapped, or bribed to leave Florida in the mid-1800s. Moved to the Indian Territories, they lived under the benign yet watchful eye of the U.S. government. The Seminoles, along with the Cherokees, Creeks, Chickasaws, and Choctaws, made up the Five Civilized Tribes, or nations, that had been resettled in Oklahoma. For the Seminoles, the bleak arid plains, the treeless expanses, and the bitterly cold winters with its arctic winds were all a stark contrast to the warm-water world of their home in the Everglades. They longed for their subtropical homeland, but treaties signed under duress after three long and bitter wars assured that these native Floridians would never return home.

The Indians of Oklahoma had petitioned the United States for their own state. But Congress, many of whose members were former military men who had fought in the Indian Wars, was repelled at the thought of an Indian state. Not only did the government turn down statehood, but it opened much of the Indian Territory lands to white homesteaders. Once again there was a long litany of broken promises made to the Indians by white men.

The Shives had some success with the native population, and they were there three years later when their first child, Miriam, was born, followed two years later by their second daughter, Ruth. By the time Lillian Naomi was born, they had moved to Giliam, Kansas, where Calvin farmed eighty acres. In 1910, they moved to Arkansas, Kansas, where their first and only son was born. He was named Paul after the apostle.

Calvin Shive's ministry would not support a young growing family, so he retired, though he continued to preach for the rest of his life.

"Daddy loved to preach," recounts Lillian Shive Padgett.

To earn a living Calvin dedicated himself to farming and, between plantings, construction. After his crop was in the field, he would seek out carpentry or construction jobs. He moved from job to job, staying in one area two or three months before returning home.

In 1901, oil was discovered at Red Fork Fields near Tulsa, Oklahoma. Overnight the little prairie town tripled in population, then tripled again, as wildcatters, roughnecks, con men, speculators, land men, prostitutes, and out-and-out thieves rushed in. If ever a town needed a bit of piety, Tulsa, Oklahoma, was it.

Carpenters were in high demand. Calvin Shive left his family in Kansas and traveled to the booming city of Tulsa, where between jobs he built a house near Kendal College, the future University of Oklahoma. With the family home finished, Calvin sent for his family.

Rhoda made their clothes and curtains; Calvin built their furniture and accessories. Together they made the Shive house a comfortable home.

When Paul was two years, old he contracted pneumonia. It was winter and his recuperation was slow. The doctor recommended that they take the child to a warmer climate. Calvin's father, Henry Clay Shive, mother, Jill, and brother, Con Shive, were living in the panhandle town of Lynn Haven, Florida, and Calvin and Rhoda bundled Paul tightly, packed up the girls, and drove to Florida. It was the first time Calvin and his family had been in Florida. One of the elder Shive's neighbors was a William Bell. He took Calvin aside and told him that he was headed for West Palm Beach, where he assured Calvin there was a lot of opportunity for a young, hard-working man. There were also opportunities in Oklahoma, Calvin informed Bell, and when Paul recuperated, the Shives returned to Tulsa.

With the attention given to Paul growing up with all girls, it was feared he would become a sissy. Instead, he showed an innate business sense early on. When the ground thawed, Rhoda Shive planted an extensive garden that bloomed through the spring and summer. When the early blooming flowers like sweet peas raised their colorful petals to the sun, Paul, with Lillian's help, gathered up handfuls of posies and made simple bouquet arrangements. Paul took the bouquets downtown and sold them directly to the secretaries. He then shared his earnings with Lillian.

"Many people sold thing on corners, but Paul marched right into the buildings and sold his flowers inside the offices," Lillian said.

Paul was eleven years old.

In March 1921, Tulsa experienced the worst race riot in American history. A vague racial incident in a downtown elevator involving a black man and a white woman escalated into a full-blown riot. Some ten thousand white men and boys descended on what was the most prosperous black community in the United States. Three days later, three hundred black Americans, many World War I veterans, lay dead. Thirty-five city blocks had been burnt to the ground. For Calvin Shive, the incident was a sign that it was time to leave.

Four years before, Calvin's parents had retired to West Palm Beach. They lived in a small two-bedroom frame house on Palm Street across from the Woodlawn Cemetery in south West Palm Beach. In the back, Calvin's brother Con had built a second house on the same lot. Realizing the opportunities presenting themselves in Florida, the senior Shive invited his son to join him.

"There is a real estate boom going on," he told his son. "People are doubling their money in a month, and there seems no end in sight."

Calvin Shive set off with his family for the Sunshine State. Florida was the place to be, the land of opportunity, the last American frontier.

Calvin had gone through one boom in Tulsa and recognized the makings of another in West Palm Beach. It was 1921, and for a retired minister with a family of seven, Florida was the land of opportunity. The optimism of the times was catching. His brother Con was building houses in Palm Beach for the wealthy, and Calvin was asked to join him. It was an alluring idea, starting a family construction business in the middle of a building boom. He was ready to join his brother, he told Rhoda.

Then temptation struck.

Along Clematis Street, all night revelers from after-hours clubs and speakeasies on old Banyan Street crossed with the early-risers seeking out breakfast restaurants, grocery stores, and butcher shops. People bought fresh meat every day since icebox ice melted rapidly in Florida's tropical heat, and refrigerators were still a luxury. A black face in the crowd meant it must be past six o'clock. The Strand movie house on Baynan Street offered the latest Hollywood silent movie starring Rudolph Valentino and Agnes Ayers. Like all theaters of the times, one feature would remain on the marquee for two, sometimes three, months. The daily newsreels brought in repeat customers. While West Palm was a city, most of its inhabitants were farmers a few years removed. People went to bed early and rose in the wee hours. There was no radio or television to distract them at night, though for the hard-core night owl an active red-light district flourished.

Calvin, always an early riser, was on Clematis Street in the West Palm Beach grocery shopping with his father Henry Clay Shive. Model T's lined the street. Parking space was at a premium. The temperature was already in the high seventies, promising a hot day. In front of the grocery store the Shives ran into Bill Bell, their acquaintance from Lynn Haven. Enthusiastically, he exclaimed that there was an incredible opportunity for someone with vision. In an Everglades town called Pahokee, a half day's journey away, was newly drained land so fertile that anyone could grow a cash crop and make a fortune. And it was for sale.

"A farmer like you could make a killing out there," Bell told Calvin.

Those were magic words to a farmer, and the next day Calvin was on the Palm Beach mail boat with Bell to see Pahokee for himself.

THE Palm Beach Canal, the only transportation link between West Palm Beach and Lake Okeechobee, cut a straight line through wetlands, water sloughs, and sawgrass prairies. Running daily from the turning basin near the railroad tracks in Palm Beach, the mail boat took four hours to reach Canal Point on Lake Okeechobee. In 1921, there was little in the way of developed land in between. For the first part of the trip, jungle leaned over the banks of the canal. There were majestic stands of cypress trees that soared to the sky, pines alongside an occasional live oak. Once past Loxahatchee the jungle ended and the cypress trees disappeared. The forest gave way to a prairie of sawgrass that stretched to the horizon. No one said a word as they gawked at the seemingly endless expanse of sawgrass. It was a new world—a wondrous watery world so foreign that the passengers stared in anxious silence.

Bell stepped up and said somewhat reassuringly, "Wait until you see the land around the lake."

There was no other sign of civilization until they reached Connersville, just east of Canal Point. Connersville, the cattle ranch of millionaire and promoter W. J. Conners, was a collection of houses and shacks that served the cowboys and help. Connors was determined to show the world how to farm the Everglades. He set out high-grade beef cattle to graze on sawgrass and pigs to forage in the hummocks. Within four years, all the cattle would be dead, the pigs would escape into the forest, and the ranch would be abandoned.

PAHOKEE was the Seminole name for the Everglades. The promoters had placed the town site on top of a sand ridge that paralleled Lake Okeechobee's eastern shore to the north and ended in the series of lake islands. The ridge was high enough to keep the town above the frequent floods that continued to plague the Everglades even after the canals and the drainage ditches had been completed. While not an eagle's perch, it was the highest point on the eastern shore of Lake Okeechobee. Rising six feet above the surrounding glades, it offered the people who built houses on the west side an expansive view of Lake Okeechobee.

The land company had a real estate office in the fledgling town of Pahokee. It had divided land around Pahokee into five- and ten-acre lots. Calvin and Rhoda found a five-acre lot with a clapboard house on stilts in one corner that was ready to occupy, a real estate agent assured Calvin. Although the area was isolated, the real estate man showed Calvin a map of the town with hundreds of lots laid out in neat rows that allegedly had been sold to people eager to build their dream house. As a bonus, along with their five-acre lot, the Shives would receive a lot in town.

The crowning point was a trip to a working farm. The real estate man dug his hands into the rich, recently plowed black soil and balled up a fist full of caked muck. Calvin sniffed at the rich and fertile earth and smelled opportunity. Other fields had vegetables and fruit trees. This had to be how the Garden of Eden began, Calvin thought.

"One look at the rich black soil and those vegetables it produced, and he went crazy," Lillian Padgett recalled eighty years later. "He just had to have some of that land."

Calvin Shive, ex-minister of the Christian Church and lately of Tulsa, Oklahoma, had found his new calling, and Bell's real estate broker had a new binder.

Anxious to begin his new life as an Everglades farmer, Calvin Shive returned to West Palm Beach, packed up his family, and in a week was back on board the Palm Beach mail boat for Pahokee.

ARRIVING at the farmhouse, Lillian Padgett could only stare in disbelief. Pahokee was an isolated area situated at the edge of the Everglades. This swampland was to be her home? Raised in Tulsa, she was a city girl. Pahokee was as foreign as the young girl could imagine with the omnipresent odor of dank muck, the exotic night sounds, and the bugs and clouds of insects humming in a deep monotone. At night the echoing bark of old bull alligators frightened her so she couldn't sleep. On the other side of the gauze netting draped over the bed, a faint two feet from her ears, thousands of blood-crazed mosquitoes buzzed. If one got into the net, it took a while to find it and kill it against the netting. She learned to use a lit candle under the netting to attract the offending insect. Whoever said "Never let small things bother you" had never slept in a room with a mosquito.

She was fourteen. At that age girls were looking for a boyfriend, dating, choosing a husband, and settling down with a family. How could she exist out there where there were no boys, no girlfriends? They were alone in a wilderness.

"All of that nature scared me," she related later.

Twelve-year-old Paul, on the other hand, loved the farm. Everywhere he turned there was wonderment. Exotic animals scurried about, birds flooded the sky, and strange new trees abounded. Pahokee was so different from Tulsa. His mother warned him about snakes, and most people instinctively killed every snake they saw. But one of the old-timers showed Paul those that were poisonous and pointed out those snakes that killed rats and other varmints. The rat snakes, especially the large, black ones, he said, should be left in rafters. They were better at ratting than a tomcat.

The Shive farmhouse, a typical wood-plank house, had one large room that served as a living room, a dining area, and a bedroom for the children. Calvin and Rhoda slept on the screened porch. It was placed on the edge of the five acres near a small drainage canal lined with a two-foot bank that they used as a walking path during the rains.

After a year, Calvin built the family a house in Pahokee on the side of the ridge facing Lake Okeechobee, and they moved into town. On the opposite side of the ridge was Noble Padgett's house. The Everglades pioneer's house was a rarity. It had two cupolas raised above the roof, one in the front and one in the back. For years it remained the largest house in Pahokee.

The Shives found the lake people to be rather clannish, and Lillian, the city girl from Oklahoma, felt like an outsider.

"I did not have my accent then, and they all spoke southern," Lillian recalled.

The Shive family liked to read, but books were scarce in Pahokee. Calvin did manage to bring his prized copy of the *Encyclopaedia Britannica*. During the school year, the other children would visit Lillian to use the encyclopedia. There were nights when the entire high school seemed to be studying on the porch.

Her popularity improved.

The first year Lillian attended the two-room schoolhouse in Pahokee. The following year an agricultural high school was constructed in Canal Point, and the Pahokee children were bused three miles along a winding road that ran along the sand ridge from Canal Point to Pahokee. There were few cars or trucks in the first years. The old sand road was used mostly for walking.

Each morning fifteen students would board the open bus to Canal Point. Lillian was in the ninth grade. The road to Canal Point crossed a ditch that drained the Stuckey family's farm into Lake Okeechobee. Everyone called it Stuckey's Ditch. Sometimes when a northwestern wind was blowing, it would push the lake up over the ditch and water would cover the road. More than once Lillian and the other students had to take off their shoes. After the boys rolled up their pants, all the children pushed the bus through the knee-deep water. For the next four years, knee-deep water became very familiar to Lillian Shive and the rest of the Everglades pioneers.

WORLD War I was over, and the doughboys fresh from the fields of Flanders and the fleshpots of France were arriving home to a changed America. These were not the wide-eyed hayseeds sent over to save the world for democracy. These were hardened veterans who had seen unspeakable horrors that they'd take to their graves. They were a silent generation who never complained but who were not satisfied with a return to the status quo. The found they were not alone; the United States was on the move. People utilizing newfound mobility packed up Model T's and hit the road in astounding numbers. There was anxiousness, an unsettling disquiet in America, as if the old rules no longer applied. Hemlines rose, illegal drinking was the norm, and immigrants with odd-sounding names, olive complexions, and pungent smells wafting from their kitchens fanned out from core city ghettos into the suburbs and country. Anyone with a new idea could cash in on the booming stock market with multiple returns. Change was in the air—big change.

With American frontiers settled, for the first time people in the country felt hemmed in. The American dream of staking out a claim in wild territories had ended everywhere but in the Everglades.

THE end of the Great War coincided with the end of South Florida's dry-weather cycle. That year, after a long dry winter, the rains returned. The summer rains of 1920 surprised even the hardiest lake-bottom farmer who had grown accustomed to floods. Water lay on the land for months, forcing settlers to move about in boats. Though they did not realize it, the Everglades farmers had been lucky, but now they were in another cycle—a wet cycle. Many of the squatters along the lakefront packed up and left as the lake waters drowned their farms.

In December, in the middle of the winter planting season, a week-long northwestern wind tide blew the lake along a continuous front up and over the bottomland along the eastern and southern shore, drowning crops and ruining farmers that had remained. Lake-bottom and sawgrass farmers were not the only victims of the rains and wind tides. Sugarcane fields at Moore Haven also fell victim to the floods. With the sugarcane drowned and rotting in the fields, the Moore Haven sugar mill, the first in the Everglades, closed its doors.

For those who survived the December wind tide and were able to replant, the spring of 1921 was a dry and profitable season. The bottom squatters returned to farm the lake's edges, cautiously at first, then with abandon they planted farther and farther out into the retreating lake, and another year of record crops was brought in.

THE MARTINS

The rains had left Loney Martin's house stranded. His only mode of transportation was his small skiff. But at least he was not alone. The arrival of his sister and her husband not only provided a reprieve from his solitude but also added much-needed help. The Martins always worked together as a clan. When threatened by nature or man, they closed ranks.

One of the few families that survived the 1920 rains was the tenacious Martins, and when the water retreated in November, they were ready to plant anew. When Henry had visited his brother and sister, a new crop was in the ground and lush green bean stalks sprouted above gleaming black soil. The rains of 1920 had been forgotten.

But the weather was not finished with the Everglade farmers. Planting in the rich muck, once considered a sure thing, was now a gamble, pervaded with risk and uncertainty. But farmers have short memories, and the rich black muck made many a farmer an instant amnesiac.

On the return trip home, visions of black soil, bumper crops, and free land danced in Henry Martin's head. Here was an opportunity to be seized. First, he knew, he had to convince Bessie Mae. She'd be concerned and, like most women, cautious of such a radical move. In West Frostproof, they had a small but comfortable house, a working farm, and a citrus grove that in a few years would be producing fair if not spectacular crops. Riding across the last miles through Polk County to the farm, Henry could only compare the poor sandy soil of Frostproof with the jet-black muck of the Everglades. The sandy land around Frostproof produced just enough to make farming worthwhile, and then only if prices were strong. Besides, in spite of Frostproof's name, a freeze like the killer frost of 1917 could destroy all their orange trees overnight.

However, images of the black Everglades muck and the crops it produced worked on Henry's mind like an opiate. He had to have some.

BESSIE Mae knew before Henry said a word that they would be moving. She saw it in his expressive eyes that told her what he was thinking before he spoke. She listened attentively as Henry described the opportunities in the Everglades. She trusted him. He was her husband and a good provider. The family never wanted for anything. If Henry felt determined, Bessie Mae would follow her man to the Everglades. Not to do so was unthinkable. Wedding vows were forever. Divorce was rare, a moral disgrace in the eyes of most Americans.

Many of the pioneers were on their second or third spouse. Not by divorce but by death they did part. Farming was a dangerous occupation. Husbands were killed on the job, in the fields, or while traveling. While men tended to die away from the house, women died in bed—in childbirth. But it was not an equal battle, as the many gravestones of wives in family plots attested.

Childbirth was not far from Bessie Mae's mind. She was a fertile woman and proud of it. Pregnancies were welcomed but feared. A women's fertility and the fruitfulness of the field were part of the farming family ecosystem. A fertile woman was a sign of a fertile field. A large family was wealth, and fertile Bessie Mae was again expecting.

Children, while not quite a commodity, had value. The more children a couple had, the more hands there were to help farm, and large hard-working families made the most money. A pioneer woman's fertility was an integral cornerstone to the family's prosperity.

"It was necessary for all who could do so to work on the land," Mutt Thomas explained. "The children worked as soon as they were big enough and when they were not in school. In those days the family with the most kids had the best farm. My mother worked beside my father as she had done in North Florida. You cleared the land by hand, and the more land you cleared, the bigger your farm. The more help a family had, the more you grew."

Everglades women were fertile, and their innate fertility was one of the reasons why so many young mothers died the night of September 16, 1928.

In the end, Bessie Mae would follow her man. She loved her tall, lanky husband with his dark serious eyes, hard hands, and quick smile, and Henry Martin openly reciprocated that love. They planned to move in two years; first they had to "prove up," or legalize, their homestead. Once the farm was proved up and they had a negotiable title, they could then sell it and with the money grubstake their Everglades land. But before the Martins were able to prove up their homestead, events in the Everglades changed their plans.

STRICKEN by a sudden illness, Henry's brother-in-law Jimmy Griffith suddenly died in 1921, leaving his wife, Bernie, a young widow, alone in the Everglades. With no interest in remaining in the Everglades, she sold Henry her squatter's rights to the land and her one-room lakefront house. That fall Henry Martin packed his tools and as many implements as he could carry and left for the Everglades, leaving Bessie Mae, who was pregnant with Shelly Ernestine, to watch over the farm and the children. He set himself up in his sister's abandoned house and planted green beans for what he hoped would be a quick cash crop along with cabbage, onions, and tomatoes for personal consumption or barter.

Henry Martin's luck held; the winter of 1921–1922 was a dry year. The lakeshore retreated back to the prerain boundaries, then even farther out. While other farmers in the United States were suffering from the lack of rain, in the damp fertile lake bottom vegetables grew well—huge, in fact. Heads of cabbage grew three to four feet across; two-pound tomatoes hung in bunches and threatened to break away from their stems. They had to be carefully tied to stakes. The few acres Henry planted brought in a large crop.

In spring 1922, with the proceeds from the sale of the crop in his pocket, Henry began improvements on the house. Like many pioneers, his sister had built a large one-room house. The kitchen, the living room, and the bedrooms were one large open area. Even though the house was large enough to accommodate his family of nine, Henry would need another room for the children. For the children he built a long bedroom that ran the entire side of the house, a storage room for tools and supplies, and a wide porch across the front facing the lake and its spectacular sunsets.

He plowed the lake bottom as far as he could up to the lake edge. It was arduous work, but he could count on help from Loney, since the Martins, as did all pioneer families, worked in teams. If a job needed to be done at Loney's house, Henry would help, and Loney in turn helped Henry clear and plow his land.

From the front porch of the house, Henry Martin could eye his fields. Stretching out before him to the lake were neat rows of freshly plowed black soil that shimmered like anthracite coal extending to the dark blue lake waters sparkling in the midday sun. The small round-bottomed boat he called *Tadpole* was beached on the muddy shore. On either side at the lake edge grew stunted elderbushes and tall grasses that had rooted in soils dry enough to grow in but too wet to farm. Maybe next year, if the lake cooperated, that land too would be dry enough to clear and farm. More land meant larger crops. For a hard-working person like Henry, the Everglades was the land of opportunity.

THE rains that summer came early and hard. Fields next to the lake began to fill with water as the lake stretched its greedy fingers along Henry's rows of green beans and then covered them. Each day the fingers crept closer to the house until they surrounded it. It rained through the fall, and the expected winter reprieve never materialized. The rains refused to stop, and again the lake rose. Many farmers wondered whether the idea of reclaimed Everglades lands was nothing but a myth.

Henry Martin waited for the rains to stop. They didn't. The winter of 1922 was one of the wettest winters on record. For three months it rained continually. Lake Okeechobee rose fourteen feet. Visitors in motorboats had no problem motoring up to his front door. From his front porch, Henry could look down through three feet of water to the lake bottom that only a few months before had been his plowed fields.

IN January 1923, Bessie Mae and their seven children arrived by train at Moore Haven. They took the mail boat across the lake to South Bay,

where Henry was waiting for them with the *Tadpole*. Evening had settled
on the lake by the time the mail boat arrived. Henry packed up his family in the *Tadpole* and in the bow hung a lantern that cast an eerie glow
across the water. Except for crossing the dredged canal, the water was
never more than four feet deep. The children huddled in the unstable little boat. Every night sound echoed across the water, and off in the edge
of the light more than one pair of animal eyes glowed back, watching
them before disappearing without a sound beneath the water.

The anxious children, frightened and excited, almost capsized the little
Tadpole.

"Be still," Henry yelled as the boat rocked to one side. "Do you-all want
a whipping?"

They poled past Uncle Loney Martin's house at the head of a shallow
dead river to their new home where Henry tied the *Tadpole* to the front
porch and helped Bessie and the children off the skiff. Bessie Mae must
have wondered what her husband had gotten them into. Like the Ne-
olithic lake dwellers in Switzerland, they lived in a poled house perched
a few feet above water level. They had to leave the house in a boat and
walk along rickety raised walks that were strung like scaffolding in front
of stores down the sides of streets in town. The scaffolding was even used
for trips to the outhouse.

"Don't worry, now," Henry told the family. "Come November the water will fall."

Bessie Mae was not so sure.

If Bessie Mae was disappointed or shocked, she did not let it show. She
was a true pioneer woman—stoic, accustomed to deprivation. However
poor they might have been, they did not have to live poorly. The day after she arrived, Bessie Mae set about fixing up the house. The floorboards
of the original house were well worn. She had them ripped up and turned
over so that the smoother side was up. The cracks in the floor and walls
were patched to better keep out mosquitoes.

That spring Henry had to plant something or, like many of the other
farmers, leave. Until the waters receded, farming the land he had bought
was impossible. Taking the *Tadpole*, he searched up the ends of the dead
rivers until he found small drier areas. They were covered in tough elderbushes and custard apple tree forests blanketed with massive growths of
moonvine. By hand the Martins cleared the growth with machetes and
axes. The vines had to be cut, pulled down off the trees, rolled up in bun-
dles, and burned. There were also the ever-present poisonous wampee
plants that gave a terrible burning sensation if touched. It was difficult
work in which the entire family participated. They had no mules or
horses. The small areas had to be cut, cleared, hoed, plowed, and seeded

by hand. They cleared one- or two-acre plots called patches. Henry Martin harbored the hope that he would be granted homestead rights to the land he was clearing. But in reality the Martins were simple squatters, and as squatters they would never have clear title to their land.

EVERY other Sunday Henry went into Belle Glade to catch up on the local gossip and farming news, buy a day-old paper, and scout for a store site. He was determined that when the family brought in two more good crops, he was going to open up a grocery–dry goods store like he had in West Frostproof. Maybe not this year, but surely the next. He was a man of the land and liked farming, but it was proving too risky even for Henry Martin.

THE Martin family's arduous labors paid off when the first crop of vegetables came in. Despite the high water that had crippled many other farmers, the Martins prospered with their crops. Because much of the Everglades land was under water, the price of vegetables was high. Henry Martin experimented with other crops such as romaine, lettuce, and tomatoes, but green beans continued to be the cash crop.

After breakfast each morning except Sunday, Henry would pack the family into the *Tadpole* and pole to the cleared patches. Together the Martins would work, weed, and build small dikes around the plots. Bessie Mae prepared lunch at the patches, though more often than not Henry would do the cooking. He liked to cook. Bessie Mae would just as soon work the fields, tend to the "youngins," and leave the kitchen to her husband.

Many times the rest of the Martin clan would join them. Farming was an extended family effort, and the entire Martin family worked on the cultivated patches out in the Everglades. Uncle Loney's and Aunt Grace's families would join Henry's family there. Together they made a success of each other's farm.

When there was no work to be done, the children played hide and seek in the fields. They dove off the front porch and swam around the house, sometimes swimming a couple of hundred yards to a large cypress tree where they could stand waist-deep on its knees. Thelma usually stayed behind because she was the only one who did not swim well. Raymond Thaddeus was a strong swimmer, and against his mother's wishes he would swim out to the old skinning benches in the lake.

All the girls except Annie Mae were tomboys. They fished, hunted rabbits, chased the hounds, and kept up with the boys.

As Nancy Martin related to Ruth Irvin, a local Belle Glade historian, "You might say we lived in a natural wonderland. Wild hogs were plentiful until the thirties. There were deer, and the men and boys went out hunting them in the sawgrass. The ducks were so plentiful, you wouldn't believe it unless you could have seen the sky black with them. They covered the lake. We ate lots of them. Wild geese came in the winter. The lake had every kind of fish, and all of us liked to fish.

"We ate lots of rabbit as they were plentiful, often catching five or six rabbits at one time. The custard apples could be pulled off the tree when dead ripe, leaving the center still hanging on the tree. This gave off a fragrant perfume that one could smell a long way off. We liked to eat the ripe custard apples, although there wasn't much to them."

From the time they could walk, all the children were expected to assist with the farm. Thelma, not yet seven years old, helped around the house and in the fields. Unable to reach the sink, she washed the breakfast and dinner dishes standing on a chair. The boys tended to the fences and outbuildings, and although amenities were scarce, food was not. Annie Mae and Nancy would rise at four in the morning, start the fire, and prepare breakfast, after which they went outside and, while it was still dark, milked cows before going off to school.

All the children walked to school along the dike to South Bay. Before there was a bridge across the North New River Canal, they had to gingerly cross along the tops of the locks. A plank walk led from the canal to the schoolhouse to keep their feet dry in the rainy season.

"The little kids had to step off the walkway, sometimes in the mud, when the big kids came along, or the big kids would push them off," Nancy Martin remembered.

A universal truth, no matter where, is that children will be children.

EVEN with the high waters, the rich Everglades soil fed its people. Food was never a problem there—the heat, humidity, and the mosquitoes were. The Martins' house had no screens on its windows; the fine mesh needed to keep out the mosquitoes and flies was too expensive. At night they closed the heavy wooden shutters against incessant swarms of mosquitoes and night bugs. Screens were useless against "no-see-'ems." These tiny swarming pests could pass through the tightest mesh screen. Only painting the screen with an odorous, sticky, used-oil-base solution would prevent the invisible pest from invading a house.

The mosquitoes were at their worst a couple weeks after the first summer rains. Pools of stagnant water dotted the land, especially under the shade of dense growth—perfect breeding spots for mosquitoes. And breed they did. Millions of millions of the buzzing, biting, blood-sucking insects would take to the air at the first sign of dark.

At times the clouds of insects were so thick the Martins had to retreat and shut themselves up inside suffocating houses. Smoky smudge pots were lit inside the houses to repel the mosquitoes that got by the boarded-up windows and closed doors. They filled the houses with an acrid, sticky smoke. Outside the mosquitoes were so bad at times that smoky fires were set at night to drive them away from farm animals. Even so, the animals suffered. The mosquitoes bit the horses and mules, and the especially nasty yellow gnats would fly into their eyes and noses. Frustrated farmers watched as their animals ran around their corrals in a vain attempt to flee the insects. The Martins lost their last "jack"—a jackass—to insects. A mass of night gnats had flown into his nose, blocked his nasal passage, and asphyxiated him.

If more of the Everglades were drained, then there wouldn't be so many mosquitoes and there'd be more land for the farmers. What the Everglades needed was water control—a dike to keep wind tides off the fields, a dike to hold water in dry season for irrigation. In a single voice the Everglades settlers lobbied loudly for a dike until even distant Tallahassee heard the clamor. Drain the Everglades! Build a dike!

CHAPTER 4
THE GREAT WALL OF THE EVERGLADES

Good fences make good neighbors.

—Robert Frost

Aside from hard work, hunting, fishing, and watching sunsets, there was scant entertainment in the Everglades. With no moviehouses and few radios, the Everglades men found little to do at night except drink or gamble. Each town had one or more stores where weekend poker games flourished in the back room. Gambling was not only illegal in this era of Prohibition and temperance, but also, in polite circles, frowned upon. Still games of chance were played in the open. Along 5th Street one block west of 4th Street, the dividing line between white Belle Glade and "colored town," games of chance and gambling bars thrived in the laissez-faire atmosphere of the Everglades. Sheriff Clarence Everett knew who was running each gaming house but seldom interfered unless the peace was physically broken.

Henry Martin, like most pioneers, was a born gambler. He loved the chance to double it all. As a farmer, each day he made the ultimate wager—he bet against Mother Nature. Whimsical weather, funguses, and plagues of insects conspired to ruin a farmer. Of course, when Mother Nature cooperated, the return was bountiful.

During one prolonged dry period, a farmer who had planted green beans in a field north of Chosen told Henry that he was about to lose everything he owned. If it didn't rain this week, he'd have to leave

Belle Glade. They both knew the extended forecast called for continued drought.

Henry listened intently and then asked, "How much do you want for it?"

"Four hundred dollars," the man said. "That would be enough to pay my people and replant."

Henry nodded, went into the small back room, opened up his safe, and counted out four hundred dollars in cash and handed it the man. No receipt, no lawyer, no witness, only a quick handshake and the deal was done. Henry Martin had bought a field of withering green beans sight unseen. It was the type of deal Henry loved, though he was not about to mention it to Bessie Mae, at least not just yet.

Three nights later it rained, and the parched fields of stunted green beans bloomed. Henry eventually brought in the crop at $1,500. Henry's luck had held. The Martins, he could be forgiven if he thought, were blessed. At least their stars shone brightly.

Henry's true gambling love was cards. He reveled in the tension of the draw, the bluff, and the call—the moment of truth. Unfortunately, he was not a good card player. Even with his poker face and sense of bluff, he was prone to taking low-percentage draws, a fact known by most of the card players in South Bay and Belle Glade.

Henry Martin was a man of his time. While the times might not have been simpler, they were clearer, the rules transparent. From the moment they were born, men and women had roles to play. Men provided and protected, while women prepared and populated. The rules of life had been set, and if not quite biblical in origin, they had been around long enough to seem immutable. A strict man, Henry had a clear-cut outlook on life. There was right and there was wrong; there was good and bad, black and white. Oaths, honor, and a person's word were sacrosanct. Honor was worn on a man's chest like a medal. For the poor, honor was their only asset. Though surrounded by poverty, houses were left unlocked. Robbery and home invasion were rarities because theft was dealt with severely. Laws were to be lived by and obeyed. Except for a band or two of Robin Hood–like outlaws and moonshiners, criminals were ostracized. Known lawbreakers were routinely chased out of town by the local sheriff. There was no probable cause. Rights were relative.

That he might be wrong rarely occurred to Henry Martin. He was not quick to say he was mistaken or sorry. He knew his place in life, and he expected others to know theirs. Growing up in southern Florida, he was a strict segregationist, though he did not abide the abuse many whites visited on the local blacks. A black man considered himself fortunate if he worked for Henry Martin. He had to work hard, but he knew he'd be paid and given decent treatment. It was well known in town that you did not harass one of "Henry's niggers." If Henry got word that anyone, white or black, bothered one of his black workers without provocation, that person could expect a visit and a terse warning. Henry understood that to keep good people, black or white, they had to be treated right.

With the children, he was a strict disciplinarian, firmly believing in "spare the rod, spoil the child." Frontier children grew up fast. At fourteen, a boy was a young man; a girl at thirteen, a woman. Henry and Bessie Mae's young girls were growing up. Annie Mae, being the oldest, was the first to attract the attention of the local boys. Cautiously the youthful suitors would come by the Martin house, especially if they knew Henry was away. They still had to slyly contend with Bessie Mae and Raymond, but at the first hint that Henry Martin was returning home they would scatter like rabbits. Woe be to any young man caught near one of his daughters alone. Henry's blood would boil if anyone even thought of dishonoring one of his women. He was a physically imposing man who knew how to defend himself. While not a man who looked for trouble, the few times he had to take care of himself physically, Henry Martin came out the better. He was a man who defended his family, his farm, and his people.

He understood better than most the temptations of youth, and like most fathers, he was determined to marry his daughters off young before they had time to dishonor the family. Henry Martin did not want one of his daughters becoming a "sawgrass widow."

True to his nature, when planting season came around Henry was ready to reinvest his entire profit and expand the next crop. Ready, that is, if it would start raining. The way each season developed, it looked like it would remain dry forever. The old-timers remained skeptical. They reminisced about the old days with month-long storms and high winds. But it was different now. The Everglades had changed. To the lake-bottom farmers, with the draining of the Everglades, the climate seemed to have gotten dryer.

FOR ten thousand years, the Everglades have been a delicate balance of water and earth. Droughts and floods were the Scylla and Charybdis of the Everglades farmer. Everglades floods were not torrential, bank-breaching deluges. Wind tides were just that—tidelike rises of lake water pushed out of the basin by wind. The water crept slowly and quietly over the land. Most floods were only a foot or two deep, at times reaching halfway up the pilings of the houses—hardly biblical in scope, though they could leave enough water sitting on the land to ruin a crop, but not enough to stop daily human activity. During floods, the bottomland farmers became like Stone Age lake dwellers with their forlorn shacks perched precariously on stilts surrounded by water. Boats were not alternative transportation but necessities. Whether a large diesel inboard, a ten-foot skiff, or a dugout canoe, everyone had a boat. With no roads and the paths mired in muck for much of the year, they were the only communication with the outside world.

In late spring 1922, it began to rain. The summer thunderstorms came early. They came more frequently; they came morning and night. The rains that season were serious. The heavens ripped open and dropped a proverbial forty days and nights of continuous rain, then threw in an additional thirty days in case they missed anything. Lacking an ark, the animals were forced to forage in belly-high water and slept on the raised canal dikes. For the Everglades, it was the year of no sun. In the flat plains of the Everglades the rainwater had nowhere to go. It accumulated where it fell. When the wind began to blow out of the west, the wind tides added the lake's water to the rain's. Together they conspired to cover hundreds of square miles of the Everglades.

The Everglades farmers were patient. With stoic resignation, they would wait for the rains to stop, or the wind to cease blowing and the water to retreat before continuing where they had left off. But the floods of 1922 sent even the hardiest muck rat scurrying for dry land. Scores of families, broken by nature's onslaught, packed up their worldly possessions and left.

Where many saw tragedy, Henry Martin saw opportunity. Even underwater, cleared, abandoned land had value. He knew if he could only hold out until the water receded, he might be able to set a claim on some of that land. If only the Martin luck would rear its head once more.

WITH the constant threat of flooding, pioneers learned early on to build their houses on stilts four feet above the ground. The better-built homes had stilts that reached down some twelve feet below the surface and were anchored to the top of the marl bedrock.

There was a delicate balance between a good rainy season necessary for a good crop and a rainy season that raised the lake level and flooded crops out. Worse was a dry summer.

In a prolonged dry season, the soil, sun-baked hard, would kill their crops, leaving dried stalks as kindling. Though water was never more than a few feet below any field, few farmers had the capital to purchase pumps and irrigation equipment. They had to rely on rain.

During the twenties, the odd years were drought years. Drought did more than destroy crops—it brought the muck fires. Rich organic muck, when dried, burns like peat, and once muck fires start, they burn like an underground coal fire and are extremely hard to extinguish. Unless drowned by a week-long soil-soaking rain, most muck fires burn until they run out of fuel.

Taking advantage of the dry season, farmers clearing land burned fallen custard apple forests, piles of ripped-up sawgrass, and their fields before plowing. Often the fires spread across to the sawgrass. If the land was too dry, the muck caught fire. In a few hours a fire could burn the muck down to bedrock. At times dozens of sawgrass fires burned, sending up a sheet of black smoke so thick that travel became impossible. The air filled with thick choking smoke. Visibility was reduced to zero. Roads were closed; canal navigation slowed as if in a fog.

The occasional thunderstorms were no relief. Instead of soil-soaking rain, they brought lightning that set off more sawgrass fires.

A muck fire is exceptionally grievous. After a fire, a forest will eventually grow back, if a city block burns it can be rebuilt, but once muck is burned, like oil or coal, it is gone forever. A muck fire leaves a sterile ash where nothing will grow. Once muck ashes moisten, they form a cement-hard substance. Hundreds of acres of land burned down two to three feet, leaves a bare limestone scar on the surface. It was not until decades later than Henry's days that the importance of keeping water levels high to preserve the muck became apparent. Unfortunately, by that time thousands of acres of prime fertile soil had been burnt or blown away.

Everglades muck had a third enemy—oxidation. Once land was cleared of sawgrass and custard apple trees and the soil exposed to the elements, the dry peatlike muck started to oxidize and blow away. This phenomenon was noted early on by Disston's engineers in the Kissimmee River Basin. Each year close to an inch of rich topsoil disappeared. Areas where the muck was a few feet deep became unsuited for agriculture in a short time. Not only was the Everglades land losing precious fertile soil; its land level was sinking.

SEBRING FARMS

Not all Everglades farmers were poor. True, for the most part, only people with nothing to lose would risk their savings, their health, and even their lives in a strange, isolated, dangerous land. However, the rich soil of the Everglades did attract a few well-off people with dreams of their own. These were the entrepreneurs with sufficient capital and vision. The potential of the Everglades was limited only by the fertility of their imagination. The coal-black muck had that effect on men's minds—like gold to the conquistadors.

One such visionary was H. Orvel Sebring, son of porcelain producer George Sebring, founder of Sebring, Ohio, and Sebring, Florida. George Sebring was enthralled by new technology and gadgets. The new automobile, he recognized, would change the face of America. During a winter stay at Daytona Beach, he fell under Florida's tropic spell. He actively participated in the automobile races along the hard sand beaches. When he founded his town of Sebring, sixty miles north of Lake Okeechobee, he made plans for a speedway that became the future home of the Sebring twelve-hour endurance automobile race.

Orvel, like his father, had a vision of opening new lands using advanced techniques. Where oranges and cattle dominated the land around the town of Sebring, Orvel dreamt of avocados growing on Lake Okeechobee, long rows of large avocado trees filled with plump, green, pear-shaped fruit rooted deep in that black soil.

Sebring bought a parcel of land near Miami Locks in 1918 from Sewell, one of first pioneers to settle on Lake Okeechobee's south shore. Carrying on the family tradition, Orvel renamed his land Sebring Farms. Orvel Sebring set out to develop the largest avocado plantation in the United States. As envisioned, it would produce thousands of crates of the fruit for the northern market. The price of avocados was high enough to warrant the three-year wait before the trees matured and produced a sufficient amount of fruit to justify shipping costs. With no roads available, he dug a canal from South Bay so as to have his own direct access to the large transportation canals.

Like bananas, avocados were considered an exotic fruit. High in vitamin C, the rich avocado flesh had more protein per pound than beef. Unfortunately, they had one major drawback: they were not hardy and were highly sensitive to frost. But the Everglades were touted as frost-free. Conveniently forgotten was the big freeze of 1917.

Sebring brought in the first tractors to be seen in the Everglades. He also built the first pumps to drain the land, large pumps driven by bulky steam engines whose boilers were fed a steady supply of Florida hardwood pine brought in by boat from Fort Myers. The local custard apple and elderberry bushes had too low a BTU-rating to produce a high enough temperature for a good head of steam.

In the end it wasn't the frost that crushed H. Orvel Sebring's dream in the Everglades; it was water. The rains of 1922 were egalitarian; they wiped out the wealthy farmer as well as the poor. Sebring was not the only farmer to abandon his farm after 1922. So many farmers left the Everglades that for the first time since the Seminoles were expelled, the population of the Everglades declined.

CHARLES THOMAS

The rains would affect another family destined to make an impact on the Everglades. While the Shives took the Palm Beach Canal mail boat to Pahokee, and Henry Martin built an addition to his recently acquired farmhouse, another family settled on Ritta Island. At the urging of his brother Richard Mays Thomas, Charles Edward Thomas with his wife, Susan Indiana, and their four children, two sons and two daughters, left northern Florida for the Everglades. A born-and-bred cracker, Charles gave up his farm in Madison, Florida, when the prices of peanuts and cotton fell after the Great War.

Richard Mays, an early pioneer, first came to Lake Okeechobee in 1910, when it was the haunt of hunters, catfishermen, and a score of wild Seminoles. He worked the big dredge that was digging the lake section of the North New River Canal. The new canal was intended not only to help drain the Everglades but to replace the obsolete Miami Canal. The old Miami Canal had been dug with a suction dredge. It moved soft muck and sands but could not dig into hard marl bedrock. This made the canal shallow in places where the bedrock rose close to the surface. When the water level fell, the Miami Canal became impassible. During the dry season, it was common to find boats and barges caught up on ledges, forced to wait for the next rains. The North New River Canal was to be an all-season canal, affording dependable passage year-round. The new canal opened up the Everglades to a steady stream of settlement from Florida's populous east coast.

Ritta Island had changed little since Willie Boots was born five years before. At that time Ritta was one of the most populous areas on Lake Okeechobee. It had a school built in 1916, and most of high ground on the island had been cleared for farming. Ritta and its sister islands—Observatory, Kreamer, and Torry Islands—had the first permanent residents in the south shore area. The islands, muck-covered remnants of the Pahokee sand ridge, were higher than the lakeshore and less susceptible to floods or high water. They were extremely fertile, and, just as important, the breezes carried away mosquitoes and gnats—just what the mosquito-gnawed pioneers coveted. But progress or development had shifted to the eastern shore. There were more boats and more people.

Lake Okeechobee was still a wild area. Occasionally, Seminoles poled their dugout canoes around the island dressed in bright, colorful, open-sleeved shirts and skirts. These were no "for tourist" Indians. They were the remnants of the undefeated tribes who had retreated into the depths of the Everglades more than a half century before. They would appear suddenly, like apparitions, trade skins and cloth workings, then quietly disappear, still wary of the white man who had tried for one hundred years to exterminate them.

Charles Thomas found a vacant house on Ritta Island. It was, he said, "made of Florida pine, consisting of a large living room, bedroom, small kitchen, back and front porch. The windows were screened with shutters, and the porches were open."

Uncle Richard Mays acquired the adjacent farm, and together the Thomases had a tract of some of the best Everglades land. Charles had an eye for good land. He envisioned the island producing a plethora of crops and immediately planted corn and a small crop of his favorite treat—peanuts.

The second crop of corn that Charles and Richard planted in the spring of 1922 had grown to seven feet, and it looked as if he was going to bring in another bumper crop when it began to rain. The tiny settlements of Bare Beach, Clewiston, and Okeelanta were underwater. Most of Ritta Island was flooded. The water rose so fast that the Thomases had to harvest their corn from rowboats.

What hurt Charles Thomas was the loss of his peanuts. It was one of the rare treats the Thomas family looked forward to each Sunday. The peanut plants were barely in bloom before they were covered with two feet of water.

The high water forced animals, snakes especially, to seek higher ground.

"Chicken snakes fell on the mosquito nets that hung from the rafters and covered our beds at night," Mutt Thomas related. "My dad would get up and throw the snakes outside. Cottonmouth water moccasins clustered around the higher grounds and the houses. They would attack chickens."

Finally, the rains proved too much even for the hardy pioneer family. The Thomases packed up and moved to Fort Lauderdale, where Charles found work as a day laborer for a dollar a day. The Thomases lost their homesteading rights.

"They had overslept their homestead," Mutt Thomas explained.

But the call of the Everglades was strong. Within a year, Charles Thomas was making plans to return and start anew.

PAHOKEE

Toward the end of 1921, a major advance in recreational activity arrived at Pahokee. On Main Street a new one-story movie theater with its own light plant was built. During the weekend show, the latest silent films lit up the screen. The audience would read the subtitles out loud. And the bored organist would at times play the wrong music for the scene.

"It'd be a sad scene, and the music would not be playing with the scenery or acting at all. Quite funny at times," Lillian Padgett recounted.

Ever the entrepreneur, Paul Shive and his best friend Peter Padgett made a deal with the theater owner. For free viewing, they would sit on the generator belt when it would go limp, using their weight as tension pulleys. There weren't too many economic opportunities in Pahokee for a youngster.

One source of excitement for the children was the arrival of the mail boat. When it docked they would jump on board and ride the boat as it turned around for the trip back to West Palm Beach. Paul got to know the crew. The captain was impressed with the well-raised, honest boy. When the *Palm Beach Post* needed a paperboy to deliver newspapers to the people in Canal Point and Pahokee, Paul Shive was recommended. Each day with his papers in a bag, he rode on the back runner of the bus as it bounced and chugged along the winding road from Canal Point to Pahokee. At each house he'd jump off, run to the front, deliver the paper, and race back in time to jump back on the bus as it labored slowly over the soft sand roadbed.

He was proud of the money he made on his own. At night he would take the day's receipts out from under his bed and carefully count them out. Few children had money, especially those who were going to school and not working the fields with their fathers, or fishing, or hunting. A natural salesman, he was always looking for deals. If he had been a few years older, he might have made a million selling Florida real estate.

MOONSHINE

In whispers and knowing nods, the news spread quickly through the town bars and stores. Down in western Broward County, moonshiner Tim Rawlings and his cousin had been found shotgunned to death and their whiskey still burned to the ground. Tim was from Fort Lauderdale and had, most assumed, mixed with bad company, what with all the gangsters and outlaws running around. Though the killings happened in Broward County, their deaths sent a shudder through the moonshine community as no federal raid could. There were many questions. Not only Who killed the two men, but Why? Was it a message or revenge? No one really knew.

What they did know was that many of the bootleggers on the coast were vying for control of the lucrative trade, not only for important Bahamian and Cuban smuggling routes but for the hundreds of small farmer-run stills that dotted the Everglades.

Illicit alcohol distillation has a long tradition in the Everglades. One of the largest sections of Lake Okeechobee was named Moonshine Bay. Surrounded by a cheap supply of sugarcane, and thousands of square miles of wilderness and impenetrable wetlands, the Everglades was the perfect setting for moonshining. The industry was active year-round, but it was in the five months between the spring and fall harvests that the stills worked overtime.

The time between the spring harvest and the fall planting was dead time for Everglades farmers. It was too wet to plant. In a land of plenty, many families went hungry during the summer. With no crops to sell throughout the summer, money was scarce. Many farmers made it through the dead summer months distilling illegal whiskey.

Sugarcane, the prime material for distilling liquor, grew like weeds in the Everglades. Everyone had a patch of cane. Some of it was used to feed the animals, especially the pack animals or workhorses and mules to give them energy during long work days plowing or harvesting. The rest was squeezed into a watery liquid that was boiled down into a brown syrupy mix that the children loved to eat. Further treatment and it hardened into a dark brown mass that was blocked. The brown blocks or sugar loaves were shaved to sweeten food.

HENRY Martin was no stranger to distilling. In Frostproof he kept a still in the woods behind his butcher shop. Making moonshine was often a communal affair. Friday afternoons, the men would disappear for a few hours to sample one another's product. When Bessie Mae's younger brother, Tommy Wells, visited, Henry taught him the finer points of brewing.

Like most who made moonshine, Henry preferred stealth to arms to protect his still. He knew the Everglades and the back alligator-clogged waterways, the isolated hummock, and the currents of the open slough. No one—federal agent or strong-arming bootlegger—could find them.

Henry squeezed the sugar cane, forcing out a cloudy syrup before cooking it down to a brown thick molasses. Some operators swore that a dead cat in the mixture added a special flavor; others, that a drop of water moccasin venom doubled the kick. That might be true, but Henry was a purist. He did not add gratuitous materials to his brew. He drank what he made and took pride that it was some of the finest 'shine in South Florida.

People regarded the making of moonshine to be an illegal but benign activity. After all, in America whiskey distilling had a long if checkered tradition. After George Washington gave his farewell speech, he retired to his farmhouse at Mount Vernon and in 1797 built a whiskey distillery that produced eleven thousand gallons of corn and rye whiskey per year. The father of our country, it is recorded, made a tidy profit of $7,500.

In 1794, the fate of an infant United States was threatened by a whiskey rebellion. Bootlegging was criminal. Most who made moonshine, however, were not bootleggers. They wanted cheap drink. Selling their product was not only an added benefit but a definite aside. There was an economy to scale. Once the still was set up and running, it cost as much to distill ten gallons as it did one. Henry had more than enough for his own consumption, and by bottling it in quart bottles, he sold his surplus to friends like Ed King on Torry Island.

The stories in the press about the gangsters and the turf wars raging in Chicago, Philadelphia, and New York seemed a world away. But everyone knew that Florida, with its thousands of miles of coastline, bays, and mangrove swamps, was a smuggler's paradise. Since Spanish colonial times, smuggling has been a tradition in Florida. So close to the Bahamas and Cuba, anyone in a small boat with enough gasoline could make a midnight run.

But it was the Everglades, wild and isolated, where moonshining reigned. Lawrence Will noted that more than once dredges cutting canals in the Everglades had to stop work while a still was moved. With so many stills operating between seasons, it was not long before the whiskey production got the attention of organized crime.

Organized crime discovered southern Florida. Chicago's Al Capone wintered at Palm Island in Biscayne Bay, New York crime families regularly visited Miami and, occasionally, Palm Beach. Illegal gambling abounded in many counties. Miami and most of southern Florida were declared an open area; no single crime family would control the area. While outside criminals and Mafia syndicates might get a foothold in the Sunshine State's urban areas, Florida crackers unquestionably ruled the swamps and palmetto plains. Buyers from the East Coast swarmed the Everglades each summer. Henry knew the potential of making moonshine, but men like Jake Mansley, who took bootlegging more seriously, were consolidating the business. More than one still operator had been found shot dead in the sawgrass.

The locals blamed the Prohibitionists and the overtaxing federal government, while turning a blind eye to the local boys who only wanted an honest drink.

THE DIKE

From his front porch, Henry Martin watched as surveyors dressed in waders and wide-brimmed hats moved cautiously along the lakeshore. Behind them they dragged shallow draft skiffs to cross dead rivers and mucky bogs. With oversized rods and tripod-supported transits, they waved arms and shouted as they staked out a line that ran across the front of Henry Martin's house.

"We're gonna lose two acres of our best land," Henry complained.

"Everyone's losing land, " he was told. "That's progress."

"We're going to have to move the house," Henry told the family at dinner.

Using tractors and mules, the house was lowered off its pilings, placed on rolling logs and moved back a hundred yards then reset on new posts. A small inconvenience, as far as Henry was concerned, for security against flooding. At least the dike was being built.

BOWING to pressure from the lakeside farmers, the railroad companies, and merchants, the Florida state legislature finally raised funds to build an earthen dike around the southern and eastern end of Lake Okeechobee. As planned, the dike was to stretch fifty-seven miles from Pelican Lake to Moore Haven.

The dike, intended to keep back summer rains and the loathed north-western wind tides, was never envisioned to circumscribe the entire lake. To the west and north lay the "sand lands"—nonmucklands, lands fit only for cattle. On the western shore of Lake Okeechobee, just north of Fisheating Creek, was the Brighton Seminole Reservation where a couple hundred Indians and their cattle eked out a living in scrub brush and sabal palm hummocks. To Tallahassee, this was nothing of importance. There was no immediate need to continue the dike around the entire lake. Indian cattle could swim; beans couldn't.

Local barge and dredge owners, the brothers Hamp and Scott Halloway, won the state contract to construct the dike. To captain one of the dredges, Hamp Halloway hired Lawrence Will, mechanic, all-around handyman, and future grassroots historian. Will had a personal stake in the dike. The 1922 floods had forced him to abandon his Okeelanta farm. With the money he saved working on the dike, Will bought a lot on Main Street in Belle Glade where he would build his Pioneer Service Station Building

Aside from the survey, few other studies were conducted. No soil samples were taken, no stress test models done. As conceived, the Lake Okeechobee dike was to be a farmers' dike, only bigger—different in scale only.

The big dredges began work at Bacom Point in January 1923. First they had to build a nine-foot levee across the mouth of the Pelican River. Immediately they ran into a problem that would haunt them a dozen times again. The river bottom soil was fine, soft silt that would liquefy when saturated. It flowed like water. The dredge operators had to carefully lift up each bucket full of silt, pause, and let it drain before swinging and dumping it onto the dike. Eventually, enough silt was piled up to dam the Pelican River.

Navigating a relatively straight line, the dredges scooped up muck and occasionally rock and sand, then dumped it to one side. The dike cut across the dead rivers, destroying one of the unique aspects of the lake: the dead rivers were the breeding grounds for Okeechobee catfish and bass. Immediately after the dike was built, the Lake Okeechobee catfish industry collapsed.

Averaging forty feet at its base, the dike ranged from five to nine feet high with a gentle bank sloping into one or two parallel canals. In the name of expediency, the dike followed the contour of the lake. It made one sharp angle at South Bay where a tongue of the lake stuck out and emptied into the North New River canal. The angle formed a funnel, making South Bay overly susceptible to wind tides blown out of the north and west.

Depth was the main factor in where the dike would go. Except for the concrete used to build the locks, little material was imported. It was built of whatever soil was dredged up. As it passed through mucklands, muck was thrown up; crossing one of the few beaches, sand was mixed in and soft silt was piled on where it crossed old dead rivers. A part of the dike crossing a dead river near Moore Haven had to be rebuilt five times. After each rain storm, the silt would wash, leaving a low bloblike mound, not a sign of a sturdy structure. Finally, in 1925, the last bucket of muck was lifted and dumped on the end of the dike three miles west of Moore Haven. The Great Wall of the Everglades was finished.

FOR the Martins, the dike radically changed their landscape and lifestyle. No longer could a boat be brought to their front yard. In front of the Martin house, the dike was five feet high and forty feet wide. Standing on the front porch of the farmhouse, Henry could still clearly see the lake.

The dike, a long, dark black scar with each end at the horizon, dominated the landscape, though within a month it was reclaimed by grass and elderbushes. Bessie Mae would miss the fiery sunsets over the lake horizon, but the dike was progress, and there was no arguing with progress.

Whatever its shortcomings, the dike performed as planned: it kept the lake at bay and opened up thousands of acres of fertile muckland to farming. Henry planted his first large crop—green beans. With the dike and the new Palm Beach Road completed, progress was rapidly arriving in Belle Glade. Farming boomed once again in the Everglades. And the Martins, having persevered against difficult odds, were at the head of the new prosperity.

THE dike was not the only progress to come to the Everglades. In 1922, the Bank of Pahokee was chartered with a capital of $15,000. A well-run bank, it was the pride of the local residents and endured the real estate boom and bust. Eventually it also survived the 1926 and 1928 hurricanes, the Great Depression, and World War II to become the oldest bank in Palm Beach County.

While 1924 Pahokee might not have resembled the metropolis promised by the land developers, it did have a schoolhouse, a bank building, and a row of sturdy houses on each side of Main Street. Men could socialize at the stores or one of the drinking establishments; the women had no place to call their own. The women folk lobbied for a women's club. Calvin Shive found a sturdy house and had it moved into town. The women had their club, and like many frontier town women's clubs, it was one of the first public buildings and often doubled as a meeting hall and a local courthouse.

NOBEL Padgett had prospered since the big freeze of 1917. He farmed a large patch of land about a mile west of Pahokee and a mile south of where the Pelican River forked—later called Padgett's Island. Padgett tried to homestead the land, but his claim was disavowed. Not willing to lose his hard-worked land, he bought the section, consisting of six hundred forty acres of rich muck lands. Though slightly higher and a bit drier than the surrounding land, it was susceptible to wind tides blowing from the south up the Pelican River.

The new dike changed the Padgetts' fortunes. With the wind tides and floods controlled, Padgett was able to bring most of his land under cultivation. His family's soggy section was now valuable, fertile, lake-bottom land. Once more good fortune smiled on the Padgetts and was to do so again.

Duncan Padgett, Noble's son, attended the agricultural school. The young Everglades-raised Padgett had a crush on Lillian Shive. To Duncan, Lillian was a woman of the world. She was traveled, smart, educated, and quite attractive. Duncan was smitten by the city girl, and he set out to win her affection. Duncan's winning formula was humor. He liked a good practical joke; few people escaped being the butt of one of Duncan's pranks. But nothing warmed his heart so much as to see Lillian smile, and he went out of his way to make her laugh. For Lillian Shive that was enough. The city girl from Tulsa, Oklahoma, fell in love with the genial class clown.

HILLSBORO CANAL AND BELLE GLADE

What was to become Chosen and Belle Glade was a collection of scattered farms and stores perched on the canal bank known as the Hillsboro Canal Settlements. There was a hotel—the Meyers Hotel—that catered to hunters and a few remaining land speculators.

The postmaster delivered the mail each day by rowboat from the Torry Island Post Office. In 1922, Charlie Riedel, a landowner in Okeelanta, bought the Meyer Hotel and the William Clark farm immediately on the south side of the canal. The floods of 1922 forced him to abandon his farm in Okeelanta.

Riedel labored like every other Everglades farmer, planting green beans and fighting rabbits, insects, and wind tides. For him and the other farmers, the new dike was a godsend. In December, another godsend was literally dropped at Riedel's front door: the new all-weather road that directly connected the Everglades to West Palm Beach and the east coast ended in the middle of one of his fields. Not one to miss an opportunity, Riedel subdivided his farm into lots and held an auction. The town of Belle Glade was born.

PUERTO RICO

When the Spanish-American War ended in 1898, the young United States was suddenly thrust into the international arena. The nation had succeeded in its primary objective of freeing Cuba from Spain. As a plus, the victor received as spoils Puerto Rico, Guam, and the Philippines. With the acquisition of Spain's possessions in the Caribbean and the Pacific, America became a world power.

Six years after the war, in the small mountain town of Toa Baja in western Puerto Rico, Juanita Ortiz was born, the youngest of ten children. Her father was a white Spaniard, her mother a black native Puerto Rican. Her father—finally tired of dealing with the Yankee invaders—left for Spain, leaving the mother alone and impoverished. But poverty did not stop her from understanding the value of a good education.

In 1917, U.S. citizenship was granted to Puerto Ricans. By the time Juanita had finished school, she had all the rights of a U.S. citizen. Those rights, she was soon to learn, varied greatly from location to location. After graduating from high school, she set her eyes on higher education. Her goal was to be a teacher.

Scraping money together, her family bought her a steamer ticket to Tampa. The ship left San Juan, stopped in Porto Principe, Haiti, and Nassau, and finally docked in Tampa. It was 1924 and segregation was in full force in Florida.

"When I got off the ship, the black porters were shocked that a black girl was on board. They hid me in a cabin for the night, brought me food the next morning, and escorted me off. So no one knew I was even there," she recalled with a smile.

It was her first taste of American segregation, but it would not be the last. After a short stay in Miami, she took a train to Alabama and began a two-year program in George Washington Carver's Tuskegee Institute.

"COLORED ONLY"

The segregation Juanita faced was an accumulation of sixty years of oppressive laws and customs. However, in the twenties segregation took on a new and more virulent form. It became more institutionalized. Local customs were codified with more restrictive legislation. Segregation was not strictly a local or state rights phenomenon. In the view of many southern and some northern whites, the federal government had been lax on segregation, especially in Washington, D.C., and federal agencies. Even though the army was strictly segregated until World War I, many federal employees were black, especially those dealing with programs to help poor farmers. Immediately after the Civil War, the party of Lincoln had elected a number of black representatives, most of whom were never to serve, as reconstructed states disenfranchised them. They were, however, allowed to labor in federal agencies. When President Woodrow Wilson, the first southerner and Democrat voted into the presidency after the Civil War, gained the White House, he institutionalized a policy of rigid segregation at the federal level. From President Wilson on, all the land, federal and state, south of the Mason-Dixon line was safe for whites.

The 1920s saw a resurgence of the Klu Klux Klan. By 1926, the KKK had over six million members, becoming a national political force to be reckoned with. This was the time of the Rosewood, Florida, massacre. Rosewood had been a small, prosperous black township near Cedar Key, Florida. In 1923, it was burned to the ground by a white mob from a neighboring town, and many of its inhabitants were murdered.

The massacre at Rosewood was unique not so much in that the number killed or the property damage was high but that the victims were so afraid of retaliation or scorn that the story of Rosewood remained untold until 1984. Segregation has a long memory.

ONCE platted, Belle Glade, like all southern towns, had itself divided. Belle Glade's "colored town" was set off from the white community by 4th Street. African Americans and Caribbean blacks began to move out of the isolated shantytowns to live in the more substantial housing in town. Belle Glade was really two towns, each a seeming continent away from the other across a great social and economic divide. To keep that divide, after closing up his Ford dealership Sheriff Clarence Everett made the nightly patrol of colored town, making sure that no whites remained on the west side of 4th Street after 10 p.m. And no sensible African American would be found in "white" Belle Glade after the witching hour.

Fewer than a quarter of the area blacks lived within the rural hamlets dotting the Everglades. Aside from strict segregation laws and Jim Crow whites, only a handful could afford the lots and better-built homes in town. For the most part, their huts and shacks sprouted in unwanted corners of the farms they worked or along roadways or canal banks. Some of the more affluent had purchased farms, mainly in marginal sawgrass lands. A few small-farm black planters, like Jacob Porter, survived in the live-and-let-live Everglades spirit. But the option for white mischief was constantly present. Taking the road of least resistance, they kept to themselves. Out of sight, out of mind, out of trouble.

PIERCE, ARIZONA—THE BOOTSES

Forced out by the 1917 freeze, the Bootses returned to the arid and mosquito-free lands of Arizona. There they began to farm the land they had left four years back. But Arizona had changed. There were more people. There were settlers who did not remember Bill Boots or the widow Mattie Mae Rawle. There were more farms. Marginal lands stretching into the desert were under irrigation. There was less water.

He had been warned that Arizona was no longer for the small farmer. But the Boots family had no choice. Working his old land, Bill plowed and planted. For extra money he worked for other farmers, mostly the larger agrocomplexes that were gobbling up the small farmers like the Bootses. At least the big farms had work. They had something else that the Bootses did not have: political clout. When new water projects came on line, water rights were assigned to the new agrobusinesses, while water available to the small farmer was subtly cut back.

Every month a letter stamped Torry Island, Florida, arrived at the Pierce Post Office. Mattie Mae read the letters from Bill Rawle scribbled religiously in his jerky handwriting, beseeching their return. The area, he said, had recovered after the big freeze, and more and more people were settling the Everglades. A new dike had been built around Lake Okeechobee, opening up new lands. Sebring had bought some of the newly reclaimed lake-bottom land and needed someone to help manage it. Her husband could have the job if he wanted it.

As tempting as this proposition was, Bill Boots was determined to make it on his own land. He had done fairly well for three years. Then a drought hit. Day after day, month after month, the sun dawned in a cloudless sky, rose, then set. As Rawle's letters bemoaned the constant rain falling in Florida, Bill Boots helplessly watched his crops wither away for lack of water. He desperately needed water, and there was only one place to get it. He had to dig a deep well.

In the intensely irrigated valley, the water table had dropped. It was now fifteen feet below the surface and sinking. Bill Boots began to dig. With each spade full of dry dirt, he could think of only one thing: all of the water just lying there in the Everglades. Forget the freak freeze, forget the mosquitoes, and forget the floods and the dour isolation. The Everglades and all that water seemed like paradise, an irresistible siren that continued to call seductively to him.

Before he could finish, a broken Bill Boots crawled out of the still-dry well a defeated man. His powerful body, which had always carried him through physical crises, had given out. Bill was diagnosed with "dropsy," a catch-all term for an array of debilitating diseases from multiple sclerosis to Parkinson's. Without water there was no future for the Boots family in Arizona. Finally, with their options exhausted, in 1925, Bill and Mattie Mae Boots packed their four sons into an old Model T Ford, hitched up their traveling trailer filled with all their worldly goods, and crossed the country back to the Everglades.

Upon arriving at Ritta Island, the Bootses lived in a houseboat called the *Estero*, which was a leftover from the Koreshan hollow earth utopian cult founded by Dr. Cyrus Reed Teed, the self-anointed "Seventh Messenger" (Jesus Christ being the sixth) who called himself Koresh, the biblical name for Cyrus. This nineteenth-century Koresh founded and built his town, New Jerusalem, on the Estero River between Naples and Fort Myers, near the Gulf of Mexico coast.

Well built by German immigrant followers of Koresh, the seventy-five-foot, narrow *Estero* was to be home for the Bootses for a year. Mattie Mae, with her usual flair made ornate curtains, decorated the cramped houseboat space, and had Bill redo the kitchen so she could cook some of her well-known recipes.

While on Ritta and the islands, Bill Boots had shown that he was a capable leader and soon was helping other farmers to supplement his income. Even though he still had bouts of weakness, Bill was hard worker whose skills and abilities did not go unnoticed. He was hired away from the Forbeses to be foreman of Sebring Farms. Bill Boots moved his family out of the *Estero* into one of seven houses at Sebring Farms, one of the same houses he had helped build in 1916.

EARLY lawmen in the Everglades were an eclectic collection of humanity, ranging from businessmen like Belle Glade's Everett to recently converted outlaws. One of the most colorful was the town of Okeechobee's Sheriff William Collins, better known as Pogey Bill. In his younger days, Collins was a hard-fighting fisherman, and he was not unfamiliar with the inside of a jail cell. However, once elected sheriff, he stopped drinking and smoking and transformed himself into a tough, no-nonsense sheriff.

Okeechobee was a rough-and-tumble place with hard-drinking, rowdy cattlemen and fishermen who lived hard and fast on payday. Like many Wild West towns, Okeechobee needed a strong-willed lawman who was not above breaking the law to enforce it. His peacekeeping, while not colorblind, did cut across racial barriers.

A new arrival in town commented that he heard Sheriff Collins was pretty hard on the colored folks.

"Not just the colored folks" was the reply.

Collins often turned a blind eye to local moonshiners. They were, after all, hometown good old boys trying to make a buck in hard times. This attitude was not shared by United States Treasury agents who had tried to put a stop to the rampant illegal distilling in Okeechobee County, where federal agents set up a task force. They met with little success and were sure Collins was tipping off the moonshiners. They targeted Collins, and he was finally arrested for accepting payments from a moonshiner. After a mistrial, he was convicted in a second trial, sentenced to six years' probation, and forced to resign.

EVEN in sparsely populated rural Florida, the Roaring Twenties would not have been complete without a genuine home-grown outlaw. With his chiseled handsome face, his swaggering walk, and his one-eyed glare (the other was covered with a black eye patch), John Ashley perfectly fit the bill.

Starting life as a hunter, John Ashley was a crack shot. He gathered around him family and friends eager to break out of the rank poverty of a frontier family. The family homestead was set deep in the poor lands of the pine forests in western Martin County. The Ashleys struggled in the harsh wilderness until John decided there was a better way.

One of John's first victims was the son of a Seminole tribal chief, Desoto Tiger. It was his body that was dug up in the Everglades by a dredge that was digging the North New River Canal. Over a dozen others would follow Desoto Tiger to the grave before John Ashley's criminal reign ended.

The Ashley gang was the original gang that couldn't shoot straight. Their list of crimes included a train robbery that was botched when the thieves couldn't figure out what to do. While robbing the Stuart Bank, an accomplice shot out John's eye. John was captured and jailed. Later his friends attempted to break John out of jail. Two people, including one of the gang, were killed. When the gun smoke cleared, John Ashley still languished in his cell.

John did finally escape and retreated into the protecting vastness of the Everglades. He organized the hijacking of bootleggers' whiskey and sailed to the Bahamas where his gang stole competing rumrunners' liquor, but John Ashley's fate was sealed when he stepped over an invisible line. He killed a police officer who happened to be Palm Beach County Sheriff Barker's nephew.

Determined to wipe out the outlaw gang, Sheriff Barker began an unrelenting campaign against the Ashley gang. One by one their hideouts were destroyed and many of their allies arrested or intimidated. Finally, realizing Palm Beach County was no longer a safe haven, John Ashley decided to flee to Jacksonville. An informant tipped off Sheriff Baker, who alerted Fort Pierce Sheriff Merritt, and an ambush was set up at the Sebastian Bridge, where all traffic to Jacksonville had to cross.

The Ashley gang approached the bridge in two cars. John rode in the second car, his rifle out of sight but cocked. They were stopped at the bridge, but before John could react, the sheriff had a shotgun in his face. John Ashley had been captured.

What happened next is open to interpretation. Police reports said that after the gang gave up their rifles, Ashley and his accomplices in the second car went for their pistols. Passengers in the front car said that Ashley and the others were handcuffed and shot in cold blood. Ashley died in a barrage of bullets and shotgun blasts. Frontier justice, while swift, was not strong on appeals.

News of the demise of the Ashley gang spread across the Everglades like a sawgrass fire. With the death of John Ashley, one violent chapter in Everglades history had been closed.

CHAPTER 5
THE YEAR OF STORMS

For every action force, there exists a reaction force that is equal in magnitude but opposite in direction.

—Isaac Newton's Third Law

Off the coast of Peru, under the frigid gaze of the snow-capped Andes, scores of fishermen, bobbing in small boats, anxiously watched the skies. Through the eternal mist that hung low and gray over the coastal desert and barren foothills, they could see the birds—millions of sea birds, winging their way from the rocky guano-stained islands to feed in the open sea. The birds were searching for the large schools of small fish, mostly anchovies, that fed off the plankton brought up from the depths by the cold, nutrient-rich Humboldt Current. The bird's presence meant that El Niño was gone. The birds meant that the fish were back.

El Niño, from El Niño de Dios, the Child of God or the Christ Child, is the Spanish equivalent of Santa Claus. It is the El Niño de Dios who brings Christmas presents to well-behaved young children on his birthday. Every seven years or so around Christmas, El Niño de Dios brings the coast of Peru a present it could do without—warm water. From the mid–Pacific Ocean, abnormally warm water is forced eastward toward the Peruvian coast. The sea surface temperature rises, and the cold waters of the Humboldt Current are pushed deep, too deep for the fish to feed. The hungry fish leave or die, and the birds follow suit. Nests are abandoned, the barren shores of Peru are quiet—the desert deserted.

For the decade and a half following 1910, El Niño had played havoc with the currents and the weather of coastal Peru. Moisture-laden El Niño–warmed air rose high into the Andes, where it cooled and condensed against glaciated mountain peaks. Massive rainstorms billowed down the mountains, through steep valleys, and out into the desert, causing floods and catastrophic landslides. People drowned in the desert. For the fishermen and their families, the world was turned on end. But this year, the year of storms, the water cooled; the rains stopped; the birds were back. And so were the fish.

El Niño's effects were not restricted to Peru. The abnormally warmed Pacific air altered weather systems around the world. Sub-Saharan Africa suffered droughts, rains inundated the Californian coast, while across the Pacific wildfires plagued a rain-starved Australia. Even the frigid air currents of the Arctic changed their pattern. In North America El Niño had drawn the subtropical jet stream farther south, causing the high-altitude westerly winds to oscillate over Florida and the Caribbean. The southern positioning of the jet stream brought drier weather to Florida. But, just as important, two thousand miles farther east, the jet stream's high-altitude winds blew the tops off of the tropical thunderstorms developing off the coast of Africa. It literally decapitated the massive megascale thunderstorms a hurricane needs to form. During El Niño years, fewer Cape Verde–type hurricanes are seen in the Atlantic Ocean, giving Florida and the Caribbean a much-deserved reprieve.

La Niña, the feminine of El Niño, does the reverse. The east Pacific waters cool, the coasts of Peru and California dry out, and the subtropical jet stream is pushed further north. Without the high-level jet stream winds to hinder their development, massive thunderstorms regroup off the coast of Africa, stretching their billowing white heads forty thousand feet high into the troposphere. Once formed, they are free to develop into hurricanes and move westward with impunity across the warm waters stretching from the Cape Verde Islands to Florida. La Niña years are hurricane years.

Hurricane-wise, until 1926, the Roaring Twenties had been quiet for south Florida. Since the series of cataclysmic storms that had hit the state in the decades just before and after the beginning of the century, there had not been an overactive hurricane season for sixteen years. The last major hurricanes to hit southern Florida were in 1909 and 1910. This exceptionally long hiatus was about to end abruptly. The 1926 hurricane season would prove to be an exceptionally active and deadly year, producing eight recorded hurricanes—four of which became killer storms. In July, a hurricane killed 287 people in Puerto Rico, followed by another in August, which struck Louisiana, taking 25 lives. The season was capped off with a late storm in October that killed 709 people in Cuba. However, it was September, the month of hurricanes, that spawned the storm that would etch 1926 in the memory of south Floridians forever.

BY the spring of 1926, the United States was at the height of the Roaring Twenties. The stock markets had reached new highs with the Dow Jones Industrial Average lapping at the 180 mark, ready to zoom to an astronomical 380 in the next two years. Real estate prices were soaring, unemployment was at an all-time low, and industrial production hummed along at nearly full capacity. There were scheduled airline routes, many businesses and some homes had telephones, the big-city liquor mobs were organizing, and women smoked in public. Florida and the Everglades were enjoying unprecedented prosperity and, like the rest of the country, were inexorably swept up in a national giddiness. America was changing. Yet the business of America remained business. Everyone was busy, and no one was busier than Henry Martin.

Spreading out before Henry Martin were green fields of ripe Bountiful beans. Between the rows of legumes were a dozen black bean pickers bent under the hot sun. Their bodies were hunched over as they grasped at the vines and, with one swift motion, pulled the beans from the stalks and dumped them into the hemp hampers they carried at their side. Once filled, the hampers were taken to the side of the field and stacked, where they were added to the picker's total. Pickers were paid fifteen cents a hamper. Entire families, from grandparents to six-year-old children, picked together. Every hand was needed. Anyone able to harvest beans worked. Survival depended on them.

Behind them the recently finished muck dike loomed above the horizontal land—a black wall sprouting tall weeds and green elderbushes. Stretching like a long, black check mark from Pahokee to Moore Haven, the dike had succeeded in keeping the Martins' fields free from crop-drowning wind tides. Luckily for the Martins, winter and spring had been dry. The rains had not flooded the seeds in the ground or the young plants. The year had enjoyed a perfect growing season. Along with Loney Martin and the black help, Henry had cleared more land—now dry, thanks to the new dike—and planted a larger second crop that he was now harvesting. For the first time in his life, Henry felt economically secure. He had land, a sturdy house, a recently purchased two-year-old Model T, a large healthy family, and money stored in a tin box hidden in the rafters. Henry also had plans. He wanted to plant more land, buy a tractor, and, most of all, start a store in Belle Glade.

In July, Henry's mother, Grandmother Martin, suddenly took ill. With no one to care for her in Frostproof, Henry packed for a two-week trip and left Bessie Mae and the kids to tend to the farm. While he was at his mother's house, Bessie Mae's brother Tommy Wells paid him a visit.

Thomas "Tommy" Jefferson Wells had served on the front lines during World War I. In the trenches of France and Belgium, he was gassed by the Germans, blown out of his foxhole in an artillery barrage, and shot. Four times he had been left on the battlefield for dead. But Tommy Wells proved to be a hard man to kill, and after the war he returned home to north Florida to a hero's welcome. Seeking new opportunities, he had made his way south to Frostproof, where his sister Bessie Mae was living with Henry Martin. A mechanic by trade like Henry, he, too, supplemented his income making moonshine.

Tommy remained in Frostproof after Bessie Mae and Henry moved to the Everglades. It was no secret in Frostproof that their local war hero was courting young Willie Emma Carter. Though short, Tommy always walked with a ramrod-straight back. Willie Emma was demure with large, warm eyes and dark hair cut short like a flapper's. Together they were an attractive couple, but she was thirteen years his junior. Though he was a war hero and a hard worker and had a new car, her parents wanted her to marry someone nearer her own age. No matter how her parents tried to cajole her, Willie Emma, infatuated with the dashing Tommy Wells, spurned all other suitors.

Henry and Tommy shared war stories, Tommy of fighting at Ypres and Verdun, and Henry of battling floods, droughts, insects, and disease. In spite of all the hardships, Henry told Tommy that the Everglades held a future for a man who was not afraid of taking risks.

"Plenty of opportunities," Henry told him.

Tom confided to Henry that if Willie Emma's parents would not give their blessing, he was planning to elope with Willie Emma—a radical and sometimes dangerous move in those times.

Bessie Mae, Henry knew, was fond of Willie Emma and reassured Tommy, like Bessie Mae had done twenty years before, "If you and Willie Emma marry, you'll always have a place to go."

As the two men talked, a few hundred miles to the east a hurricane crept steadily toward the northwest. It had south Florida clearly in its sights. Even with dozens of Weather Bureau observation posts scattered throughout the Caribbean and the Bahamas, early hurricane warning was still an iffy venture at best. The National Weather Bureau depended on immediate observation from their on-site weather watchers, who would radio in the temperature, cloud coverage, wind speed, direction, and barometric pressure. Land-based observatories were supplemented by weather reports broadcast from ships on the open seas. The National Weather Bureau, fearful of exaggerated, inaccurate, or—worst of all—conflicting reports, discouraged local weather bureaus from issuing their own forecasts without approval from the capital. All information was sent to Washington, D.C., where it was compiled and then relayed back to the local stations with Washington's predictions—a process that was cumbersome at best. Uniform weather reporting was too slow to react swiftly to rapidly forming localized atmospheric phenomena. Thus, on the morning of July 26, Florida had little warning when a hurricane plopped its center off the coast of Palm Beach.

That morning in Frostproof, the winds were blowing steadily from the north. Henry heard that a storm had struck the Bahamas and thought that if winds from the storm were hitting Polk County from all that way it must be a big one. But not until the next morning when the wind and rain slashed across Frostproof did he become concerned for Bessie Mae and the children. Recalling the stories of the hurricanes that had struck Tampa years ago, he wondered whether this could be a hurricane. How would he know? Neither he nor anyone he knew had experienced a full-blown hurricane. Hurricanes were scary events, and the local boosters, hoteliers, and developers did not want anything to scare the tourists. The local news reported the hurricane as a tropical storm. The word *hurricane* was never mentioned—it remained the unspeakable word.

Torrential downpours inundated Belle Glade. Inside the Martin house, Bessie Mae huddled with the children. Wind-blown rain angrily slapped at the windows, and the tin roof roared. Though dry with plenty of supplies, Bessie Mae was worried. The house was built beside Cooper's River. The old riverbed, thanks to the dike, was now dry and part of the Martin fields. However, it was a couple of feet lower than the surrounding ground and was the first area to flood with rainwater. The first feeder bands of the storm racing over Belle Glade dumped an inch of water in one hour. The low land of Cooper's River filled up and began to spill over its old banks. Then the Cooper River did something it had not done in two years: it began to flow.

Bessie Mae watched the river rise around the house. She told the children to pack blankets and food in case they had to leave. By the time they had gathered a few things, the water was already up the porch steps. A neighbor, James Register, who lived in a sturdy house a mile away, sent one of his farms hands to fetch the Martin family. Bessie Mae and the children crossed the flooded fields to the Register house.

During emergencies, people banded together for common support. Neighbors inclined to support each other in times of crises. A woman alone could count on family and friends. Community in sparsely settled areas is always strong.

THE eye of the July hurricane remained well to the east of Okeechobee, sparing Belle Glade most of its fury. However, it was a "rainy" hurricane carrying an enormous amount of water. Within a few hours after the Martins had left their house, nearly twelve inches of rain fell on the lake. As the hurricane made its way north along the Palm Beach coast, the winds blowing in from the north changed to the west, directly off the lake. Like a massive wind tide, the winds drove the lake waters against the dike.

From the Registers' kitchen, Annie Mae and Nancy Martin watched as the waves lapped over the top of the dike. The yard was covered with water and floating debris. The children watched with glee as logs and uprooted bushes floated by. The chickens trying to roost in the trees and on the roof were blown down into the water, squawking as they fought to keep from drowning. Nancy and Roy jumped into the water and swam after the chickens, which they brought back to the kitchen. Some were killed and cleaned, but the others were let loose in the house. The water reached up to the floor and crept into the house. Roy helped James Register throw a bed on top of another, then place all the small children on the upper bed.

Waves dove over the top of the dike, and torrents of muddy water washed away the soft muck. The soggy muck along the old dead rivers was the first to give way. The part of the dike that crossed the Cooper River melted away, throwing the lake water upstream. The flood came in a series of continuous bores, or waves, each reaching higher than the one before. Branches and trees were swept along as a mighty river suddenly appeared around the Registers' house. Black water rose another two feet inside the house.

By nightfall, the winds had died down and the water retreated back toward the lake. At first light, with a foot of water still on the ground, Bessie Mae returned to the farmhouse. She found an inch of silt muck covering everything inside and outside the house. When she opened her water-soaked linen box, a red shirt sitting on top of the clothes had run and stained all the whites a sordid pink. Without pausing, Bessie Mae and the children began to clean up. The boys gathered in the animals, and the girls cleaned out the house. Making a mixture of lye and lemon, Bessie Mae scrubbed the clothes clean and as white as the day they were stitched.

Meanwhile, an anxious Henry Martin was forced to wait in Frostproof. News was scarce. The telegraph lines were down, and he had no real information about what had happened in Belle Glade. When the winds and rain died down, he drove all night along darkened roads to Okeechobee. From there he took the rutted dike road washed out by heavy rains, through Pahokee to Belle Glade. The next morning he coaxed the truck through axle-deep mud up to the house where he found Bessie Mae and the children sweeping out mud-covered floors. The house and farm had suffered water damage, but his family was safe and sound. Except for a few of Bessie Mae's chickens, all the farm animals had survived. They had survived, they believed, the worst Mother Nature could throw at them, and so they could be excused in thinking they could survive anything.

THE July hurricane had not been a killer storm. Rather, it was a reminder and a warning. The two-year-old dike had given way to a minimal category 1 hurricane. With stoic resignation, people picked up where they left off and went on with their lives with scarcely a comment. The question was never asked: What could a large storm do?

MIAMI

The 1920s was an exciting time for the Miami black community. Florida was experiencing an economic boom, and work was available for everyone. Money even flowed into the black communities, usually the last to feel any benefit from the trickle-down effect. The black community had a new vitality. New stores sprouted on each corner. Some black people were quietly getting rich. Most kept a low profile—no use offending the sensibilities of Jim Crow whites. But there was wealth being made in black Miami.

Taking a hiatus from the Tuskegee Institute, Juanita Ortiz returned to Miami, where she married Charles Wilson. The newlyweds built a two-story building on the corner of 19th Street. A dry goods store was situated on the first floor and a two-bedroom apartment on the second. Juanita was adjusting to life in America. Even though she could not accept segregation, she found she could live with it.

By 1926, the Miami real estate boom was showing disturbing signs of stalling. Florida was inundated with too many projects and reams of bad publicity. Investor wariness grew as the prices of land and building supplies soared. Then suddenly, at the height of the building boom, everything changed almost overnight, precipitated by the very institution that had made Miami a major city: the railroad. Alarmed at the damage the increase in rail traffic was doing to its railroad beds, the railroad shut down its Florida line for repairs. This decision could not have come at a worse time. Huge orders of building materials piled up in warehouses on the side of tracks. The few building materials that arrived came by sea, until a ship loaded with lumber sank in the channel, blocking the entrance to Miami. Miami was in effect blockaded. Construction ground to a halt. The delay in building contracts made an already-spooked market more wary. Many contracts were breached, loans defaulted, and builders fell into bankruptcy. Land purchases were forfeited, and the Ponzi pyramid began to crumble at its base.

Real estate, like the stock market, is notoriously cyclical. Miami was overdue for a "market correction." However, on September 11, the single factor that sealed Miami's and much of southern Florida's economic fate for the next twenty years was churning twenty-two hundred miles to the east, preparing to make a sprint to the west.

MOORE Haven could unquestionably claim the title of the largest town in the Everglades. It had two theaters and many finely designed buildings, and its streets were bordered with red-blooming Royal Poincianas and stately water oaks. A power plant moaning in the distance provided a continuous stream of electricity.

Before the dike was built, rains and high water had plagued Moore Haven. Too often Main Street lay for days under two feet of water. During the 1922 rains, crops drowned, sugarcane rotted in the fields, and loan losses caused the Bank of Moore Haven to fail. Like the rest of the Everglades, a dike became the top priority for the people of Moore Haven.

In 1924, Moore Haven found itself at the end of the recently finished mud dike. Farmers planted with abandon right up to the dike. The feared rains and the wind tides would bother them no more. With paved streets, a railroad, and a lake-taming dike, progress had truly reached Moore Haven.

After an exceptionally dry winter and spring, the summer rains of 1926 had been heavy. The July storm had dumped an additional twelve inches on Lake Okeechobee. The lake waters were high, lapping two feet below the top of the dike. Rain continued to fall through September. One day during the second week of September, an exceptionally heavy rain fell, and the lake rose another foot. Water managers were begged to lower the level of the lake, but they preferred to warehouse water for the coming dry months.

The section of the dike between Liberty Point and Clewiston on the south side was low and had been weakened by the July storm. There had been no funds for reinforcing the dike that year. The water managers finally opened the locks on the Caloosahatchee River. Water streamed out as fast as it could, but it was not enough. The lake level continued to rise, yet farmland around Moore Haven remained dry. The dike, it seemed, was working—too well, perhaps.

ON September 16, after crossing a thousand miles of open Atlantic waters, the fast-moving hurricane pummeled the sparsely settled Turks and Caicos Islands with winds in excess of 150 miles per hour. The low-lying islands were no strangers to hurricanes. But not even the islands' storm-hardened veterans were prepared for the ferocity of the storm. Ten hours later, much of Grand Turk was leveled.

The storm's path took it over open ocean, far from the evaluating eyes of the weather watchers. It skirted Cuba, keeping just out of sight of Weather Bureau watchers, who reported a tropical storm of medium strength churning off the coast. Moving forward at a rapid nineteen miles per hour, the hurricane stormed through the Bahamas. The last communication with the Bahamas at one o'clock indicated a storm was approaching Nassau, a big storm, but exactly how big and where it was headed no one would know until it was too late. A few hours away in Miami blue skies with light breezes blessed the afternoon.

The *Miami Herald* ran a story about the storm but added that it was not expected to hit Florida. Wary of offending tourist and investor sensibilities, especially during a downturn in the real estate market, the paper never referred to the storm as a hurricane.

Seated behind his desk, Richard Gray, the head of the Miami Weather Bureau, was growing more anxious by the hour. Weather forecasting, while not an exact science, did need information, and Richard Gray was laboring under a lack of data. With the sparse information available, he had tracked the storm across the Atlantic into the Bahamas. The lack of communication from Nassau might be from bad lines, or it might be from a storm knocking out radios and generators. One was a common nuisance, the other a potential disaster. He had to wait. False alarms made the weather people look foolish and diminished the public's concern for real alarms. Orders from the Washington, D.C., headquarters of the U.S. Weather Bureau were clear and specific: err on the side of caution. Officially, therefore, the category 4 hurricane was still a tropical storm.

As night fell, a large squall line soaked the city. Then the barometric pressure dropped rapidly, as low as Gray had ever seen it. Alarmed, Gray could wait no longer. Without Washington's OK, he had to take action. On the roof of the weather bureau building he raised the square twin red and black hurricane flags. But it was late and it was dark. Few people knew where to look for storm warning flags, and even fewer knew what they meant. Fewer still would have even understood what a hurricane was. For many, secure in their progress, new homes, and wealth, it would have been the chance to watch an exciting natural phenomenon. In essence, Miami was struck unaware and unprepared.

IN Moore Haven, Fred Flanders, state engineer for the southern Everglades, received a telegram from Miami that a hurricane was due to hit the coast. Flanders, like most of the townspeople, regarded the warning as another storm threat. He showed the telegram to others, who shared his assessment.

Flanders made an inspection of the dike near the power plant and along the fish docks. It was raining, and the lake had risen another foot. Waves were lapping at its top. A few more inches, and water would start flowing over the dike. Flanders sounded the alarm. The cry of the fire siren brought nearly every able-bodied man to the lakefront. All through the night they placed sandbags on top of the dike. At daybreak they realized their efforts were in vain, and the people of Moore Haven resigned themselves to another flood. What they were about to get was much more.

AT their home in Miami, Juanita Wilson followed what sparse information she could cull on the storm from a few newspaper articles and broadcasts from a radio in a local store. She worried about her family in Puerto Rico. Over the centuries, the island had suffered greatly from hurricanes. Lying in one of the most traveled paths for tropical storms, the residents of the island commonwealth understood the horrific power of a major hurricane. So it was with great relief that Juanita read reports that the tropical storm had done little damage to her home island. Reports now placed the storm somewhere in the Bahamas.

Along with most people, the Wilsons got much of their news from nightly newsreels at the movies.

"We went to the movies and were watching newsreels on the damage the hurricane did to Nassau," Juanita said. "When we left the theater, we were in it."

They were at the 11th Street Theater and tried to make it back the eight blocks to their house on 19th Street.

"The wind blew the rain straight down the streets. We fought our way to one street corner, then another where we waited for a lull, then we raced to another corner," Juanita remembers.

The howling wind raged in the night. Boards, windows, and shutters slammed against the walls. Just after six in the morning the wind stopped. People came out to survey the damage. Some were stunned, others curious as they walked the littered streets of Miami. The sky was partly clear, the sun was shining, and the dawn air glowed a pale yellow. But the thin air had an unnatural resonance to it.

Downtown, Richard Gray watched in horror as hundreds of people strolled down First Street toward Flagler Boulevard and the bay front. He ran out of the building exhorting the people to return to their homes—the storm was not over.

Few believed him.

Then the back wall of the eye hit Miami. Winds racing at one hundred thirty-five miles per hour whipped through the city. People running through the streets were knocked down by flying debris. Glass windows shattered. Corrugated metal roofing flew threw the air with decapitating force. A sixteen-foot storm surge swept over Key Biscayne across the bay, carrying debris and boats, before slamming into the Miami waterfront. The Miami River was lined with small freighters, fishing boats, and a few luxury yachts seeking shelter from the oncoming storm. A nine-foot tidal wave bore careened up the Miami River, lifting boats and docks, throwing them aside like play toys.

Even though much of the weather equipment was destroyed, the National Weather Bureau stated that the wind speed was the "highest ever recorded in the United States."

The Wilsons had lost their home and store.

"It was flattened just like a crushed eggshell," Juanita said, crushing an imaginary egg in her fist.

Yet the Great Miami Hurricane had not done its worst. It was saving that for Moore Haven.

In Moore Haven, the scant reports of a possible hurricane off the Florida coast did not worry anyone. Hurricanes did not come inland. Radio stations that might have broadcast warnings had no electricity, and their towers were down.

Early that morning, winds roared in from the northeast across Lake Okeechobee straight at Moore Haven. Four-foot waves topped with angry whitecaps churned across the lake. To the south, the eye of the hurricane moved westward across the Everglades, sucking up water, blowing down trees, and flattening the sawgrass. As it passed just south of Moore Haven, its winds hit Moore Haven from the north directly off the lake. The wind drove the water against the dike. Part of the dike that had been built over a dead river began to wash away. Dozens of breaks widened, sending black lake water careening down the streets of Moore Haven. People scurried to their roofs. House were lifted off their foundations and then thrown against neighbors' houses, crushing both homes and their occupants.

"By midmorning," Flanders recalled, "the full fury of the hurricane broke upon us, and the water from the lake was rushing through the town like swift rivers; the air filled with rain, the crest of waves, and flying debris. Visibility, due to the flying scud, dropped to a few hundred yards. . . . Looking toward town, some houses had disappeared, and others were slowly floating out of sight. No dry land was visible in any direction. By midafternoon, the wind had reached a howling, shrieking maximum of an estimated 120 to 135 miles an hour."

MIAMI lay in ruins. There wasn't a street that did not have a damaged building. Ocean-going ships lay on land, some a mile from the open sea. Groups of idle men loitered on the street corners, in parks, or on the stoops where their houses once stood. Its citizens were shell-shocked. The vibrant city was laid prostrate, down and out for the count.

Homeowners, unable or unwilling to rebuild, lived in ruins. Few people had insurance. There was no work. The Miami building boom had ended. People got into their cars and left, never to return.

Slowly Charlie and Juanita Wilson began to rebuild their house and store as best they could without funds. Much of the lumber was salvaged from piles of wood dumped in now-empty lots. They rebuilt part of the store, but the enthusiasm, the hope that had seemed unbounded a few days before had been drained away. The store shell stood as a parody of its former self. Juanita's husband did what little work he could find. As in all disasters, the poor had been hit the hardest, and they would take the longest to recover.

The official Red Cross report issued October 9, 1926, asserted that 43,000 people were left without homes, 6,381 were injured, and 373 were killed. No rounded numbers. This was the time of science. Exact numbers were required since they gave any report more exactitude and believability. Only the bodies physically recovered and counted were included in the total. The number of dead, however, was underestimated. The report failed to take into account the 811 people listed as missing and presumed dead, many of whom were unidentified migrant farm laborers who worked on the edge of the Everglades.

Stagnant, scum-laden water covered Moore Haven. People waded through it nonetheless. In-town cesspools overflowed, raising the real fear of an epidemic. The National Guard ordered the entire town of Moore Haven evacuated.

Within a week, Red Cross relief workers arrived, but their efforts were hampered by disorganization. Volunteer contributions flowed into the Red Cross coffers for the hurricane victims, but the funds were slow in reaching the residents of Moore Haven, and the Red Cross was roundly criticized. Months after the storm, people were still waiting for funds to rebuild. Reacting to critics, the Red Cross took measures to reform its entire organization.

THE MARTIN FARM

George Walker, a farmer in Belle Glade who was in Moore Haven during the storm, stopped at the Martin farmhouse. "That water piled up and broke the dike in the Moore Haven area," he told Henry.

"Over here, the wind had swept away the water from this side of the lake, and it was dry for a mile or so out," Henry said.

The storm had acted like a gigantic wind tide, blowing the water from one side of the lake to the other. In Pahokee, during the height of the 1926 hurricane, a surveyor standing on the dike braved gale-force winds and focused his transit on the lake. He was amazed that the surface of the lake had actually shifted and was tilted at an angle. In front of him, the lake was blown dry for three miles.

Again Henry and Bessie Mae cleaned out their lake house. Henry thought it had done them well and survived two hurricanes in one year. The stilt house was stronger than it looked. His moonshine still did not do as well. Democrat Hammock had been washed clean. There was no trace of his still except for a bare black patch where the fire had sat.

Henry took it as a sign. He had enough money to start his own store. Bessie Mae could not have been more pleased. The still was a constant worry to her, and due to recent criminal activity on the coast, she was afraid it might reach Belle Glade. Plus, she knew that deep in his heart Henry longed to own a store, a chain of stores. Henry wanted to be a merchant, and he had a building on Canal Street all picked out. But first he had to organize the farm to where it would function without his constant supervision. His main obstacle was help. He needed good reliable field hands he could trust to work the farm if he set up a store in town. Each family or group of men he hired would stay until the harvest was finished; then they'd move on. Henry Martin needed a family to live permanently on the farm.

MIGRANTS, by their very nature, had no vested interest in any one farm or area. The season was short and most had to make what they could in a few short weeks. They went where the work was and the pay the best. There were no salaries; they were paid piecemeal. If they could make a cent or two more somewhere else, they left. Farmers were not above offering more to another farmer's field hands if he had a crop he had to harvest in a hurry. A farmer might find he had no hands to work the fields one morning and end up cursing his bad luck and what he saw as the perfidies of the black race.

Bessie Mae had more luck. She was helped around the house by Tempie, a black woman who had drifted in from Georgia with her five children in tow. Though Tempie never talked openly about her husband, it was rumored he had been lynched during a land dispute. Carl, her second boy, had been born with the umbilical cord wrapped around his neck and suffered brain damage. He was, as they said, "slow."

None of Tempie's children went to school. Only Tempie ever wore shoes. They helped their mother in the fields and in white people's houses, earning whatever money they could to survive. Even Carl could be seen lugging hampers loaded with green beans during harvest time. Bessie Mae did what she could for Tempie. She insisted that Tempie stay in the best of the "colored quarters" houses and gave her the clothes Bessie Mae's own children had outgrown. Tempie was fortunate in having Bessie Mae as a benefactor, and she reciprocated with loyal hard work.

Henry, on the other hand, had a difficult time keeping reliable help. The migrant workers who filtered in and out of Belle Glade never stayed long enough to help him finish the backbreaking work at the end of a harvest. A few lived on his farm during the picking and planting seasons and were obliged to work for him first, but once the work slackened, they packed up and left, many times without a word. Carrying all the prejudices of the times, Henry considered them lazy and unreliable.

Finally, in the fall, Henry found a young black family that agreed to stay over the summer. There was no work in the other depressed areas of Florida. As an enticement to stay, Henry built them better living quarters—nothing elaborate, just enough to make them comfortable, dry, and warm: "Don't want to spoil them." No farmer wanted to pay their workers any more than was necessary. They begrudgingly housed them in makeshift shacks constructed from leftover wood and tin. A farmer who did too much for his workers was resented by the other farmers and, worst of all, might be called a "nigger lover"—an epithet no true white southerner would tolerate.

With a large amount of land under cultivation, Henry realized he had to mechanize. He needed a tractor. He had hesitated because he did not have the money to purchase one outright. Henry, like most pioneers in the twenties, had an aversion to banks, preferring to keep his money at the farm and later in the big safe at the store. He also did not believe in debt. He had seen too many people lose their farms and homes to banks.

"We don't want to be obliging to nobody," he often said.

But times were changing and he had to compete with the other farmers, many who already had tractors working their fields. A tractor was a symbol of a successful farmer.

Henry purchased a Fordson tractor from Clarence Everett's new Ford garage in Belle Glade. He bought it on credit. It was the first time he had ever taken out a loan and the first time he had gone into debt. With the tractor he could plow more land, clear more trees, and uproot and plant more sawgrass. His productivity skyrocketed.

By the new planting season, Henry had enough capital saved to open a store on Canal Street. The one-story clapboard building, with windows looking north over the Hillsboro Canal, was a sturdy if squat structure. Its shelves were stocked with dry goods, canned food, farm tools, and a scattering of exotic fruits like bananas and avocados in bins by the front counter.

Henry's store had plenty of competition. Grocery and dry good stores dotted Belle Glade. There was Badger's, Belle Glade's largest store, also housing the post office to draw in customers. Most of the stores were small merchants selling goods out of the front of their homes as supplementary income. Henry was convinced that by offering good supplies, attention to customer relations, and hard work, he would prosper, and Henry Martin was not afraid of hard work.

Many of Henry's customers were the "new people." Actually, most of the people now living in Belle Glade were newcomers. Many settled in town and regarded the original settlers as quaint. The poor farmers were called muck rats. They'd come into town barefooted, feet black from the muck dust, clothes unwashed, and permanently black-stained fingernails. Henry Martin had a soft spot for the muck rats. He had been one himself, and he understood the difficulties they faced. He recognized in many the same hope and aspiration for the better life he had worked hard for and achieved.

Occasionally on Sundays, Bessie Mae would bring the family to the store. She would help Henry cook and attend customers in the front while the children played in the back. One Sunday Sonny fell sick. He wasn't eating solid food, and Bessie Mae gave him a banana. Imported from South America, a banana was a luxury item. The yellow fruit was always a special treat for the Martin children. Watching her brother eat one of the delicious fruits, Ernestine thought it was only fair for her to have one also. When no one was looking, she took one and ate it behind a pile of boxes. Her father found the banana skin and her transgression did not go unpunished.

"It wasn't a big walloping," Ernestine said. "Just enough to let me know I'd done wrong."

By the end of the year, the 1926 hurricane season was relegated to the past. The dike was repaired, and farmers planted with renewed vigor. To prove it had recovered from the Miami hurricane, Moore Haven threw a town festival on Christmas Day. The Everglades were ready once again to prosper. Although the 1926 hurricane season was the worst in recent memory, it was only a minor foretaste of the fate that awaited the Everglades.

CHAPTER 6
THE TWENTIES ROAR
1928

That summer was hot. The stock market was hot. Everything was
hot. Nothing, it seemed, could cool the collective exuberance. It
was as if the old rules no longer applied.

—James E. Edmonds

The 1926 Miami hurricane season had been a wake-up call for the Everglades. The storms had exposed the stark inefficiencies of the dike in its present state. A new, larger dike was proposed, but money for the project was not rapidly forthcoming. Florida was in the middle of a major recession, and tax revenues were drastically down. For two years the Everglades farmers lobbied the state for funds to strengthen the dike, and each year the Florida legislature, sitting securely in Tallahassee four hundred miles away, voted down money for a new dike. The latest reverse was a bond issue that failed to garner enough votes to pass. Once again in 1928 Everglades farmers were assured that money would be approved next year. The memory of the 1926 hurricanes was, at least in Tallahassee, fading. After all, that was two years ago, and in politics, two years was ancient history.

January 1928 brought Belle Glade more than its share of hope, expectations, and new resolutions. The town had reason to be optimistic. There were two paved roads connecting Belle Glade to the outside world: the Palm Beach Road and the Connors Highway from Canal Point to Okeechobee. A group of investors led by Charles Riedel wanted to build a large electric plant to supply electricity to the entire town. Belle Glade had a water system that brought water to many homes, and though it was darkish and odorous, it was water. Main Street was clogged with cars and trucks; along the sidewalks, pioneers vied for space with new people and strangers; the sound of hammers and saws resonated throughout the town. Progress brought change and a sense of excitement.

For Bessie Mae Martin, 1928 began with high expectations. Her younger brother, Tommy Wells, had finally arrived with his new bride. Unable to get Willie Emma's father to give his blessing, and much to the scandal of Frostproof, Tommy Wells and Willie Emma had eloped. After a two-month honeymoon driving across Florida, they arrived in Belle Glade with two trunks and Tommy's oversized toolbox. They moved into John Hooker's bridge tender's house. Situated a dozen yards west of the Main Street bridge, the Cape Cod–type house was perched up high on the north bank of the Hillsboro Canal almost directly across from Henry's store, on the opposite side of the canal. The bridge tender's house was considered one of the sturdiest structures in Belle Glade. With the arrival of Tom and Willie Emma Wells in Belle Glade, the Martin clan was nearly one score strong, making them one of the largest clans in Belle Glade.

Using Tommy's mechanical skills acquired in the army, he and Henry planned to open a repair shop.

"There're more cars and tractors here than in Palm Beach," Henry exaggerated to make a point.

And if there wasn't enough work, Tommy figured he could rebuild one of Henry's old stills.

TOMMY'S arrival was not the only reason for Bessie Mae's excitement—Nancy Rachel was getting married. At five foot six, thirteen-year-old Nancy was not only tall for her age, she was a determined young lady. A twenty-one-year-old farmer, Josh Carver, had been courting Nancy for over a year. He had a Model T and a job working for Roscoe Braddock on Torry Island and was as good a prospect for a young Everglades girl as any. When he finally got up the courage to ask her to marry him, she immediately said yes. Her parents only asked her to wait until she was fourteen.

Henry Martin might not have been pleased with Nancy's early marriage because he knew too well the hardships a young couple faced in the Everglades. He consoled himself that it was better they got married than disgrace the family with an out-of-wedlock baby. Try as he might, Henry knew he could not patrol his farmhouse, especially with his attention directed at the store and other business in town. Josh Carver had a job, a car, and a place for Nancy to move into. It was more than he and Bessie

Mae had started out with. Henry understood that a frontier girl matured early. Boys were not far behind. By the time they became teenagers, they all had long lists of responsibilities that had to be completed before school. Childhood in the Everglades was short.

Nancy and Josh Carver married and moved into a house close by the Martin farm. "Walking distance," Nancy assured her mother. That first year, rain or shine, Nancy trekked every day along muddy rutted trails and across bean-covered fields to and from her mother's house. Bessie Mae must have smiled to herself. Married or not, her oldest daughter still had a lot of weaning to do.

BELLE GLADE

Walter Greer was a man with vision. A big man, with bright blue eyes, wavy hair, and a large, flowing mustache that drooped at the ends of his mouth, he was a blacksmith by trade. A Missourian by birth, he settled in the Everglades in 1911 with his wife, Tina, and lived in a small plank board house near Tedder's hotel. Though he continued to ply the craft of being a smithy in town, he, like everyone else in the Everglades, farmed. As one of the early settlers, he had suffered the privations of frontier life, the isolation, the lack of facilities, the droughts and floods. He was a hard-working, persistent man who was determined to bring the benefits of progress to Belle Glade. Patience, however, was not one of his virtues. Through his efforts the first church was built in town, then a school. He lobbied for a road to connect Belle Glade to Palm Beach. He helped organize a drainage district to oversee the pumping of the land, and he pushed the state for an agricultural experimental station. Belle Glade was growing and it needed a leader. He knew how to organize and usually got what he wanted. What he wanted now was to incorporate Belle Glade.

Pioneers by their very nature are individualists. They believe in self-sufficiency and are suspicious of authority, especially governmental authority. Few of the early pioneers saw any need for Belle Glade to incorporate into a town. They wanted no mayor "lording over them," but Greer argued that Belle Glade was growing. It needed services. It needed water, electricity, telephones, and the organization to provide, or bring, those services to town. Walter Greer was determined to bring progress to Belle Glade.

A town meeting was called. After a quick head check of those present, it became clear to Greer that the idea for incorporation would be voted down. Instead of voting to form a town, he first had those present vote on a board to study the possibility of incorporating. The backwater Machiavellian nominated some of his major critics. Once a board was elected, an attorney who just happened to be present informed those gathered that the formation of a board constituted incorporation. Thus on April 10, 1928, the town of Belle Glade was born.

While such rough tactics might not have made Greer many friends, everyone knew that his unbounded energy was good for Belle Glade.

THOUGH not allowed to attend the town meeting, Walter Peterson was as interested in Belle Glade's future as any white person. The Petersons had arrived in the Everglades in 1925, from the northern Florida town of Jasper. They had followed migrant work down the center of the state until finally stopping at the literal end of the road—Miami Locks. Walter and Dina were tired of the migrant life. They had six children, five girls and a seven-year-old son, Ardie. Two of the grown girls were married and their husbands lived in the same house. Dina Peterson would never hear of one of her children living off by themselves until they were well enough off. The Miami Locks house might be crowded, but the Peterson family ties were strong. Walter and his sons-in-law did farm work at Sebring and other area farms until in 1927, seeking more space, he moved his family from Miami Locks into Belle Glade.

The nascent village's "colored town" was expanding. A large influx of migrant farm hands and other laborers had given the black community a vibrant social and economic life. While there was still no school for black children, and, as in all southern towns, it was always whites first, the convenience of "city life" proved too strong an attraction to live anywhere else. Belle Glade was, as everyone said, the future, and Walter Peterson had a vision of a better future for his children.

MIAMI LOCKS

Lying flat and straight with its banks overgrown with elderbushes and hyacinth clogging its channel, the Miami Canal had slowed down. The first canal to connect the populous southeast coast cities to the Everglades was a pale reflection of its former self. Though still deep enough to swim in, the Miami Canal, like the entire Everglades, was suffering from a lack of water. South Florida was in the grip of the worst drought in its history. Life-giving pools dried up, leaving their bottoms littered with the bodies of fish and tadpoles. Animals that were able migrated in search of water. Alligators dug holes in the muck seeking enough water to keep their skins moist. Lake Okeechobee's shoreline retreated half a mile behind the now seemingly redundant muck dike. The lake dropped to its lowest recorded level. A pall of heavy omnipresent acrid muck fire smoke hung in the air.

When spring ran into summer and there was still no rain, the Everglades played a waiting game. The farmers waited for rain to plant. Wildlife waited for rain to breed. On the big lake, cargo waited on docks. At train terminals, empty boxcars waited for freight. The entire Everglades slumped into a haunting state of suspended animation.

THE LAKE LEVEL AND WATER POLITICS

On August 7, the hurricane that had ravaged Haiti and the Bahamas crossed over the Florida Straits and made landfall at Fort Pierce. By the time its outer edge reached the Everglades, it had degraded to a category 2 storm. While it killed two people in St. Lucie County, before it struck the Everglades it veered north, sparing the people of Belle Glade any gale force winds. Nevertheless, it was a wet hurricane and in one day it dropped five and a quarter inches of rain, which swelled the Kissimmee River and dumped enough water into the lake to raise its level from 13.1 feet to 14.2 feet. The canal outlet at Palm Beach was only partially opened at the time. So much water dammed up that it began to flow westward, back into Lake Okeechobee.

By mid-August, the drought-plagued Everglades had stopped waiting. For the next three weeks, massive afternoon thunderstorms fueled by summer heat dropped lakes of water in a few minutes. Thunderbolts scorched the land with hundreds of lightning strikes. For the newcomers who had never weathered a Florida summer, thoughts of Noah and his Ark must have flooded their minds. Occasionally the sun would shine and blue skies would raise hopes, until the clouds regrouped, darkened, and dropped more rain. The incessant summer rains had raised the water in Lake Okeechobee to its highest level since 1926.

The high level of the lake did not go unnoticed.

"Spillways should be open at the outlets of the drainage canals!" read a banner headline in the July 27 edition of the *Everglades News*. Publisher and editor Howard Sharp railed against the Everglades Drainage District. "Fred C. Elliott of Tallahassee, Chief Drainage Engineer of the Everglades Drainage District, does not expect overflow conditions in 1928. . . . [H]e will hold onto the old policy of closed spillways at the outlet ends of drainage canals and will produce a high lake level." He continued, "He (Elliott) did not expect the flood in 1922 . . . he did not expect the flood in 1924 . . . he did not expect the flood in 1926 which came before the [Miami–Moore Haven] hurricane.

"The chief engineer never expects any overflow conditions."

In early August, Pahokee resident Thomas Hunter summed up the trials of the thankless job of district drainage engineer by stating, "There is a conflict of interests between upstream dwellers and downstream dwellers. The cry downstream goes, 'You are flooding us down here, close the dams!' But when the cry is heeded, then in a very short time the upstream portion of the canal becomes likewise filled with surface drainage."

Again, in the September 7 issue of the *Everglades News*, Sharp wrote, "On August 14, 1926 [the year of the Miami hurricane], the lake level was at an elevation of 17.5 feet at Canal Point. It took a hurricane to raise it to an elevation of 19.1 feet."

That height reached by September 9 was to anyone's eye, even an untrained eye, a dangerously high level.

CHOSEN: THE CHOSEN LAND

Belle Glade's sister town, Chosen, lay a scant two miles to the west. It was founded before, situated better, and promoted harder than its rival. Yet by 1928, Chosen was running a distant second to Belle Glade. It had let its advantage in geography and seniority lapse, allowing the younger upstart Belle Glade to bypass it within a couple of years. Although founded by preacher-promoter J. R. Leatherman, Chosen, true to pioneer suspicion of government, big and otherwise, had never incorporated. What Chosen lacked was a leader with vision—like Belle Glade mayor Walter Greer.

Rather than a village, Chosen was a series of scattered farms. Clans of related people who lived within walking distance of each other and farmed their own plot of land. The Burke family lived in a one-story house close to the dike. A hundred yards across the road lived brother Ray. On weekends the sound of harmonious piano music emanated from the Burke house.

The Schlecters, with their eight children, lived even closer to the dike. Nearly every day after school, and especially in the summer, the children of Chosen swam in the lake.

Isaac West had placed his store as far to the east as was possible, yet remained in Chosen, hoping to attract customers from both towns. Like many businesses, his store was directly on the Hillsboro Canal. West had built the large, sturdy structure from the top down. Wanting his living quarters on the second floor and needing a place to live, he first built the second floor before finishing the ground-level store

A half mile up on the south side of the Hillsboro Canal, Fritz Stein, the lake lock tender, lived in a large two-story house with a sturdy brick chimney on one side. When he wasn't in Fort Lauderdale, Captain Stuart Holloway called Chosen his home.

Bill Hunt brought his new bride, Lois, to his one-story home near Isaac West's store. He carried her over the threshold into a dingy house that retained its drab appearance even with a fresh coat of paint. It took Lois Hunt one week to brighten up with curtains, a new bed, and a dining table.

Not far from the Hunts' home, the Morris brothers lived in a modest one-story house surrounded by five acres of bean fields. The brothers took frequent trips out of state, and while they were gone, a neighbor, John Elliot, kept an eye on the house. In Chosen, as in most small rural communities, neighbors helped neighbors. But within a few weeks this small community of family villages would suffer through ten hours that would change it forever.

JACOB Porter swore. Silently, of course—no true Christian man, especially a member of the African Episcopal Methodist Church, ever swore openly, but it was still an oath. The old brown mule was acting up, as mules are known to do. He would have preferred a horse, an even-tempered, easy-riding animal. But the heat and the humidity and pulling a plow through the back-breaking muck would kill a sane horse. So he used mules. Unfortunately, their hooves were narrower than a horse's and sank deeper into the damp black muck. They had to be fitted with muck shoes called "muck steppers," foot-round iron plates with insteps and leather straps for the mules' narrow hoofs.

Jacob tightened a mud shoe on each of the mule's hooves. The mule protested, quickly raised his head, and stomped one of the heavy shoes near Jacob's bare foot. But Jacob knew better than to leave his foot near a mud-shoed animal.

Jacob Porter had been farming the muck lands for five years, making him an old-timer by Everglades time. He did not own his own land. He cleared and plowed the land, planted seeds, and then shared the crop, or profits, with the owner. He would have liked to farm one plot, but the owners would raise the rent, give the plot to another, or decide to plant themselves. White folk could be terribly capricious, as he well knew.

He hitched a single-bladed number two plow to the mule's harness and set off down the first row. It was back-breaking work. While Jacob Porter pictured the crop that would spring from the ground in a couple of months, he also dreamed of one day owning one of those new Fordson tractors developed to work in the muck. Some of the white farmers had tractors, and one day he'd own his own.

Jacob Porter feared and hated white men. He resented the way he was forced to act dumb and shiftless in their presence, especially with poor white trash. Jacob was one of the ten black farmers working plots of land up against the dike. He also worked at Sebring Farms. His foreman, Bill

Boots, gave him leave to plow and plant as long as he made the time up later. Boots also lent him tools and the plow. Bill Boots was a good man—good for a white man, that is.

Jacob had arrived in Belle Glade as a migrant farmhand, traveling with the seasonal crops. He and his family had traveled as far north as North Carolina, picking crops as varied as tobacco, apples, lettuce, strawberries, and oranges. The first migrant workers in the Everglades were white men whom the locals called "fruit buzzards" as they scurried up and down trees on long wooden ladders picking oranges and grapefruit. When vegetables replaced fruit and green beans became king, the back-breaking work of bean picking was taken on by black field workers. The blacks migrated with their entire families, living in huts and shacks supplied by local farmers. Planting his own crops even if he was sharecropping would give his family stability. Hopefully they would not have to migrate at the end of the season.

Through hard work, Jacob proved his reliability and was given the chance to sharecrop.

Jacob was worried. He was behind schedule, and it was going to cost him time and labor. Most of the farmers who plowed their fields early had already planted, and he would have planted earlier except his first obligation was to work the fields at Sebring Farms.

The slosh of the mule's muck shoes made a sucking sounded with each step. It was slow, hard work. But Jacob Porter was a hard-working man. A pioneer had to be, and even more so if you were a black pioneer.

Behind him the muck dike loomed. It had been abnormally dry all summer until August. Then the skies opened up. With all the rain the lake was high. Without the dike, the land that Jacob was plowing would be under five feet of water. One mile east the thunderstorm, dropping its deluge on Belle Glades, had just missed Chosen. Dark clouds rolled overhead, a few raindrops had left darkened wet spots, and the wind had picked up some. But there was nothing more. This thunderstorm would miss them, but they'd get the next one, Jacob thought, staring at storm clouds. He had to finish today and was grateful for the reprieve.

Jacob lived with his wife and three children in one of a half dozen clapboard shacks that dotted a small canal near Chosen. He had replaced the tarpaper roof with corrugated metal so it didn't leak. Around back, his wife, Sara, had planted a little garden of vegetables and herbs for the kitchen. At harvest time his older son, now seven, would help pick the beans, as would his second son when he reached seven, and his baby daughter when she was seven. Every hand in the Porter family was needed at harvest time. It was a hard life for a black family in South Florida after the Great War, but Jacob Porter had hope. He also had something few of his fellow migrant laborers had: hidden inside the shack in an old rusted coffee can was $432, hard-earned money Jacob Porter had saved for a farm of his own.

He returned home just before sundown. Though it wasn't much, it was his place, far from the prying eyes of whites, surrounded by other African Americans, where he could finally relax. There was no acting, no fear that a casual incident with a white person would escalate into a confrontation that he could only lose. He could talk freely, smile, and listen. Watching the sun set from his narrow front porch, he enjoyed his time, time with his family, and, God willing, in time he'd soon have a place of his own.

DR. WILLIAM J. BUCK

Throughout the spring and summer of 1928, people poured into the Everglades. After the real estate collapse of 1926, a wave of East Coast people, "new people," moved to Belle Glade to try farming. Farms were bought and sold at an unprecedented pace. The same people who had looked down contemptuously on Everglades dirt farmers— calling them damned crackers and swampers—now wanted a piece of their land, to be their neighbors. At least farmers didn't starve to death. Not here in Florida. Not here in the muck.

Perhaps the most heartily welcomed of the new people to Belle Glade was Dr. William J. Buck. Until he arrived in April 1928, there was no other medical doctor between Pahokee and Moore Haven. Dr. Buck was the only doctor for six thousand widely dispersed people.

Medical attention in the Everglades was sparse. Treatment was limited to an array of home remedies. A common local cure for snakebite was a foul concoction whose main ingredient was creosote. With no doctor, it was the druggist who prescribed medicine. Even after the road was built, patients still had to be transported to the hospital in West Palm Beach. Many never made it.

Dr. Buck was born in Illinois. He studied general medicine at Northwestern University. After graduation, he joined the army and was stationed near the Mexican border. Mexico was in the throes of a vicious civil war they called their revolution. Combatants on all sides regularly attacked not only military targets but civilians as well. At times villages were punished for supporting another side. On March 9, 1916, the Mexican Revolution spilled over into the United States. Pancho Villa, with four hundred eighty-five men, attacked Columbus, New Mexico. Though the Villistas lost ninety men when the Thirteenth Calvary, which was garrisoned nearby, counterattacked, the Mexicans did kill eighteen Americans and made off with over a hundred horses and three hundred Mauser rifles. The United States could not allow this affront to go unpunished. President Wilson ordered the army to find, and capture, Pancho Villa.

Under the command of General John "Black Jack" Pershing, a punitive expedition of ten thousand men supported by tanks and artillery was sent into Mexico to subdue the countryside and capture Villa. As part of the medical team, Dr. Buck accompanied the expedition into Mexico, where he became friends with General Pershing.

Dr. Buck had a knack for languages. He quickly became fluent in Spanish, which helped him treat not only American soldiers but the local Mexican population as well. As the expedition moved farther into Mexico, Villa fled deeper into the Sierra. After a year, the Americans returned to the United States, having failed to capture their elusive prey.

Soon after the Mexican expedition, the United States found itself at war with Germany and Austria. Dr. Buck married his high school sweetheart just before receiving orders to report to a base in New Jersey. In 1918, while examining soldiers ready to board ships for France, his wife died from influenza, one of the twenty million people who would die in the worldwide epidemic. There was no time to mourn her death. His duties were such that he hurriedly buried her in New Jersey before sailing to France with his contingent.

In France, he was assigned to the Eighty-second Division's base hospital in Le Mans, France, where he rose to the rank of major. Much to the delight of the local population, he quickly learned French. In spite of long hours examining soldiers and civilians, Dr. Buck was able to reorganize the hospital into an efficient operation. For his efforts he received a personal commendation from General Pershing and a promotion to colonel.

After the war, he stayed in the army and was transferred to Panama, where he worked on tropical diseases. Once resigned from the army, he settled in West Palm Beach and opened his private practice. When the new Palm Beach Road opened, he drove to Belle Glade. There he was awed by the natural wonder of the Everglades. The bustling town with its pioneer spirit intrigued Dr. Buck, and when he learned that there were no doctors between Pahokee and Moore Haven, he decided to settle in Belle Glade and to open a practice. Soon the citizens became accustomed to seeing meticulous Dr. Buck near his office on Main Street dressed in a spotless white tunic.

"If he soiled his jacket treating a patient, he would take it off and give it to his houseman to clean while he put on a clean jacket," Abby Zumpf, his assistant for twenty years, recalled.

Finding a number of World War I European veterans in Belle Glade, he organized a local American Legion post and was voted its first commander. Most of the veterans were grateful for someplace to congregate, to share their experiences, and rekindle the camaraderie they had experienced fighting in the trenches of Europe.

The United States government had not been kind to its returning veterans. After the war, the soldiers who had fought in the gas-poisoned trenches of Verdun, Ypres, Argonne, and the Somme were demobilized, verbally thanked, and sent on their way. There was no G.I. Bill. There was no Veterans Administration, and they would have to wait, the federal government told them, forty years for their promised pensions.

Once home, the ex-doughboys found a country in the throes of a depression. The economy had not shifted smoothly to peace. Factories that produced munitions, artillery, and tanks were closed. Cattle and produce prices were down from their wartime highs. Country boys returned to failing farms. Unemployment was rampant. With few prospects at home, tens of thousands of young men set out across the country, some in buses, some hitch-hiking, while others rode in the same box cars that had carried them off to war. The term *hobo* became a household word. Social services were few, and the American Legion was the one organization that veterans felt lobbied for their concerns.

Dr. Buck did a lot of pro bono work, never refusing a patient even if that person had neglected to pay him for the last visit. To Dr. Buck, for a doctor to refuse a patient medical care was a sacrilege, a breaking of the Hippocratic oath.

During his stint in the army, he had learned to command. Running a field hospital loaded with wounded and gassed men, he had to make split-second decisions each day. The lives of hundreds of young boys depended on the precise organization of the hospital. Dr. Buck might have known how to organize a battalion-sized hospital with nurses, orderlies, and doctors, but he did not keep his own records until 1943, when he hired an assistant, Abby Zumpf, R.N.

Spending day after day surrounded by death and mutilation weighs on a person. After long hours in wartime operating rooms, Dr. Buck liked nothing better than to sit at a table with a few fellow doctors and enjoy a glass of smooth French cognac. It helped relieve interminable nights and the tension of the operating room.

After the death of his young wife and the trauma of war, Dr. William Buck welcomed the chance to be a simple small-town general practitioner.

THE SHIVES

Death was nothing new to the southern shore. Until men began to bring their wives and families, death was more common than birth. There was no cemetery in the Everglades. Since a corpse would bloat up and its casket float out of its grave in the waterlogged muck, the dead were taken and buried in the Woodlawn Cemetery in West Palm Beach. Sometimes it was a week before a person was safely interred. In the tropics corpses decomposed rapidly. Some old-timers were doused with alcohol to preserve them a day or two longer, much to the chagrin of the other fishermen. A few men, those with no family or friends, were left to the lake, the catfish, and the snails.

The end of each summer would find Calvin Shive preparing the car for the yearly pilgrimage back to Tulsa, Oklahoma. Inside, Rhoda and the girls packed and prepared food for the three-day journey. This year Paul had other plans. Two weeks before, he had made a trip with a friend in his father's truck to Georgia, where he purchased a load of peaches, brought them back to Pahokee, and sold them. After paying for food, lodging, gas, the peaches, tire repair, and his friend, he had made a nice profit and was anxious to return. He begged his father to let him stay. Finally, Calvin Shive reluctantly gave in, and the family left for Tulsa without Paul.

Paul packed up his things for the long drive to the Georgia peach orchards. At that time of year peaches were plentiful in Georgia and cheap. Floridians who had tired of oranges, guavas, and even bananas longed for the taste of sweet succulent peaches and paid a good price for them. This was a wonderful opportunity for an enterprising young man.

Once the peaches were loaded, Paul and his friend set off for Florida as the aroma of peaches filled the passenger cabin. To Paul it was the sweet smell of profit. Once across the state line, they drove all night down the narrow two-lane highways to Ocala when one of the old tired tires gave out; a common occurrence with thin pneumatic rubber inner tubes. Paul undid the tire, patched the tube, pumped it up, and had the tire back on the truck within fifteen minutes. As he got back into the truck, he noticed that one lug nut was still loose. He took the jack handle, stepped back down, and gave the nut a tightening twist. As he stood up and opened the truck door, he saw an oncoming car, but did not see a speeding roadster coming up fast behind him. The roadster swung around to pass the parked truck and drove straight into the path of the oncoming car. To avoid a head-on collision, the roadster swerved to the right, clipping Paul as he stood on the running board of his truck. The roadster took off the fender where Paul had rested his hand. It dragged the young man a hundred yards before dumping him on the road with a broken neck. By the time his friend reached him, Paul Shive was dead.

The Shives had left Oklahoma in a three-car caravan to return to Pahokee. Calvin and Rhoda Shive drove one car, Lillian and Duncan were in another, while her sister, Ruth, and husband, Dan Carpenter, brought up the rear. Ruth was seven months pregnant with her first child. She had even picked out a name—Milton, if it was a boy, after the blind poet. The caravan maneuvered slowly over pot-holed roads. At each rut and bump, Dan Carpenter slowed down so as not to jar Ruth and her baby.

Long-distance automobile travel was still an adventure and was often done in caravans. Tire punctures were common on long stretches of lonely roads, while engine troubles were a chronic nuisance. Traveling in a group ensured a more secure journey.

At Baton Rouge, while waiting for the ferry to cross the Mississippi River, the group received a message that Paul had died. Calvin and Rhoda rushed on ahead to Ocala. By the time they arrived, Paul's body had already been embalmed on orders from a doctor friend in Pahokee. It was shipped by train to Pahokee and three days later buried in Woodlawn Cemetery in West Palm Beach.

Calvin fell into a deep depression. The man who had consoled so many people over the years could not forgive himself for letting Paul stay behind. He blamed himself for his only son's death. Both parents grieved so that Lillian and Ruth thought they would get sick. The family tried to distract them with activities. Calvin busied himself fixing up his house, while Rhoda worked with the Salvation Army. The activities kept them from dwelling on Paul's death. Within a few of days the entire Shive family would have more than they could want to keep them busy.

BELLE GLADE

For the residents of Belle Glade, the first weekend in September approached in typical fashion—a thunderstorm drenched the landscape. Legally the muckland town was just over five months old. Henry Martin had been at the first contentious town meeting and had backed Charlie Reidel and Walter Greer. Henry recognized that the Everglades were growing. Progress required planning, and to plan, Belle Glade needed to incorporate. He understood those that opposed incorporation. The total population of the mucklands was nearly six thousand people. For many of the original pioneers, it was getting crowded.

Henry and many of the other whites were concerned that the black migrant farmworkers had not moved on as they had in other years. There were so many of them, too. When he had first arrived in 1919, outside Moore Haven, only a few dozen black farm hands lived in the south Everglades, and they were glad to get work. Not like those today who worked for a few days then disappeared, Henry suspected to get drunk.

Having a large available labor pool benefited the local farmers. Help would be easier to find, and the competition would drive down wages. But was there work for so many people? And what would they do if they did not find work? Sheriff Clarence Everett ran the more obvious black vagrants out of Belle Glade. Most kept out of sight in and around the fields, never bothering anyone, giving the sheriff no excuse to drive them to the town line with stern orders not to return until next year.

And there were all the newcomers who crowded the streets with their new cars. Henry was uncomfortable with all these new people buying up the land, seeming to have unlimited funds. They were buying land that had been earned—cleared with sweat and blood of the original pioneers. The newcomers were people who did not understand the Everglades like they did; some were even Yankees. He could tolerate most as long as they bought food and dry goods at his store. As the weekend came, Henry Martin's cash register rang sweetly, soothing any anxieties he might have about progress and population growth.

BELLE GLADE

By September, most people who opposed incorporation had accepted the fait accompli. They could console themselves with the obvious progress that happened in the ensuing months. Telephone lines, strung from West Palm Beach, brought service to a few stores and homes. A new state road to Clewiston was being built. Florida Power and Light was building a new generator that promised uninterrupted electricity for the entire area. Belle Glade was progressing, and if there is anything Americans love, it's progress.

While Belle Glade was preparing to celebrate its fifth month of official existence, five thousand miles away an easterly wave of superheated Sahara air shimmered westward across Africa. It was hardly unique. During any given year, an average of sixty waves form. Most meander across the Atlantic, changing air temperature but doing little else. But it was September. The Atlantic waters were warm. In a swath from the coast of Africa to the Gulf of Mexico, the SST was eighty-five degrees—as warm as it would ever be.

As the hot, dry wave passed off the African coast, it encountered water—lots of warm water. Evaporating the surface water, the clear air began to cloud. Puffy white cumulus clouds, fair weather clouds, billowed skyward. A warm-air updraft lifted more moisture into the air, carrying it higher and higher. The surface air pressure fell. By the time the wave reached the Cape Verde Islands, it had formed into a well-defined low pressure. Though cloudy, it stubbornly refused to give up any moisture. It hoarded its water like a miser and passed over the islands without leaving a drop of rain, much to the consternation of the people below. Once past the Cape Verde Islands, it encountered the westerly trade winds blowing from the northeast. The low pressure drew the winds slightly to the south, toward its center. The winds pushed the clouds together into a tighter circular pattern. The winds blew at a breezy twenty-five miles an hour. Cumulus clouds swelled into cumulonimbus clouds with massive anvillike heads. High-altitude moisture condensed, releasing latent heat into the air. Droplets formed. Now it gave up its water. It had more than enough to spare. It had an entire ocean.

As the thunderstorm reached higher into the atmosphere, the low's surface air pressure dropped further. The westerly winds began to curve around it until they had formed a circle. More thunderstorms formed. The low-pressure area had morphed into a tropical depression.

Four hundred miles west of the African coast, the depression's thunderstorms stretched their heads skyward until their tops brushed the troposphere. Encountering no contrary winds to disperse its upward movement, it rose further, creating drowndrafts and heavy rains that warmed the air, further forcing its clouds to rise higher still. Air pressure in its center dropped. More air rushed in. The thunderstorms closed circle and spun around the depression. The wind speed jumped from forty-five to a gusty sixty miles per hour. The thunderstorms began to organize into a distinct circular form. A hole opened up in its center like a yawn, or more like a baby's cry at birth. It was the seventh of September, the first day of the storm's life.

CHAPTER 7
MOTHER NATURE GIVES BIRTH

Saturday, September 8

Warm air rises; cold air falls.

Hurricanes are classified on the Saffer-Simpson scale. Divided into five categories, the scale quantifies a hurricane by its destructive capacity and wind speed. A tropical storm officially becomes a hurricane, a category 1 hurricane, when its winds reach a sustained speed of 74 miles per hour over one minute's time. In a category 2, sustained wind speeds range from 96 to 110 miles per hour. Above 110 miles per hour, a hurricane becomes a category 3 and is considered a severe hurricane. A category 4's winds top 131, and a category 5, or a catastrophic storm, has sustained winds of 155 miles per hour or greater.

Only one category 5 hurricane struck Florida in the last century, and that was the Florida Keys 1935 Labor Day hurricane. The force of the wind actually sandblasted skin off people's bodies. The deadliest historical hurricanes, however, were category 3's and 4's.

When the winds reach eighty miles per hour, they actually act like a vacuum cleaner, sucking up thousands of gallons of water from the ocean like dirt off a carpet. At a hundred and ten, it actually lifts and shovels water into the air. Fish caught on the surface are carried aloft. Wind will pick up objects and fling them like missiles—metal, wood, glass, and bricks. In the 1900 Galveston hurricane, a one-inch steel hull of an ocean-going freighter was pierced through with a piece of lumber.

Wind velocity often dictates the size of the eye of the storm. The larger the eye, the stronger the centrifugal wind forcing the clouds that shape the eye wall outward. The eye of a hurricane can vary from 5 to 110 miles wide. The strength is usually, but not always, indicative of the size of the eye. In 1992, Hurricane Andrew, the most destructive hurricane in U.S. history, was a compact powerful hurricane with a small eye.

As violent as a 150-mile-per-hour gust of wind, moving air is not the major killer in a hurricane. It is the giver of life, the universal sol-vent—water—that takes most lives. A storm might dump one to two feet of water on any given area, causing devastating flash floods, but the single event that takes most lives is the storm surge. Until coastal evacuations were organized, nine out of ten hurricane deaths resulted from the storm surges.

A storm surge is not a storm wave or a tidal wave. It is a fast-moving dome of water that will continue to move with the storm as long as it does not en-counter land. A major hurricane will generate a storm surge well over fifteen feet high; a category 5, over twenty. Along the coasts, another four to ten feet can be added depending on whether the storm hits at low or high tide.

Many factors determine the size of the storm surge. Wind is the most important. The circular wind near a storm's eye herds water into a con-centrated area and holds it, dragging it along as it moves. The air pres-sure decrease at the center of a hurricane acts like a vacuum cleaner, actually lifting the water up thirteen inches for each one-inch reduc-tion of atmospheric pressure. When Hurricane Camille came ashore at Mississippi in 1969, it produced a twenty-five-foot storm surge. Flat Florida, with its thousands of miles of coastline, is especially vulnera-ble to storm surges.

Not all hurricanes are created equal. Some are windstorms, some rainstorms, others both. A strong or severe hurricane may or may not have a lot of rain. While rated as only a tropical storm, Claudette dumped forty-five inches of water near Alvin, Texas, in 1979. Yet Hur-ricane Andrew was a relatively "dry" hurricane that dropped only six inches as it sped through southern Florida. In mountainous area, rain-driven flash floods are as deadly as the storm surge. Most of the ten thousand people killed in Central America by Hurricane Mitch were flood victims.

From the vantage of a weather satellite orbiting twenty-four thousand miles above the Earth, a hurricane is a thing of beauty. It's big and round, and it moves with silken, studied grace. Its white clouds pirouette like a ballerina with long elegant arms stretching hundreds of miles, embracing all within its reach. Viewing a hurricane is seeing something that is alive—it moves; it breathes; it vibrates; it pulsates. And it has an eye, a large, round, clear eye that stares unblinkingly at the heavens. A hurricane's fury—the waves, the wind, the lightning, the low black clouds, and the rain—are all choreographed to create awe. With feeder bands of clouds reaching out in a galactic stance, for those caught in its grasp, a hurricane is a universal unto itself. It is godlike, in both scale and beauty. And like God, it holds life and death in its hands.

CAPE VERDE ISLANDS

Along the main streets and the central plaza lined with brightly painted stucco facades, the sound of staccato Portuguese chatter filled the air. The streets of Praia, the capital of the Cape Verde Islands, were lined with distinctive Portuguese colonial design buildings. The people, an eclectic mixture of Mediterranean and African, moved in deliberately paced steps, conserving energy in the heat.

An archipelago of ten volcanic islands and five islets, Cape Verde hovers off the African coast like an afterthought. While Dakar, continental Africa's westernmost point, is its closest neighbor, the Cape Verde islands are farther east than Iceland—a redoubt of land in a water world.

Colonized by Portuguese and African slaves, the islands were an important stop for Portuguese traders. During the early fifteenth century, the visionary Prince Henry of Portugal sent his privately financed carracks down the coast of Africa, probing each river and inlet. He hoped to find a way around Africa to the rich spice lands of the East. Cape Verde became an important way station in that endeavor. Prince Henry's efforts began a century of exploration that would culminate in the European rediscovery of the Americas.

With little to keep them home, Cape Verde's young men migrated. During the 1800s, they became sailors, whalers, and ship captains. In Herman Melville's time, most of the New Bedford "colored" sailors were Cape Verde Islanders. They labored side by side with other able-bodied seaman. New England whalers were America's first truly integrated enterprises. If you feared God and the whale, you were given a berth.

The whalers and sailors knew of the great storms that formed in the southern North Atlantic. They knew hurricanes, and they knew the big storms had a season. They knew it was dangerous to whale in the equatorial Atlantic waters off the Cape Verde Islands during August and September. Yet the islands themselves were safe from their namesake storms. Cape Verde hurricanes never strike the Cape Verde Islands.

When the Portuguese discovered the islands, the green slopes were a welcome change from the stark Sahara coasts. Over the centuries, man's intrusion along with climatic change rendered Cape Verde a desert. Once stripped of its forests, the winds from Africa conspire to keep the islands dry. The green slopes of colonial times were now barren and brown. Still, the islands were very livable because aside from the stark beauty of the volcanic mountains and the sea, the westerlies—the northeast trade winds—tempered the temperature of the Cape Verde Islands. And it is into these westerly winds that hurricanes are born—Cape Verde hurricanes.

While only 60 percent of any year's Atlantic tropical storms are Cape Verde–type hurricanes, they account for nearly 85 percent of the major hurricanes. The two greatest natural disasters to strike the United States—the Galveston and Okeechobee hurricanes—were Cape Verde storms, as were the Miami, the New England, and the 1935 Labor Day hurricanes. Most Cape Verde hurricanes form later in the season, favoring September. And the Okeechobee hurricane was right on schedule.

HENRY MARTIN

Henry Martin's plans for expansion took a quick turn in August. The Southern Sugar Company wanted to set up a store for its employees and needed a reliable experienced person to run it. For a salary, part of the profits, and the right to sell his own produce in the company store, Henry agreed to set up and manage Southern Sugar Corporation's commissary in South Bay.

Henry had to spend most of his time in South Bay setting up the new store. He left the day-to-day management of the Belle Glade store to Arlin Woodson, a Martin cousin who had recently arrived from Frostproof.

The first weekend in September found Henry Martin still stocking his new store in Miami Locks. He knew if you wanted something done right, you had to do it yourself. He hated delegating responsibility. At least the black family that lived on the farm were good workers and responsible. For the first time Henry felt he could leave the fields in the care of someone else. Also, Raymond was old enough and could make the rounds in the fields while he was at the stores.

Even with reliable help, Henry Martin still worked seven days a week. He knew if he didn't have what a customer wanted, then he'd lose that customer. A grocery store needed the owner's strict attention to detail. Listen to the customers' wishes and quickly supply what they want and they will return. It was like cooking. Use the right ingredients and you had a meal; if not, you had slop fit only for hogs.

Henry was personable and good with names and faces. He greeted each customer who came through the door. The bell hanging over the top of the store entrance rang its melodic jangle as the door opened, and even before it closed he usually recognized the figure silhouetted by the bright light streaming in from the street.

One of Henry's customers was Edna Hughes, the Miami Locks school-teacher. She had recently moved her houseboat to Miami Locks. For two years she lived with her husband, John, and their young son Paul in their houseboat docked on the Bolles Canal.

During the school year, every morning she would row Paul and herself in a small dinghy to Miami Locks—a three-mile trip. There she tied the boat to the dock and walked to the schoolhouse. In the afternoon she would row home. Thunderstorms often caught them out in the open, at times filling the dinghy so full with water that it threatened to sink.

Edna knew all the students and their parents—the Bootses, the Thomases, and the Lees. All good kids, hard-working kids, though some obviously believed that schooling was a waste of time. Mrs. Hughes never had a disciplinary problem. One implied threat of a note to their parents was enough to tame even the rowdiest child.

Most of the parents realized that some education was good for their children; however, everyone, teachers and parents, understood the realities of living in a rural area; planting and harvesting were even more important. So the school year was customized around the seasons. She realized most of the lake children were destined to be farmers, but they'd be better farmers if they could read, write, and calculate. Against the odds, a few of the area children had already gone to college. Roscoe Braddock Jr., from Torry Island, was a sophomore at the university who had returned home to help his parents clear land before the new semester began.

Edna liked Henry Martin. He was one of the few men with whom she could talk kitchen. He was always polite and extremely respectful. She ignored the rumors that he made moonshine. Edna had never touched a drop of liquor in her life. She did not condone its use, though she was not preachy about her temperance. She had witnessed firsthand what unfettered drunkenness could do to a family, especially the children. Some of her students had alcoholic fathers, and the children were always the first to suffer.

The Hughes family hoped this would be the last year they had to live in the houseboat. Though cozy, it was cramped, and at times the walls seemed to close in on them—and the humidity as well. It was always damp on board. With their combined incomes, they would soon be able to afford a farm of their own.

The canal system begun by Disston and Broward still drained millions of gallons of Everglades water daily, though with the railroads and new highways to Palm Beach and Okeechobee, most water transportation was reduced to milk runs across the lake. Below the South Bay locks a small fleet of houseboats, barges, and tugs were securely moored to the docks. The two large barges belonged to the Huffman Company. One was a massive work barge whose dark rusting hulk dominated the canal. The Huffman Company had collected many of its boats and barges at South Bay to support work on the Clewiston South Bay Road construction. The work barge had been converted into a quarterboat to house the workers building the new Clewiston road.

Tied up to the dock directly behind the quarterboat was Bill Rawle's tug, *Fox*. The Forbes family had a contract to support the Huffman Company boats when they needed to be moved. Rawle was one of the most experienced captains on the lake, but lately he was becoming worried about his future. With the new roads to West Palm Beach and Okeechobee, and the railroad in Belle Glade, boat transportation was becoming a thing of the past. The last passenger boat ran to Fort Lauderdale in 1920 and to West Palm Beach in 1922. Each day less and less cargo seemed to travel by boat. Bill Rawle knew there was little future in water transportation. Even though he had invested in land on Torry Island with Felix Forbes, his father-in-law, he knew this might be the last year he captained on the great lake. The great era of the graceful double-decker Everglades barge boats was drawing to a close.

THE HORSE LATITUDES

At first it moved slowly, as most tropical storms do against the equator, with a top forward speed of ten to twelve miles per hour. Forward motion had carried it six hundred miles farther west, slowly getting its sea legs. Like a young dancer taking her first steps across the world stage, it had not gotten its rhythm. It was awkward, uncoordinated, off balance, not quite symmetrical. It wobbled from one side to the other like a slow-spinning child's top. Continuously fueled by the warm summer waters, it became more organized. The air at its center rose, its air pressure continued to drop, and wind speed increased. Thunderstorms spun around the eye in a neat circle, creating a wall of clouds, the eye wall. It flung its arms farther out to its sides, a hundred miles at first, then two hundred, embracing more air, more moisture, and more warm water—everything it needed to grow. By dawn the next morning, with sustained winds topping seventy-five miles per hour, it was now officially a hurricane—the god Huracan reborn.

Carried confidently by the North Equatorial Current and the Northeast trade winds, it headed west, due west, sandwiched between the equatorial doldrums and the temperate horse latitudes. Deep in the Atlantic, far from the busy shipping lanes, it attracted little attention. But that was soon to change.

BACK at his farm, no matter which way Henry Martin did his store's books, he must have been pleased. With the combined income from the crops and the stores, they would make a tidy profit. Next month was the last payment he'd have to make on the loan he took out for the Fordson tractor that he had purchased in 1926.

"Well, Kid, one more payment and the tractor will be ours," he said proudly to Bessie Mae.

In the summer of 1928, Henry and Bessie Mae Martin had every reason to be optimistic. They had eight healthy children, two stores, and some of the best land for growing produce in the state. Finally, after years of hard work, they were living the American Dream—property and prosperity.

SUNDAY, SEPTEMBER 9, ATLANTIC OCEAN

Captain Samuel Kruppe was on the bridge of the SS *Commack*. The American flagship had inadvertently sailed into a storm. The waves were rising in a high chop, occasionally sending white angry water over the bow. Visually the captain judged the wind velocity by the feel of the seas and cloud movement. Sea drift sailed off the wave tops like ghostly white banners waving in the wind. More helpful were the roar of the wind and the sound it made through the guidelines; both tones can give a seasoned captain a fairly accurate wind velocity. He calculated the storm was almost a hurricane. If a barometer reading was taken, it wasn't recorded.

The captain was not worried. He had made scores of trips across the Atlantic, both North and South. The 390-foot, 5,111-ton SS *Commack* was headed from Bahia, Brazil, to Philadelphia, its home port, with a cargo of bananas when it encountered rough seas and strong thunderstorms. The wind was out of the northwest. The ferocity of the storm surprised Captain Kruppe. He, like most Atlantic captains of his day, believed that hurricanes were mostly creatures of the Caribbean. He was well aware of the summer storm season between the Cape Verde Islands and the Caribbean, but he was, he thought, too far east to encounter a full-fledged hurricane. He radioed in the position of the storm. Captain Kruppe had just made history; he had just informed the world in real time of the eastern-most recorded hurricane to date.

A TYPICAL EVERGLADES SUNDAY

Sunday in the Everglades was God's day, or at least Sunday morning was. Depending on the weather, people went to church. Most towns had one church that might call itself Baptist or Methodist but in reality was an all-denomination house of worship. Everyone was welcomed except Jews and Catholics.

Sunday afternoons were times to play. And baseball was the all American sport.

At Bacom Point, where the sand ridge ended just south of Pahokee, was a large sandy area. It was flat and offered a good natural field when it wasn't flooded. Spectators spread blankets along the first and third base lines. Pitchers of lemonade and sandwiches were passed around. The men and boys paired off, choosing sides led by the better players. There were teams. Pahokee was to play Canal Point next month. All the large farms, the sugar mills, and towns sponsored teams. Each farm had a star player who received special privileges as far as what jobs he held. Everyone knew he was there to play ball. Some of the farm teams took the game too seriously. Fierce rivalries developed between the farm teams, sometimes ending in physical confrontations. But mostly it was a time to relax and enjoy playing and being seen.

While baseball was played in Pahokee, the residents of Torry Island, lacking a large sand field, had to settle for a fast game of croquet at the BeaDer house. Early in the morning the children set out the croquet hoops and stakes. Captain Ed King had bought the colorful wooden set before he went blind. The ground was a bit soggy from all the rain, but the bright sunny morning promised to dry out the lawn. It was the prime time for the youngsters to get together. The girls flirted and the boys roughhoused under the watchful eye of their parents.

Elizabeth BeaDer hoped that Frede Aunapu would pay a visit. The men had been busy working on the water pumps. She was sure that if no more water pumps broke down, then Frede would be there. Even so she kept her fingers crossed. Last night Frede had paid a visit to the BeaDer house, and they had sat for hours on the front porch ignoring the insects. Though he hadn't asked yet, she was sure he was the man she was to marry.

The Aunapus were early settlers on the islands. At the turn of the century, Frede's father, John, had emigrated from Russian-held Estonia. He farmed and ran a successful canal-side store on Byrd Island. The Aunapus lived in a large two-story house that they built after John sold the Byrd Island store. Along with farming, they, like most island residents, spent much of their time maintaining the large water pumps that kept their fields dry. The new dike, while keeping water off the reclaimed lands on the mainland, raised the water level on the lake and around the islands. The islands were now even more susceptible to flooding. Heavy rains and wind tides during the first weeks of September kept the island men busy around the clock.

TUESDAY, SEPTEMBER 11

The storm moved in a mechanically straight line along the fifteenth parallel—the middle of the Intertropical Convergence Zone (ITCZ). With pig-headed determination, it had not changed course since its inception. The first land that would feel its wrath was to be the twin islands of French Guadeloupe. Packing sustained winds of over one hundred miles per hour, the storm jumped to become a category 2 hurricane. With perfect conditions and a clear path, it had no intention of stopping there.

For most of the Caribbean islands, weather forecasting in 1928 was a hit-and-miss affair. Only a dozen stationary weather stations dotted the Caribbean and Bahama Islands. Some open-ocean information came from ships at sea, those that had good radios. Others related their observations when they reached port. A few ambiguous reports reached the Leeward Islands. Those tiny mountain specks precariously perched at the very edge of the Caribbean were always the first to greet tropical Atlantic storms. Like the Cape Verde Islands, many of the Leeward Islands had either active or dormant volcanoes. Some islands, like Guadeloupe and Montserrat, regularly spewed smoke, ash, and lava down their steep flanks. Islanders liked to say that living in paradise, you pay—the devil gets his due twice: volcanoes and hurricanes.

WEDNESDAY, SEPTEMBER 12

The bottom of the weather column of the *Palm Beach Post* read as follows:

```
TIDES AT GUS BATHS High: 6:33; low: 1:05
STORM WARNING

By the Associated Press
Washington. Sept 11—The weather bureau issued the fol-
lowing advisory storm warning at 8 o'clock tonight.

    Tropical disturbance of considerable intensity cen-
tral near 16 North 14 West—moving west or west-north-
westward. Its center will likely pass over Lesser An-
tilles North of Martinique, Wednesday.
```

GUADELOUPE

With rain forest–draped mountains reaching to the sea and a warm climate seasoned by the trade winds, the island of Guadeloupe could easily be confused with paradise. It lay in a direct path of the ITCZ nearly on the exact latitude as the Cape Verde Islands—the cradle of the Atlantic Ocean's killer hurricanes. Locked at the elbow of the Antilles, Guadeloupe juts out into the Atlantic Ocean as if daring the Atlantic. Basse-Terre, its provincial capital, is the exact latitude as Praia, the Cape Verde capital, with nothing in between except for 2,150 miles of warm open ocean.

By Wednesday morning, the storm had drunk its way across the Atlantic and was about to encounter its first land. The storm came ashore in the morning, and by noon the eye had settled directly over the island. The weather station recorded a barometric low of 27.76 inches and winds of 120 miles per hour. The storm had reached category 3, an intense storm. But it wasn't supposed to be here. The latest weather bureau report had the storm tracking for Martinique, one hundred and twenty miles to the south. The fickle storm had taken a slightly more northern path than predicted. With all communications down, the rest of the world could only sit back and wonder.

MONTSERRAT

The island of Montserrat, a speck of land positioned at the northeast edge of the Caribbean Ocean, could boast some of the world's best climate. Steady year-round ocean breezes tempered its warm tropical days. While its ten thousand residents enjoyed a nearly ideal climate, at times weather had not been kind to this tiny island. With no warning four years before, a vicious killer hurricane had struck the island in the dead of night with a frightening fury from which the island economy was just recovering.

It had been a very hot summer even for tropical Montserrat. The usual cooling sea breezes failed to temper a series of intolerable heat waves. Wednesday, September 12, brought slightly cooler air carried by fast-moving north winds. By noon, the north wind began to increase in strength. The cooler air , the islanders knew, was not bringing relief. Just the opposite.

This time the island knew a hurricane was fast approaching. The Weather Bureau in Washington, D.C., had broadcast a warning that a storm of "considerable intensity" was headed that way. From atop St. George's Hill above Plymouth, the capital, the British administrator, Commissioner Peebles, sounded alarms, urging the residents to prepare for a storm. At five o'clock that afternoon, the hurricane struck. It raked the island for ten hours with wind gusts reaching 140 miles per hour. In its wake it left forty-two people dead and five thousand homeless—half the population.

By Wednesday morning's light, the storm had moved off shore. It spun on toward the west, aiming its fury on the straight course it had kept since forming off the Cape Verde Islands. With the exceptionally warm summer, the waters of the Caribbean were warmer than usual with an SST of over ninety degrees. The warm water further energized the storm, giving it more strength. The thunderheads reached higher into the heavens, the barometric pressure dropped in its eye, and the winds increased. Shifting into a higher gear, it gained forward velocity as it headed westward.

THE MARTINS AND STORM RUMORS

Six-year-old Minnie Lucy Martin cringed as her sister Nancy sat her down and carefully parted strands of her hair. Monday, while helping in the fields, her hair had gotten infected with redbugs. Her scalp was a blotch of red welts and scabs where she had scratched and picked at them. Nancy had cut back her impossibly tangled bright red hair in spots so she could directly treat the bug bites with a smelly ointment. Minnie Lucy looked like a Raggedy Ann doll. To make her hair neater, Nancy took a pair of shears and gently trimmed the rest of her hair short like a boy's.

"It'll grow out," Nancy reassured her.

At first Lucy thought it was horrible, then after glancing in the mirror a few times, she began to like it. No long hours combing or drying it after a swim in the lake. Still, outside the house she wore a scarf.

After her marriage, Nancy Martin spent over half of each day at her mother's house. After all she was still a girl; Bessie Mae still had a lot to teach her daughter, and Nancy knew it.

As he did every morning except during harvest and planting, Henry Martin left the farm right after breakfast for the store in Belle Glade. Planting was over and school terms were beginning. He had to make sure the store was stocked with erasers, pencils, and foot-long wooden rulers. A couple times a week Bessie Mae came to cook and clean the store. In general, Henry preferred that his women stay on the farm. Someone might curse, and Henry would have to remind them that there were women present. If he persisted, the offender would be escorted from the store, and that was not good for business.

The first whispers of a hurricane approaching Florida reached Belle Glade on Wednesday. Some people, with the Moore Haven hurricane in mind and an eye to the high lake level, had made rudimentary evacuation plans. Bill Rawle had arranged with Bill Boots to take his mother and the Boots boys to South Bay where they could ride out the storm on board Rawle's tug, the *Fox*. The work tug was docked just below the North New River Canal locks. It was commonly thought that boats and barges secured tightly with wire cable to the docks were the safest place to weather a hurricane. At least they floated. Most people planned to pack up their automobiles and take the only two exits from Belle Glade east to West Palm Beach or north to Pahokee and Okeechobee. Pahokee, built on the sand ridge, was considered high safe ground. No one wanted to spend a major storm in the low lands of Belle Glade and South Bay. To others, thought of abandoning their homes or their livestock overrode any fear of a hurricane, and they battened down their houses to wait out the storm.

The more cautious made ready to leave on a minute's notice. They'd gas up, top off the fluids, and charge the batteries of their cars. Some planned to literally ride out the storm in their flimsy automobiles. For those who would ride out the storm in their car, it would be their last night alive.

The 1926 hurricane that destroyed Miami and Moore Haven had brushed by Belle Glade with severe rain and wind—little different from a prolonged summer thunderstorm. Many considered the 1926 hurricane an aberration, a freak storm that couldn't happen again in another ten years. And what about the dike? The Everglades farmers, like all who make a living off the land and nature's bounty, were an optimistic people.

Few gave any consideration as to what the black migrant workers would do. They had nowhere to go and no cars to carry them to safety, they could not travel on the barges, and they had no relatives in high and dry places. They would have to take their chances in their flimsy shacks built of scrap wood and tarpaper, most no stronger than poorly built coffins.

WEATHER BUREAU ADVISORY. Washington D.C. September 12.

Advisory 8:30 p.m.—Hurricane central above 50 miles south of Saint Kitts moving west-northwestward. Its center will pass south of Virgin Islands Thursday morning, short distance south of Puerto Rico during Thursday and probably south of Mona Passage in late afternoon or early night, and over southern Haiti Thursday night. Great caution advised vessels near path of hurricane.

CHAPTER 8
THEY LOST THE STORM

Thursday, September 13

The signs are all there, they're just read wrong.
—*Rudyard Kipling*, Captains Courageous

SS *MATURA*

Sixty-five miles southwest of the American Virgin Island St. Croix, the SS *Matura* struggled against roller-coaster seas. The 376-foot Bermuda-registered freighter rode low in the water, its 4,556 tons heavy with spare parts for the large Texaco refinery in Trinidad. For the twenty-year-old freighter, this was another milk run, a voyage it had made more than a hundred times. Straining against each wave, it groaned as its steel plates protested the pounding. Each crew member had to wonder whether the old ship could take much more punishment. Still, it was a good ship, a strong ship, a ship that had seen many seas—but none as vicious as these.

Captain Richard Harwich, dressed in a long Macintosh, stood behind the first mate as he struggled with the wheel. They had turned into the wind and would remain in that defensive position until the storm had passed. While he was not overly concerned, he was peeved that the storm would delay his arrival.

The night before, the freighter had encountered large successive ocean swells, a rarity in the Caribbean Sea, which was soundly protected by a string of islands and two continents. By midnight, the wind picked up and the seas had begun to chop. Captain Harwich ordered all the bulkhead hatches sealed. Now, thirty- and forty-foot waves rose and fell in nauseating rhythm; some were higher than the wheelhouse.

Last night's sunset had been brilliant—brick-red brilliant—an ominous sign that dispelled the old sailor's refrain: "Red skies in morning, sailor's warning; red skies at night, sailor's delight." All on board knew that this brick-red evening sky was no delightful portent. As for a dawn warning, there was no dawn, just low, fast-moving black clouds against dark gray skies. Storm skies.

Captain Harwich had read the U.S. Weather Bureau's storm warnings. Though he knew that a major hurricane had struck Guadeloupe the night before and was headed in his direction, he had not thought to change course. Changing course, for any good captain, went against his grain. He had weathered hurricanes before. But he had never experienced such high seas. This was more than a hurricane, he thought. Faced with overwhelming force, he had turned the ship into the storm, into the waves. The first mate tried to keep the boat slicing through waves at a slight angle, but the contrary winds made that difficult. Gusts were so strong that as the freighter topped each wave, it swayed in the wind like a sailboat.

The ship came down hard on each wave. The water, for a second, parted; then it rushed in over the deck, trying its best to sink the irritating anomaly. Captain Harwich watched the enraged white water break over the bow, then roll up at the wheelhouse window until his vision was blocked by rabid foam. The wind was out of the northwest, blowing, he estimated by the humming of the wire stays and the angle of the rain and sea spray, at 135 miles per hour, maybe more. He preferred the more conservative figure. He was a sea captain, and sea captains, unlike fishermen, were not prone to exaggeration.

Through the driving rain, he could just make out the next wave. At the top of each wave, visibility was a few hundred yards. In the troughs, it was zero. The freighter rolled and pitched hard to starboard. A ship is vulnerable on its flank. If caught sideways by a large wave, it is tossed and, depending on the center of gravity, will roll on its side, reaching for the breaching point—the point of no return. Unlike the wooden sailing ships that could right themselves when breached, steel-hulled ships sank like stones. Captain Harwich knew they would not breach. Their cargo was too heavy; their point of gravity was too low. If they went down, it would be structural failure. In these seas, structural failure was a real possibility.

All captains understood that while the sea was their mistress, it was also their master. Captain Harwich must have wondered whether he had met his master. While he would not say he was lost, he could not swear to the exact coordinates. The storm had pushed them far off course. The waves seemed to reach higher; the wind blew more strongly. The caps of the highest waves were blown off, decapitated, leaving a horizontal trail of steely froth whipping the air.

Suddenly, the ship broke through the rain and clouds into brightness and then sun. The wind had stopped. The sea still swelled up, but a clear sky shone blue. Though he might be lost, Captain Harwich knew where he was. The SS *Matura* was in the eye of the storm. He grabbed his sextant and went outside. Placing his feet far apart, he braced himself and made a reading on the sun. He noted the coordinates in the log. Then he made a reading of the "glass," as a barometer was then called. The mercury-filled tube registered 27.50 inches. Incredulous, Harwich flicked his finger against the glass tube and took another reading. It was still 27.50 inches. Although he knew different, for a moment he let himself believe the instrument was broken. That was the lowest reading he had seen in twenty-six years at sea. It was the lowest reading he had ever heard any ship's captain make. The pressure in the center of the storm had fallen 0.26 inches in less than twenty-four hours. The hurricane was growing—and growing fast.

The SS *Matura* rolled hard with each wave. He could see hope in the faces of his crew as they gazed at the clear skies. But Captain Richard Harwich knew this was a fleeting moment and would quickly pass. Twenty minutes later he saw a monstrous wall of dark swirling clouds five miles high rising before him. Captain Harwich knew they were still in for a stormy ride.

ST. CROIX

For the eight days of its spectacular life, the storm had been spoiled. Everything was going its way. Atmospheric and oceanic conditions were perfect, and it was nearing the height of its powers. Nothing had dared to challenge it in its due west drive. Yet as it approached the continent of South America, for the first time it felt resistance. Neither a wall nor a push, but rather a gentle, firm obstacle that distorted its symmetry, forcing its leading feeder bands more to the northwest. The storm had encountered a high-pressure system from the South American landmass that covered much of the southern Caribbean. This hulking, slow-moving, invisible giant, backed up by the massive Andes Mountains, confidently challenged the storm. The high stood its ground. Like most bullies, the hurricane took the route of least resistance and bent its path to the northwest. It was now aimed straight at the soft underbelly of Puerto Rico.

First, however, it had to deal with the Virgin Islands—tiny specks of land in warm shallow water that energized the storm. The powerful category 4 hurricane aimed its right uppercut at the American islands. Ten terrifying hours later, the Virgin Islands lay in ruins. Entire villages were flattened. Radio towers lay in tangled heaps. When the seas retreated, dozens of boats lay on Christiansted's docks high and dry. Tens of thousands of people were without homes. Yet this was only a glancing blow. Unsatisfied, the storm rapidly moved toward Puerto Rico.

The storm's forward movement was a speedy nineteen miles per hour. That gave the Weather Bureau little lead time to predict its course. Even with good communications, it would have made the Weather Bureau people extremely nervous. With communications down, there was no way to inform the world that the hurricane had shifted course.

PALM BEACH POST, September 13, 1928:

> The hurricane concerning which warning was issued last night is moving, according to reports, at a rate of approximately 450 miles a day. Its present course, if maintained, will carry it south of Cuba and thence into the Gulf of Mexico. No indications of an approaching storm were evident off the Florida coast last night. Local barometers were holding at normal and no fear was voiced by weather-wise persons that this section would feel the effect of the storm.
>
> Tides at Gus Baths. High: 8:13 p.m.

HENRY MARTIN

After a breakfast of eggs and bacon, Henry had left the farm just after sunup for South Bay. Three dozen still-warm eggs, well packed in old newspaper, sat on the passenger seat. In the back, milk sloshed in a half-filled twenty-gallon can. Henry had left Raymond at the farm to oversee the workers; he'd check the fences and the fields and make sure the seedlings that were beginning to break through the soil had just the right amount of water.

Once they had finished the planting, Henry was free to concentrate on the stores. He alternated between the Belle Glade and South Bay stores. While he had good help, Henry Martin did not trust even close relatives with the day's receipts for too long. He understood temptation, and the less placed in front of people the better. He was not an overly religious man, but he knew all the classes of temptation the devil could place before a man. Therefore, he rationalized, the less temptations, the less sin.

Technically, the new store in South Bay was not Henry's. It belonged to Southern Sugar Company. At the insistence of the company, it was run like a company store. The sugar workers were paid in tokens and chits by the sugar company, which they exchanged for goods in the store. Townspeople paid in cash, and sometimes Henry would barter or trade with those who had no cash. Henry stocked the store with items ordered in West Palm and Fort Lauderdale and with fresh produce from his own and other local farms. The store smelled of onions stored in low-lying bins, well-oiled leather goods, various medicinal swabs and libations, and kerosene oil for the brass and glass lanterns that had not yet been given the name hurricane lamps.

Farmers like Henry who lived close to the muck dike were well aware of the level of the lake. It was raining very hard. The month before, 13.7 inches of rain had fallen, and it had not stopped raining since. The lake was over the nineteen-foot mark—a record level.

Rain or not, Henry Martin looked forward to making a good weekend in the stores. He also looked forward to a good card game of poker at Griff's Club in South Bay.

School was to start on Monday, and he needed more children's clothes, notebooks, and pencils. Henry had to prepare the store for Saturday, payday. Henry would man the store; then Sunday he would work at the Belle Glade store.

At the farmhouse, Ernestine Martin could hardly hold back her glee. She twitched and wiggled as she watched her mother dress and fit her sisters in their dresses for the new school year. Bessie Mae had been working all week, measuring, cutting material, sewing, and fitting the girls' dresses. Now they were ready. Draped carefully across the arm of the wooden chair was Ernestine's dress. To Ernestine, the bright, rich colors were like a princess's gown, and she couldn't wait to try on hers.

Annie Mae held baby Robert as she paced beside the sewing table. She hefted him up on her hip, balancing him there while she watched Bessie Mae work. Robert was big and heavy for a two-year-old, and Annie Mae fretted, wondering whether he would ever lose his baby fat. As long as she had the baby, she did not have to do the other chores around the house, especially the outside chores that she detested. She envied her sister Nancy who had made the break by getting married. She had escaped the drudgery of constant housework, tending to children, and an overbearing, strict father. Annie Mae dreamed that one of the young men who cautiously circled the house would one day rescue her and take her away. But her father, like the dragon at the gate, chased off suitors with threats and roars.

As if reading Annie Mae's thoughts, Bessie Mae looked up and smiled before returning to her work. She put the last stitches in Minnie Lucy's dress. Her plump, round face beamed as her youngest daughter turned around, showing off her dress. With her bright red hair and new dress, she looked like an angel. Monday was to be her first day at school—the first grade. Her little baby girl was growing up.

PUERTO RICO

On Thursday, just before the end of their noon siesta, the people of Ponce on the southern coast of Puerto Rico were awakened by the erratic peal of church bells. It was the day of San Felipe, the Saint of the Hopeless. Rung by strong winds blowing through the centuries-old high belfries, the bells toiled a sardonic melody. Waves of angled rain poured down on the city. Majestic palm trees bowed low as if praying. Along the beach, heavy surf pounded the shore. No one had to be told that the hurricane that had devastated the West Indian Islands of Montserrat and Guadeloupe had arrived.

Puerto Rico, the rich port of the Spanish Main, was no stranger to hurricanes. Since Columbus's fourth voyage, the incredible destructive forces of hurricanes had been recorded. Given warning, the people—even those living in the flimsy shacks and huts that blanketed the hills and were built on bamboo stilts over the water—could seek shelter. Though Puerto Rico had been a United States protectorate for thirty years, it was mired in perpetual poverty. After its initial settlement by the Spanish, Puerto Rico passed into redundancy. The more important colonies of New Spain, Nuevo Granada, and Peru, were generating tons of gold and silver for the coffers of the Spanish kings. Within a hundred years of its founding, the rich Spanish port began a four hundred–year decline and was now called the "poor man of the Caribbean."

The storm's sudden turn to the northwest caught most people on the island by surprise. With approaching 150-mile-per-hour winds and gusts to 170, the storm crashed ashore. It threaded itself between Ponce in the south and San Juan in the north, Puerto Rico's two most populous cities. Even the island's formidable mountains did little to lessen the storm's impact as it descended on the north coast. At 2:30 p.m., the San Juan Weather Bureau recorded winds of 132 miles per hour before the anemometer was blown away. Gusts were calculated at 150 miles per hour. The storm was the worst to hit Puerto Rico in recent memory. It was not only an extremely violent hurricane but also a highly electric storm. Lightning bolts lit up the night sky like an accelerated strobe lamp.

In San Juan, the roofs of both the Hotel Palace and the exclusive Union Club were blown off. Thousands of homes in the capital city were flattened. At the harbor entrance, the large steamer SS *Helen* sat on the jetty rocks. Other smaller boats littered the docks, or lay drowned in the bay; some were carried four blocks inland by monstrous seas.

In making its turn to the northwest, the storm had slowed to ten miles per hour, allowing it to dwell for an hour longer over the rain-drenched island. Like a ball striking against a solid object, the storm turned into itself. For a moment the winds of the north side of the hurricane were the strongest, not from the northeast quadrant, as is normal. As it straightened out, it rebounded and grew larger, faster, and deadlier. Its cyclical outer feeder bands stretched over five hundred miles from its center, embracing an area of nearly one million square miles. A violent, swirling vortex spun up from its center, sucking the very air from the ground. At the eye, the updrafts stormed up to fifty thousand feet.

Damage was enormous. Over two hundred thousand people were without homes. Food and medical supplies had been destroyed. Villages in the mountain regions had been cut off as bridges and roads were washed away. With little warning, saturated hills slid into rain-swollen rivers, carrying hundreds of homes and many of their occupants to watery deaths. Famine and disease became a real possibility.

Because of the devastation wrought by the hurricane, it was given a name—the name of its saint day, San Felipe. In the Spanish lands, only hurricanes worthy of remembrance were given names, and when they retired, their names, like the numbers on star athletes' jerseys, would also be retired forever.

The storm, now classified as "a dangerous storm," worried the Weather Bureau, which feared it might be as big as the Miami Hurricane of 1926. Actually, it was bigger, but there was no way they could confirm its size, its strength, its speed, or its possible path. The Puerto Rico Weather Bureau Office had been completely destroyed; radios were down, and equipment for measuring wind speed and barometric pressure were wrecked or blown away. Without up-to-date information, the Weather Bureau labored dangerously in the dark—truly blinded. Lacking reports from Puerto Rico on the strength, the direction and the barometric pressure, the Weather Bureau could only make guesses based on day-old information. At its present speed, the hurricane could cover four hundred miles in a day. At any moment the hurricane could change direction. That could place the storm eight hundred miles farther than the meteorologists might calculate. That was not a comforting thought.

The Weather Bureau advised gingerly on the evening of the 13th that it had no reports east of longitude 71—the western end of Cuba. "However," it cautioned, "the hurricane was probably centered near the southwestern point of Puerto Rico, moving in a west northwest direction and was likely to pass over, or near, Santo Domingo on Friday morning." It ended by stating that the "greatest caution is advised for vessels near that path. This is a dangerous storm."

It was a *dangerous storm* that they had lost.

JUANITA

Pacing in the partially finished living room in Miami, Juanita Wilson was sick with anxiety. The bold lettered headlines of the morning's *Miami Herald* blared out disaster for Puerto Rico, Juanita's homeland. She read all the news reports and listened carefully to the radio. The lack of information was extremely frustrating. She wanted to know whether her family was safe. Her mother, sisters, and cousins lived in the little village of Varge, high in the mountains of eastern Puerto Rico. On her dresser was the only photograph of her family taken in the plaza in front of the old colonial church. Her mother, in her Sunday dress, stared out with the dark eyes of a nearly pure-blooded black, and her lighter-skinned sisters favored their Spanish father.

She had tried to call the village town hall, which had the only telephone. Someone would relay the message. However, all telephone lines were down. For all practical purposes, Puerto Rico was incommunicado. Unable to wait around helplessly, Juanita made a fateful decision.

"I have to go home," she told her husband.

He knew better than to try and persuade her from going. Juanita was the most determined, strong-headed woman he had ever met. In the face of adversity, the one thing Juanita Wilson found impossible to do was nothing. That's why he married her.

Packing a few necessities, she took a taxi to the steamship line office in downtown Miami. She was determined to take the first boat to Puerto Rico. At the steamship line office the ticket vendor told her he could not sell tickets to "colored," pointing to a neatly painted sign that said "No Colored."

Explaining she had to get to Puerto Rico because of her family, Juanita was told she would have to travel to New York or Baltimore before she would find a steamship company that would sell a ticket to a black person.

Back home, Juanita could only wait out her frustration. Inactivity grated on Juanita's nature. She had to do something, but what? While she waited, Juanita Wilson was unaware that the storm was barely six hundred miles away and fast approaching the coast of Florida. She was also unaware that the hurricane that had devastated her native island home was soon to pummel her adopted home state and would forever change her life.

WASHINGTON, D.C.

In Washington, U.S. Weather Bureau forecasters anxiously awaited news from its weather watchers in Puerto Rico. All radio communications with the island commonwealth were down. The few ham radio messages that reached the outside world confirmed the scale of the natural disaster. But the data the Weather Bureau needed—wind speed, accurate rainfall, and storm direction—were frustratingly unavailable. Where were their people? More important, where was the hurricane headed? Where was its next landfall? No one wanted to start a panic; they had to be sure. A severe weather alert had been issued for Cuba. The one indisputable fact they had was that the hurricane was an exceptionally large storm—larger than any of the forecasters had ever experienced.

Leaving Puerto Rico prostrate, the storm skirted Santo Domingo's north coast, dropping ten inches of rain in ten hours. Mountain streams and brooks swelled by torrential rains raged downhill, washing away hills, forests, and villages. Shantytowns built on the steep rises of coastal towns slid into the sea. Parts of the Santo Domingo coast were washed clean as if scrubbed by a mammoth Brillo pad. Keeping to its northwest course, the storm blew across the channel directly over the low-lying atoll islands of the Turks and Caicos and the shallow warm waters of the Great Bahamas Bank. Sustained wind speed now topped 155 miles per hour. Surface air pressure dropped to below 27 inches. It had graduated. It was now a dangerous category 5 hurricane. It pulled weather into its heart from a million-square-mile area. Even the air over Florida felt the distant disturbance 700 miles away. It was plotting a path straight for the sunshine state, but Florida would have to wait. The storm had the Bahamas to contend with first.

HENRY MARTIN

The passenger train from Fort Pierce arrived each day at the railroad station in Chosen. A young man, standing five-foot-ten, with light brown hair, blue eyes, and a kind face, stepped onto the platform with a well-worn brown leather suitcase in hand. It was hot. A lot hotter, the passenger noticed, than the weather he was accustomed to in Dearborn, Michigan. Laboring during summer in the Ford Automobile Company's Dearborn automobile factories was extremely hot work. It was the winters that were pure hell for a Florida-born boy.

Standing on the platform, he felt a reassuring bulge around his waist. Buckled tightly around his waist was a soft alligator-skin money belt. Only a trained eye could make out the slight telltale bulge around his gut.

Zipped securely inside the belt was his life's savings. The money he had slaved and sweated for in the assembly lines in Michigan, one thousand one hundred forty dollars he had earned while working in the automobile factories, was money with which he was going to buy his dream—a farm to grow vegetables in the rich Everglades muck.

Aaron Martin was Henry's first cousin, and with the address of the store in hand, he set out on foot along the Hillsboro Canal. He was not about to spend any of his hard-earned cash on a taxi when he was perfectly able to walk.

Henry would have picked him up at the station if Aaron had spent the money for a telegram, but he hadn't. While walking along the canal bank, Aaron's nostrils were assailed by the omnipresent fragrance of freshly plowed muck, the unique odor of rotten vegetation and rich earth found only in the Everglades. He breathed it in like a fine perfumed essence— the essence of life.

It took him an hour, but he reached the store where he was warmly welcomed by Henry and cousin Arlen Woodham. After a quick lunch, Henry drove Aaron Martin home. The following day with a local friend, Cecil Warner, he stopped by Henry's store. Aaron informed him he was looking to buy a farm.

"Land has gotten quite expensive around here," Henry told Aaron.

Aaron lifted up his shirt and removed his money belt. He took out a wad of bills and flashed it front of Henry.

"One thousand forty dollars," he stated.

"That'll buy a real nice piece of land," Cecil said. He had never seen so much cash at one time.

"I'd put that away if I was you," Henry told him. He did not like flashy displays of money, especially in front of nonfamily members. Henry was a firm believer that the less others knew about the family, and his business, the better. Yet he had to admire the young Aaron. Hard work had paid off.

FLORIDA EAST COAST

Beginning in 1920, the small fleet of boats that sailed in the waters off the Floridian coast had grown into an armada. Not since the glory days of the Spanish Main had as many boats plied the waters between the coast of Florida and the Bahamas. Any boat that could make the hundred-mile passage was pressed into service. The sheer number of craft overwhelmed the United States Coast Guard. The Coast Guard was undermanned and outpowered by new, fast, streamlined speedboats.

Clematis Street, the 200-300 block, West Palm Beach, 1925. This street was the center of real estate activity in Palm Beach County; most of the land in the Everglades was sold along Clematis. Note the Palm Beach Land and Investment Company in the foreground. (*Courtesy of the MOSAIC collection, Florida State Archives*)

Belle Glade's first store and post office. Anchored nearby is Captain Benjamin's boat *Lil.* (*Courtesy of the Glades Historical Society*)

One of the array of dredges used to dig the Everglades canals. (*Courtesy of the University of Florida Special Collections Archives*)

The Martin Clan clowning for a photograph. Armed with pistols, rifles, and moonshine whiskey are Haught Walker, a Martin friend; Henry Martin with rifle; Thomas Jefferson Wells in campaign hat and shorts; and Edward (Buck) Carter, Tommy's soon to be brother-in-law. Though all men and most pioneer women knew how to use arms, the Martins preferred stealth to force to protect their back hummock stills. Belle Glade, Okeechobee Lake, July 1926. (*Courtesy Bob Wells*)

Bessie Mae Martin. Henry called her "Kid"; her children called her "5x5." Bessie died September 16, 1928. (*Courtesy Louise Betts*)

Water spouts over Lake Okeechobee near Okeechobee City, taken during first August 1928 hurricane. (*Courtesy Tom Markham. From the Lovvorn collection.*)

West Palm Beach at the height of the 1928 hurricane. (*Courtesy of the Florida State Archives*)

West Palm Beach, 1928. The desolation and extensive ruin south of the court-house. The large building is the former Dixie Hotel. Compare this photograph with the one of Clematis Street, West Palm Beach, 1925. *(Courtesy of the Florida State Archives)*

The remnants of Lawrence Will's Pioneer Service Station on Main Street in Belle Glade after the 1928 hurricane. In the background is George Tedder's Glades Hotel, the only structure to survive intact in Belle Glade. *(Courtesy of the Florida State Archives)*

Flooding around the experimental station at Belle Glade following the 1928 hurricane. (*Courtesy of the University of Florida Special Collections Archives*)

Mrs. George Tedder in front of their house before the storm. (*Photo by George Tedder*)

Four bodies floating in a canal. The corpse in the foreground is tethered to the bank. (*Courtesy of the University of Florida Special Collections Archives*)

Bodies being burned in the sawgrass near South Bay. Fifteen to fifty bodies were burned at one time. (*Photo by Lawrence E. Will; copyright © The Glades Historical Society; enhanced by Ann Tyler*)

Woodlawn Cemetery in West Palm Beach during the funeral ceremonies for over six hundred of the hurricane's victims. Most were buried in a mass grave trenched by the railroad tracks. Note trees denuded of leaves and branches. (*Courtesy of the Florida State Archives*)

A "cemetery detail." The truck is loaded with hurricane victims; the man on right is a swimmer who recovered bodies from the water. The men in the truck are blacks who were pressed into service to handle the decaying corpses. (*Courtesy of the Florida State Archives*)

A gang of 175 blacks forced to clear debris along the Pahokee road after the 1928 hurricane. (*Courtesy of the University of Florida Special Collections Archives*)

Pine coffins piled up by the Hillsboro Canal. George Tedder's Glades Hotel is in the background to the right. (*Photo by Lawrence E. Will; copyright © The Glades Historical Society*)

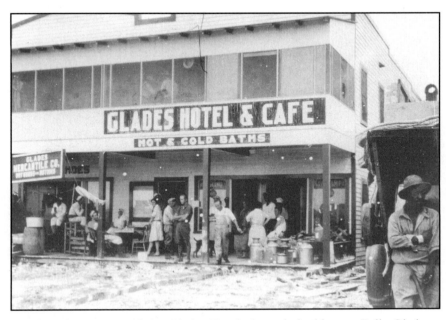

People gathering around the Glades Hotel, the only building in Belle Glade to remain intact. Doctor Buck, Tommy and Willie Emma Wells, and Ardie Peterson were among the 150 people who crowded into the Glades Hotel at the height of the 1928 hurricane. (*Courtesy of the Historical Society of Palm Beach County*)

People searching among the wreckage of their home for belongings. For months after the hurricane, people lived in tents donated by the Red Cross. (*Courtesy of the Historical Society of Palm Beach County*)

For decades after the hurricane, bones of its victims were plowed up. Farmers would remark, "Well, I plowed up someone's bones today." (*Courtesy of the Glades Historical Society; enhanced by Ann Tyler*)

Occasionally they captured a hapless rumrunner, but for the most part, with good timing, an experienced crew, and cooperating weather, the rumrunners got through.

"We're interdicting 10 percent" was the best guess of the local Coast Guard chief. "When we get lucky," he failed to add.

That meant 90 percent of the boats got through—odds that any risk-taking gambler would take with thanks.

Through the night waters, only the white V-shaped wake of the sleek low-lying speedboat was visible. The boat's extra fuel tanks gave it an extended range to make the Bahamas-to-Florida run without stops. It was a sleek wooden boat painted black to blend in with the night. It rode heavy in the water, weighed down by sixty-three cases of scotch whiskey snugly stored in the hold and tied down on deck. The gunwale was barely two feet above the water. The three-man crew fought to keep the boat from swamping. They had passed through a sudden squall line of thunderstorms, and only by bailing constantly had they kept the boat afloat. By the time they spotted the coast of Florida, just north of Hallandale, their fuel had been contaminated by seawater. The powerful boat puttered along at one-tenth speed, which was an agonizingly slow speed for the three wet and cold crew members shooting furtive glances across the horizon.

No one had to tell them that the figure silhouetted on the horizon was not good news. As it approached, its white bow wake glowed in the moonlit waters. Suddenly daylight burst over them. The beam of a high-powered searchlight drenched them in a harsh glow. Across the water echoed a barely audible siren whining like a newborn baby. The Coast Guard had gotten lucky.

Within a month, with its engine repaired, the sleek watercraft would now be used against its former allies. The newest member of the Coast Guard flotilla, CG2260, was christened with a touch of pride the *Black Maria*. It was commissioned to chase down, capture, or corral smugglers until the larger Coast Guard ships could arrive. However, within six days its first assignment would take it a hundred miles from its intended area of operation, far from the open ocean. The mission would be one of mercy.

FRIDAY, SEPTEMBER 14

According to the best information the Weather Bureau had, the storm was passing over the Bahamas, traveling three hundred miles per day. Its forward speed had slowed, making it even more dangerous as it dwelled longer over any one area.

The Bahamas is an oceanic country. Made up of a string of over a thousand islands and keys stretching from Great Iguana Island off the western tip of Cuba in the south, to Little Abaco Island due west of Palm Beach, it is a large area composed mostly of shallow seas, small islands, and smaller keys. A hurricane could almost get lost there, but this was not a normal storm. It was a category 5 hurricane. No one loses a category 5 hurricane. However, it seemed that the Weather Bureau had.

That the storm was lost would have been news to the Bahamians. At the very moment Weather Bureau bureaucrats were frantically waiting for information, the storm was striking murderous blows at the island nation. Over Andros Island the storm began to veer more to the north, which was bad news for the Bahamians. Its new path was to carry it directly over their more populated islands.

When a hurricane turns, it becomes even more unpredictable. Many hurricanes react like a slingshot; once they make a right turn north, they gain speed. Once it made its northward turn, the New England hurricane of September 1938 moved at an astonishing fifty-six miles an hour. It struck New York and Rhode Island with little warning, leaving over six hundred dead.

THE Weather Bureau's nightly report maintained:

```
The West Indian tropical hurricane is central tonight
about 75 miles southeast of Turk's Island and moving
northwest at about 300 miles a day. It will probably con-
tinue moving in the same direction for the next 24 hours
at least. Because of the dangerous character of this
storm, vessels in the vicinity of the Bahamas Islands
should exercise the greatest caution.
```

This put the storm far to the south of the Bahamas and on a track that would bring it over the southern tip of Florida, threatening Key West, but away from Palm Beach and the Everglades. Many in Belle Glade who read it were reassured they no longer lay in the path of danger.

SATURDAY, SEPTEMBER 15, 1928—THE THOMASES

Early Saturday morning, Charles and Susan Thomas set off for West Palm Beach. Driving their Model T Ford along the Palm Beach Road Highway, they crossed the new steel bridge at Six Mile Bend and then drove due east to Belvedere Road, the entrance to West Palm Beach. With the new school year beginning Monday, they needed to buy school supplies and clothes for the children. Charles had read in yesterday's newspaper that the Antilles hurricane would more than likely miss

Florida. The storm's track was thought to be to the south, affecting Santo Domingo, Haiti, and Cuba. While the headline asserted that the storm might hit Florida, it also stated it was still too far away to affect Florida. There was a good chance it would continue to the south or turn to the north, sparing Palm Beach County.

In West Palm Beach, he bought a copy of Saturday's paper. While the headline blared "Florida May Feel Storm's Wrath," the weather report at the bottom of the page was more reassuring, forecasting "mostly fair Saturday and Sunday, increasing cloudiness, showers Sunday afternoon or night: gentle east and northeast winds Saturday increasing northeast Sunday: probably becoming strong off the northeast coast by Sunday night."

If he had read further, Charles would have seen a small ominous box printed in the right-hand column that stated, "Wind reports indicate HURRICANE likely to strike here." The Saturday *Palm Beach Post* covered so much contradictory information that it was hard to know what to believe. The editors were just as perplexed. They were inundated with conflicting reports and felt compelled to print them all. Radio station broadcasts were more optimistic. They reported that the storm would not hit Palm Beach. The last thing anyone wanted was to panic and scare off the tourists and damage the winter season on which so many people in South Florida depended.

Before returning to Belle Glade, Charles was told by friends and associates that they were sure the storm was to pass to the north and spare the county. By the time they headed back to Sebring Farms, Charles Thomas was convinced that there was no hurricane threat.

SEBRING FARMS

When his parents left for West Palm Beach, Mutt, along with Roy, Virgil, and Vernie Boots ran over to watch the construction work on the South Bay to Clewiston Road. The Huffman Company had a large drag line working on the pilings for the bridge over the South Florida Conservation Drainage Canal. The bridge was part of the new road being built to connect South Bay and Clewiston. Mutt watched, mesmerized as a massive piece of machinery dipped into the muck, pulled, and then lifted a ton of muck, rock, and water, which it dumped onto the road. He watched as the pile driver drove the pilings. Blam, hiss, blam, hiss, blam. Steam spouted out of the sides like a fairytale dragon—a mechanical monster, a fascinating creature of iron and steel.

Barefoot, the boys horsed around, slipping in the mud. Vernie knew his mother would not be happy with their muddy clothes. A quick dip in the canal would clean most of it off.

The clouds and wind blew in a steady stream to the south. It had started to drizzle, making the deck and the muck banks slippery. The men on the drag line quit for the day and retreated to the protection of the quarter-boat in South Bay. Mutt and the other boys ran home.

When the Boots boys arrived home, they found their mother and father packing blankets, food, and supplies. They were going to South Bay and ride out the hurricane on Bill Rawle's boat. Bill Rawle had sent word to Sebring Farms that he thought a hurricane was coming, and he wanted them safely on his large tug. He shared the common belief that a boat was the safest place to be during a hurricane. Bill and Mattie Mae Boots gathered up the children into their Model T and drove to South Bay.

Rawle had cleared a couple of the bunks for his mother and stepfather. The boys could sleep on the table in the galley or on the floor. The Bootses made themselves as comfortable as possible in the cramped spaces aboard the tug. After a few hours, reports on the radio and from neighbors assured them that the storm was blowing out to sea, and even though there was a steady north wind blowing, they repacked and returned to the comfort of their home in Sebring Farms. Tired, the boys went straight to bed.

It was a cool night for September. The steady north wind had cooled the evening—a good sleeping night. Vernie, sleeping with his brother, tugged at the bedsheet and tucked it under his chin. He turned on his side and listened to the pitter-patter of rain on the metal roof as it lulled him to sleep.

LATE that night, the Jupiter radio station reported that the "hurricane center would likely pass near, or slightly north of, Nassau on Sunday morning. The hurricane was central about latitude 23.30 north and longitude 75 west, moving northwest at 300 miles per day at 9 o'clock last night. Northeast storm warnings should be displayed between Miami and Titusville. Wind was blowing at 110 miles per hour on Wadling's Island at 9 o'clock. At Nassau at 10 o'clock wind was blowing 40 miles per hour, northeast with a barometer reading of 29.46 inches and falling.

FIRST WARNINGS

The Seminole Indians in the designated Brighton Indian Reservation area on the northwestern edge of the lake knew a big storm was coming. The daylight was filtered in an unnatural eerily bright, yet pale, glow. The stilled air had a harmonic quality; sound waves seemed to hang in suspended animation as if even the air itself feared the coming onslaught. They watched wild animals scurry into protective borrows, or bed down in trees. Flocks of wading birds disappeared towards the horizon.

The fields were white with sea gulls. No birds were flying, cattle lay in the fields, snakes moved to high ground or into trees, and fish schooled deeper in the lakes and canals. None moved. To move, it seemed, was to die.

For a few moments everything stopped, even time, as some might imagined—everything, that is, except for the unsuspecting white man and his machines. The Indians shook their heads in dismay at the foolish white people who stayed in their lowlands that were once under the great water—Lake Okeechobee.

Heeding the signs, the Seminoles retreated to high hammocks to wait out the storm they knew was coming. The Seminole Indians were very wary. They had been heavily battered in the hurricane of 1926 with a dozen dead and many head of their precious cattle drowned. They understood the power of a hurricane. Tales of whole villages swept off islands in the Everglades were related in oral traditions told around campfires and in their open-sided, palm-covered chickees.

"There is going to be high water," they told Clarence Miller. He was black and one of the few non-Indians they trusted.

Few Indians would have even thought to warn a white man.

HEEDING the general consensus that the hurricane would bypass Florida, Henry remained at the South Bay store. That night he counted his receipts, locked up the store and went home. Tomorrow he would open the store in Belle Glade. He looked forward to a big day. He expected heavy sales in school supplies.

SATURDAY evening a gentle breeze blew from the north—a summer zephyr, actually. The air was unseasonably cool, a relief to the residents of West Palm Beach. By evening, the wind picked up. Along the tree-studded streets of Palm Beach, the palm fronds, battered by a steady north wind, all pointed in one direction—south.

CHAPTER 9
A HARD RAIN'S A-GONNA FALL

Sunday, September 16

It's a hard, and it's a hard, it's a hard, and it's a hard. It's a hard rain's a-gonna fall.

—*Bob Dylan, "A Hard Rain's A-Gonna Fall"*

At the Bacom Point house, Lillian Padgett and her sister, Ruth, had just prepared a hearty breakfast of bacon and eggs. Though she was seven months pregnant, Ruth still moved rapidly about the kitchen like an oversized ballerina. The two women set the table for three. Ruth's husband, Dan Carpenter, joined them while ten-month-old Donald Padgett and his father rested together in the back bedroom. Duncan, still weak from hookworm treatment, had spent the morning in bed. Any exertion, even standing, left him exhausted and out of breath. Outside, low clouds paraded in files across the sky. It was dark one minute; light, the next. The lake was steely gray, almost angry, with white-capped waves bobbing and swooping just behind the house. The three adults had sat down for their Sunday breakfast when they heard a car crunching the gravel in the driveway.

"It's your father," Dan said, glancing out the window at the Model T.

Calvin Shive knocked quickly and then burst in through the front door; he was clearly agitated.

"Don't y'all know there's a hurricane coming?" he said. "We heard it on the radio. You can't stay here."

Lillian glanced outside. It was raining, and every few minutes a gust would bend the branches of the large cypress trees out front. That was normal. Across the lake, she could see blue sky and the sun's rays brushing across the water. Was a hurricane really coming? Would the house flood or blow away, she wondered? There was no time to answer these questions. She and Ruth gathered up blankets and some food while Dan and Calvin helped Duncan to their car. As Lillian closed the door to the house, she wondered whether they would have a home to return to tomorrow.

With Duncan lying in the back seat, she followed her father up to Duncan's parents' house. By the time they reached the senior Padgetts' home, the sky had turned an ominous gray and the wind blew in stronger, more persistent gusts. Treetops swayed while leaves and other loose debris blew around the yard. A downpour nearly soaked them as they ran to the house from the cars.

The entire Shive family gathered at the Padgetts' house, which they all considered the safest structure. While Calvin Shive's house was well built, it was on the lake side of the sand ridge. Like Lillian's house, it had a pleasant view of the lake and evening sunsets from the back porch. But it was low, against the lake, and susceptible to flooding. The back yard of the Padgett house sloped gently down to freshly planted fields that were, before the muck dike was built, the bed of the old Pelican River. A large chicken coop built on blocks stood about thirty yards behind the house—close enough for an easy walk to gather eggs every morning, but far enough to keep the flies away.

By midafternoon, the wind gusted at gale strength. There was no doubt a hurricane was on its way. Outside the wind tore squawking chickens off their roosts and flung them to their death against the house, or a heavy rain washed them off the roof to the ground where they drowned. Calvin and Dan ran outside and gathered up as many chickens as they could. They were brought inside, and the women plucked and cooked them so as not to let them go to waste. Within a couple days, cooked chicken would be the only edible food available.

WEST PALM BEACH

At hardware stores, dry-goods stores, and lumberyards, there was a rush on candles, food, boards, and kerosene lamps. Residents boarded up their houses and then reinforced their ornamental trees. Most people planned to hunker down in their homes. Others gathered together at one house to help and support each other, strangely similar to the hurricane parties thrown by people half a century later.

Though people prepared, there remained a sense that the storm was not *really* going to strike. Richard Gray, the noted meteorologist and head of the Miami Weather Bureau, had said that the storm would pass north of Miami and Palm Beach, sparing them a direct hit, though the southern edge might cause damage. Later the Weather Bureau in Washington, D.C., reported that "winds on the extreme lower east coast of Florida will increase and probably reach gale force Sunday—*between thirty-nine and fifty-four miles per hour.*

"There was no indication last night that Miami or vicinity will be in the path of dangerous winds. Indications were that when the storm reaches a position due east of Miami Sunday morning, it will be 170 miles to sea, and winds during the day should shift to the north and diminish as the storm moves up the coast."

Enough information to give hope if anyone preferred to believe they were not in harm's way; enough information so as not to panic the populace.

THE MARTIN FARM

Ernestine looked up at the dark, low "flying clouds," as she called storm clouds. She was worried; it looked like it was going to storm. Tomorrow was the first day of school—her second year at the South Bay school. She loved school because it meant a chance to be with other kids, the teacher, and free time away from the drudgery of work. Her mother had spent the last two weeks pumping away at the Singer sewing machine making new clothes for the girls. Ernestine could not wait to show off her new dress the first day of school. It was beautiful, composed of bright colors with a tie bow in the back. When she tried it on, she felt like a princess. However, the storm might spoil it all and prevent them from going to school.

In the kitchen, Bessie Mae slowly read a copy of Saturday's *Palm Beach Post* that Loney Martin had left. The conflicting reports about the Atlantic storm making a turn to the north or south did not help her anxiety. Outside the wind had not varied from its steady north direction. The clouds looked darker and lower and were moving fast. For the first time that morning, Bessie Mae was worried. Near noon, Raymond drove up in front of the house. Henry had sent him to take the family to Tommy Wells's house in Belle Glade. At least this time she would not ride out the storm alone.

Tommy Wells's house, built on spoils dumped along the bank of the Hillsboro Canal, was perched higher than most houses. The old bridge tender's house, according to its former owner, John Hooker, had never flooded. Bessie Mae would feel more secure there, and Henry would be nearby. Just before they left, Loney Martin rode over to the house. He told her that he had boarded up his house and brought in the animals. The clouds were just like those when the Moore Haven storm hit, he told her. Bessie Mae told him they were going to Tom Wells's house and asked him to come with them.

"Nothing's going to happen," Loney said before leaving. Words that would later echo in Bessie Mae's mind.

What was she going to do with all her chickens, she wondered. If the farm flooded like it did in 1926, then they would all drown. If they sought to roost in the trees, they'd be blown down and killed. The horses and cows could swim, but her chickens were susceptible to storms, her precious flock that she had worked so hard at building up. She had struggled to protect them against chicken snakes, foxes, skunks, and hawks. It seemed that every varmint in the Everglades wanted a free meal at the expense of one of her chickens. She had built a roosting platform in the tree where they sought protection at night. Now, though, it seemed they were doomed to die. She threw the rest of the cracked corn out on the ground for them. A few hungry birds pecked at the feed, but the rest stayed hunkered down against the rains and wind, afraid to lose their perch. She then brought the cows into the front yard, closer to the house where they might find protection in its lee side.

Ernestine had seen a car drive up to the house and then heard her mother call out. When she got to the house, Bessie Mae was packing up food and blankets.

"We're going to Uncle Tommy's," she said.

Now Ernestine was really worried. She was sure she would not be able to wear her pretty dress tomorrow.

Bessie Mae had one of the black hands board up the lakefront windows. Then she placed her linens on top of the dresser, out of the high water level, she hoped. A heavy squall sent water roaring against the house. Then it stopped. During the lull, Bessie Mae and Raymond loaded the children into the car. Pools of water were forming around the house and in the fields. As the car drove away, a trio of black farmhands waved and then disappeared behind the house. Bessie Mae looked back at the farmhouse standing like a lone sentinel in the water-soaked fields, wondering whether her linens would get soaked again. She hoped that if it flooded, there would be little damage. Rounding the bend toward Belle Glade, she glanced back one more time. Hers would be one of the last pair of eyes to ever see the Martin farmhouse again.

AT Sebring Farms, Vernie Boots walked along the top of the dike. Dark, low clouds marched in single file across the sky. A few rain showers had soaked the land. Yet the sun poured through a few bright blue spots, and where it hit the lake, the water glistened like diamonds scattered on a table. More than likely the Sunday afternoon baseball game would be canceled. Aside from church, the Sunday afternoon ball games were the only time all the neighbors got together.

From where he stood, Vernie saw his house and the other six houses that made up Sebring Farms over to the left. He was practically looking down on their house, and just beyond was the raised bed of the new road connecting South Bay and Clewiston. From his vantage point on the dike, he could make out the four tall, ramrod-straight royal palm trees of the Bolles Hotel at Miami Locks. The lake was high, a scant two feet from the top of the dike. Weeds, elderbushes, and grasses covered the dike, and in places fresh muck had been dumped to reinforce low spots—about the only maintenance being done. He liked to watch the white egrets and great blue herons fishing for frogs and minnows along the dike's banks. Today there weren't any birds. They had gone somewhere, somewhere safe, safe from the coming storm.

The size of the lake never failed to amaze young Vernie. Stretching out to the horizon in three directions, it was to him the ocean, as big as the Pacific he had seen with his family when they worked in the groves in California. The wind had picked up, and the stimulating smells it carried foretold rain. Waves slapped along the bank of the muck dike. Frosty whitecaps dotted the water.

The weather had been too bad to go to church in South Bay, and there was no work to do. It was vacation time. Precious free time that a farm boy rarely had. Tomorrow, free time would end. It was the first day of the new school year. He liked school and he liked the schoolteacher. She always encouraged him to be curious even when he asked exasperating questions. The teacher, his parents, and his friends all knew that Vernie Boots had an active, inquisitive mind. Vernie loved machinery. He had an innate curiosity—the need to know how something worked, what made it go around, and how to improve it. He loved to take things apart—anything, a discarded plow, an iron, if lucky an old rusting truck transmission. Then he'd reassemble it, figuring how it worked and how it might be made to work better—an innate curiosity that would develop half a dozen practical inventions years later.

From the porch of the house, Roy and Virgil called to him. In their hands he could see the wooden propellers they had been carving the day before. He ran down the bank to the back yard. With his brothers, he drove wooden pegs into fence posts and attached the propellers, stepped back, and watched them spin in the wind. And spin they did, as fast as any of the boys had ever seen them.

Vernie watched the wind spin the propellers, gusts messing his hair. He imagined that if he could attach a belt or chain to the twirling propellers and hook them up to a pump, he'd have free energy. Or he might connect it to an electric generator like the one at the hotel in Belle Glade, and then the family would have electricity. He imagined the house lit up with a light bulb in every room, and a radio. As the rapidly spinning propellers rocked against the restraining dowel, an acrid odor tingled Vernie's nose—the wooden propellers were spinning so fast they were burning. Vernie looked away from his propellers and his dreams of bringing light to Sebring Farms and glanced up at the sky. Above him dark, low black clouds strode in an unending procession due south. Vernie wondered where they were going in such a hurry. A rain squall threatened to drench them as they took temporary refuge under the eaves of the house. The wind blew even stronger. Returning to the propellers, he thought if he could count the revolutions per minute, he could tell how fast the wind was blowing. But the propellers were spinning so fast, it was a blur. Vernie Boots knew they were in for a real storm.

Another downpour caught the three boys before they could reach refuge under the eaves. They shivered and were now soaked down to their underwear.

"Boys, get in here right now!" they heard their mother yell from the back door.

They raced each other across the yard leaping over large puddles. Their mother held the door open as they rushed up the back stairs into the kitchen and the safety of the house.

TWO doors up, at the "wrong side out house," the Thomas family had returned from their island farm. As was the custom, for a Sunday treat they had harvested half a hamper of raw peanuts, which were taken back home and boiled. Though breezy, the morning had been sunny and bright. With the oncoming clouds and the rain, the rest of the day promised to be gloomy. Charles had one way of beating the gloom. The Thomases gathered in the dining area to feast on the peanuts. Charles had a copy of the *Palm Beach Post* that Thirsk had left at the house when he had finished reading it. The storm was still in the Bahamas but had moved closer to Florida. That was not what the people in West Palm Beach were saying yesterday. Could they have been wrong?

A wind gust rattled the windows, and Mutt glanced out the window. He could see leaves and small branches wind chased along the ground. He also saw waves crest over the top of the dike—dark, angry waves.

NASSAU

The wind had finally died down. Not completely dead—thirty-mile-per-hour gusts still blew debris into the air—but the worst was over. Like a casual island-hopping tourist, the storm had jumped from island to island until it reached Nassau in the early morning hours. Downtown Nassau had taken the full brunt of the storm. The harbor and boat channel were littered with sunken boats, broken hulls, and snapped masts. Along the rip-rapped shoreline broken boats and bodies were wedged in between large boulders. Cautiously, wide-eyed people ventured out of their hiding places. Most moved as if in a hallucinogenic daze, bewildered that they had survived. Bay Street was strewn with broken lumber, roof tiles, lampposts, and automobiles. Dead horse carcasses lay tangled in the broken debris. Hundreds of broken, wet-feathered birds lay in the street. The few concrete buildings stood with all their windows blown out. Few of the older quaint wooden buildings stood at all. Bahamians were accustomed to hurricanes, but this storm had left more dead in one day than all the other storms for the entire century.

To the northwest, Grand Bahama Island along with like Great Exuma, Eleuthera, and Cat Island lay flattened. The entire island was underwater as a brackish mixture of rain and sea sloshed across the land. Many of its one thousand inhabitants were homeless. Entire villages were swept out to sea leaving no trace that man had once inhabited these shores. The sea had taken back its own.

The Bahamas with its seven hundred islands lived from the sea. Boats were its lifeline. Now there were no boats. No fishing boats, no mail boats, no rumrunners—all had been sunk, thrown miles inland, or crushed. The telephone poles and telegraph towers lay like broken toothpicks. For all purposes Nassau and the other islands were isolated, cut off from each other and the rest of the world. There was no way they could warn the world of the massive hurricane that was headed their way.

MARTIN STORE

Henry Martin was worried. Not so much about the storm itself—how many bad storms had they weathered in the last two years? But the storm was keeping customers away. Early in the day he sold out of candles, oil, and some canned goods, but little else had moved. He would have to return tomorrow to make up the business that he was going to lose. He thought about his saturated fields. They would probably flood like in most storms. It should be over in a day, not like 1920 or 1922 when half the farmers were flooded out and left. Today they had the dike. They had the large pumps that could pump a field dry in twelve hours; if it stopped raining, the crop should make it. At least Raymond had taken Bessie Mae and the children to Belle Glade. They were just across the canal. If he looked out the window of the store, he could see Tommy's house.

Leaving Arlen with the store, Henry went to Main Street. At Lawrence Will's gas station he heard that the storm was likely to move to the north. People, mostly men, milled around the stores trying to keep dry and obtain news of the storm. The few radios were turned up full volume. They strained to hear any news through the crackling static caused by the lightning of distant electrical storms.

WHEN the Martin car pulled into Tommy Wells's yard, Bessie Mae said, "We can't leave Tempie."

She sent a car back for Tempie and her five children.

As Bessie Mae and the children settled in, Willie Emma brought out two-week-old Edward. It was the first time that Bessie Mae had seen young Edward. He looked so small, and his broken arm was wrapped in a tiny splint. But he hardly cried. A very stoic baby. Bessie Mae could not help but think of Sonny when he was a tiny baby wrapped in a handkerchief for a diaper.

When Tempie and her children arrived, they gathered together in the kitchen. The children ran to the window to watch the storm. Branches of the big trees were swaying, leaning to the ground and then shaking like a dust mop. They brushed the cloud-black sky like an artist painting the mouth of hell.

At the store, Henry gazed out of the store window. Bursts of rains obstructed his view. At times he could not even see Tommy Wells's house across the canal. Water began to pool in the streets. The storm was worse than he was led to believe. Should he bring Bessie Mae and the children here or let them ride out the storm at Tommy's? Tommy's house was more comfortable than the Spartan store. He'd wait at little longer. Obviously there would be no more customers that afternoon. He checked for roof leaks and settled back to wait out the storm in the store. He had inventory to protect.

IN THE GULF STREAM

After leaving a devastated Nassau, the storm shot across the narrow sea lane directly at Florida. It slid slightly to the north but did not make the sharp turn hoped for by the Weather Bureau and local forecasters. There was no front moving down the Florida peninsula to guide it northward and away from land; the jet stream was too far north. There was no high for it to bounce off. With its path clear, the storm aimed all its collective fury straight at the heart of Palm Beach County.

Beneath the storm, the sea had risen eighteen feet. A combination of low air pressure, winds, and hurricane speed formed a hundred-square-mile dome of agitated water topped by waves fifty and sixty feet high. Out at sea the dome of water was like a large hump in the middle of the ocean. It was barely noticeable among the towering waves. Once the storm surge came on shore, however, it would trip on the beach, spilling a wall of cascading water miles inland. Anyone or anything that survived the incoming surge risked being swept back out to sea when the winds changed direction.

JUANITA WILSON

Juanita Wilson had to do something to keep her mind from thinking about her family in Puerto Rico. She still smarted from being denied passage because of her skin color, but she was not a person to mope about. She knew that after the hurricane left, the Red Cross would be sending aid to Puerto Rico as they had in 1926. She thought she might be able to get there as a Red Cross volunteer. She was determined to do something, and Juanita Wilson, once her mind was made up, got things done.

JUPITER LIGHT

At the northern-most end of Palm Beach County and a half mile inland from the coast, the ninety-foot Jupiter Lighthouse loomed massive and vigilant over the Loxahatchee River. It was designed by George Meade of Fort Meade and Gettysburg fame. Finished in 1859, it is the oldest structure in Palm Beach County. Only once in its history had the light not blazed its bright warning to mariners. During the Civil War, to prevent Union ships from spotting blockade runners, Confederate sympathizers raided the lighthouse, dismantled the lamp, and hid it for the duration of the conflict. After the war, it was restored and had shone faithfully ever since. Keeping the light burning was always a point of pride for a lightkeeper. Captain Charles Seabrook, Jupiter lighthouse keeper, carried on that proud tradition.

The light had recently been converted from mineral oil to a more reliable electric lamp. The rotation table that turned the light was also electrified. Progress. Modern conveniences. There was even talk about not needing lightkeepers anymore. Captain Seabrook did not put much faith in those stories, but he did doubt that his fourteen-year-old son, Franklin, would carry on the lightkeeper tradition. It was lonely work, and today's youth were more interested in exciting things like automobiles, radios, and music called jazz.

From the balcony at the top of the lighthouse, he could see the Atlantic Ocean, the dark seas, the darker clouds, even the white foamed waves pounding on the sandy beach. A storm was definitely in the making. It was during storms exactly like this one that the light was most needed. Ships lost in a storm, alone out at sea and unsure about dangerous waters, needed a guiding beacon, and the Jupiter light had guided thousands of vessels to safe harbor. Still unsure that this storm was the reported West Indian hurricane, he carefully descended the stairway grasping the railing tightly. His hands were sore and swollen. He had cut himself two days before, and blood poisoning had set in.

The life of a lightkeeper and his family was a lonely existence. The first keepers lived in isolation. Even seventy years later, the only neighbors were residents in the three-year-old town of Jupiter on the opposite bank, with a winter population of three hundred. The Loxahatchee River was nearly as wild as when the Jeagas Indians fished for snook with sharp bone hooks off its banks and enslaved ship-wrecked Europeans.

Storm warnings had been issued, and the flags fluttered in the gale strength wind. It wasn't until just after noon that confirmation from the nearby naval station that the killer West Indian hurricane, which had devastated Puerto Rico and Nassau, was headed straight for Palm Beach. From the flagpole, two red and black square hurricane flags whipped in the wind. Captain Seabrook could only offer a silent prayer for any seaman caught in the storm.

After dusk, a violent gust tore down the cables carrying power to the lamp. The lighthouse was thrown into darkness—an unbearable sight to Captain Seabrook. Running to the storeroom, he tried to start the auxiliary diesel generator, but it had sat unused too long and failed to start. Refusing to give in, he found the old obsolete mineral oil lamps, carried them up 105 feet to the light, set them in place, and lit them. The only other lights in the sky were a few pale warning flares from the naval station.

Seabrook nearly collapsed. His hands were swollen, and bright red streaks shot up the veins in his arms. The physical strain had inflamed the blood poisoning. He needed to rest, but his work was not done. The light had to be turned, and with no power it could be turned only by hand. Franklin volunteered to hand-turn the light. He climbed the swaying tower with two other men. He set his feet on the rain-soaked floor, and together they began to slowly turn the oil lamps. The Jupiter light shone once again.

While the Jupiter lighthouse was twenty miles from the eye of the hurricane, when the storm passed over the coastline, it placed it in its northeast quadrant—the quadrant that spawns tornadoes. Half a dozen tornadoes, stretching like eerie fingers across a blackboard, dropped from the black clouds. According to Bob Boyd, "At the height of the storm, an apparent tornado moved the tower top seventeen inches off center and squeezed the mortar from the bricks. We figured the wind gusts had to be about 250 knots (288 miles per hour)."

One of the tornadoes spawned by the storm probably struck the lighthouse. The light tower swayed violently. The lighthouse was in danger of collapsing. Yet through the storm, Franklin Seabrook never faltered. As the glass enclosure imploded, sending splinters of heavy glass flying into the room, he kept turning the light. Captain Seabrook might have had doubts that his son would continue in his footsteps, but there was no doubt that the young Franklin, under impossible conditions, carried on the tradition of his father—the tradition of a lightkeeper.

CHAPTER 10
SUNDAY AFTERNOON

And while I was looking I saw the tide suddenly rise fully four feet in one bound."

—Dr. Samuel O. Young, Isaac's Storm

A crowd of anxious people gathered in the Alston Drugstore on Main Street. At least one member of every family who had chosen to remain in Belle Glade milled about the crowded front room. The five-month-old town still had no town hall or meetinghouse. Important gatherings were held, depending on the size of the crowd, at the most convenient location. In this case, it was the drugstore, strategically positioned between the town's two sturdiest buildings—George Tedder's Glades Hotel immediately next door and the Belle Glade Hotel across the street. Lawrence Will had walked over from his service station. Henry Martin left his nephew, Arlin Woodham, in charge of the store and ran the two blocks through the rain. Charlie Riedel had joined the crowd. Noticeably absent was George Tedder. He was at the experimental station three miles away keeping an eye on the instruments monitoring the storm. Foremost on everybody's mind was whether the dike would hold. No one wanted to think that they might suffer the same fate as Moore Haven two years ago.

The drugstore crowd looked to their recently elected mayor for guidance. Mayor Walter Greer was a big man. A blacksmith by trade, he had a smith's imposing build. His six-foot frame, two-hundred-pound size, and round stout face framed by an imposing handlebar moustache instilled confidence.

The rain came down in drenching bursts, let up some, then poured again as sickle-shaped feeder bands swung their hundred-mile-long arms across Belle Glade and the lake's southern shore. It was gusting hard, at times very hard, but it was the rain that worried the people the most— the rain and the water, the lake water, and the frail muck dike that stood between them and disaster.

What had anyone heard? Should they leave? Where should they go?

Hoping to calm everyone's fears, Mayor Walter Greer took it upon himself to examine the dike personally. Accompanied by two of the town's remaining officials, they drove to Chosen to examine the dike. They parked their car and walked up to the seven-foot-high, mud-slick bank. Along the top, they were buffeted by strong winds and soaked by drenching squalls. The lake was high; waves lapped less than two feet from the top of the dike. The dike looked to his untrained eye as sturdy as it had always been. As the wind blew against his face, causing him to squint hard, he knew it was a serious storm, but Walter Greer felt the dike would hold. It *had* to hold. The thought that it might not was beyond his imagination.

What the people needed at this time was a calming, reassuring leader, not an alarmist message that might cause mass panic. The three men returned to the drugstore. The mayor wouldn't lie. He told them that he wasn't going anywhere. He and his family were staying and that would be that. Plus, the latest radio reports had the storm veering well to the north. In reality, the mayor knew they had no choice. Most of the people had no means of leaving at this late date. If they tried to leave by the Palm Beach Road, they would be driving exposed in the flat open Everglades directly into the oncoming storm. The road north to Pahokee and Okeechobee was paved, but part of it was built along the lake dike. Anyone trying to make that drive risked being blown into a canal. Either way, they might be caught out in the open with a full-blown hurricane. Like the true pioneers they were, most would stay and tough it out. Though vaguely reassured, they all understood they had no choice. That morning there had been a chance to leave. Not now.

Reassured or not, the meeting broke up, and people returned to their homes, resigned to wait out the storm. There some made basic preparations. Others went to one of the two hotels, which were larger and built of sturdier materials than most of the one story houses in Belle Glade. There was comfort in a crowd. A group of people could offer help and much needed company during the long night that everyone knew was coming. Charlie Riedel crossed the street to the Glades Hotel, the hotel he had built and just sold. It was nearly dark, darker than it should be for 5:30. At least the hotel generator hummed above the occasional gale force gusts, giving a comforting familiar sound. There at least he would find light.

HENRY Martin pulled his hat down tightly on his head and ducked out of the drugstore into the rain. A cold, hard squall caught him as he turned the corner down Canal Street to the store. Large, irregular puddles covered the street. He leaned his head into the wind. He stopped on the stoop of the store and looked at the Hillsboro Canal. The barges and houseboats docked along its side bobbed nervously at their tethers. The water was high and moving swiftly out of the lake. Current waves almost reached up to the steel bridge spanning the canal. Bessie Mae and the children were on the other side of the canal at Tommy Wells's house. Henry wanted them with him on this side of the canal.

Inside the store, he shook off the rain and called for Raymond.

"Go fetch your mother and the kids," he said.

Without bothering to button up his rain slicker, Raymond dashed into the rain and disappeared in a downpour.

Henry knew he had to prepare quickly for possible flooding. He assessed the damage a flood might do to his inventory. He and Arlin began to put bags of flour, sugar, cornmeal, and other perishable goods up on barrels, higher shelves, and makeshift benches. He pictured the water a foot, or at most two, covering the floor of the store and tried to decide what would get wet.

Raymond ran down the street along the Hillsboro Canal and across the canal bridge to Tommy Wells's house on the north side of the canal.

"Daddy says we gotta go to the store."

Bessie Mae gathered up the children and the baby, threw a shawl over her head, and followed Raymond back to the store. Tempie and her children followed close behind. Tommy Wells, ever the doughboy, said he'd prefer to wait out the storm in his own house. But within two hours, he would be forced to change his mind and retreat with his wife, Willie, and little Eddie to the Glades Hotel.

Henry and Arlin were securing shutters and doors when Bessie Mae arrived. Chairs and tables were set up and a pot of coffee was brewing in the side kitchen The family settled down to wait out the storm. The few blankets were passed out. Annie Mae looked anxiously around the store, hoping they could return to the comfort of their own beds before it got too late.

Tempie and Hattie with the other children settled on bags and boxes off to one side. Outside, the wind bellowed like a mad animal howling to get in. Tempie huddled closer to her children.

Henry thought of his brother Loney Martin at the farm next to the dike. If the storm were as big as the reports indicated, then Loney and his family would be in danger. But it was too late to send anyone to get them. They would have to trust in their house. The farmhouse did make it through the two 1926 hurricanes.

The rain rattled the windows as the wind howled and shook the store. Then the lights went out, and they were thrown into darkness. Henry and Arlin lit kerosene lamps and hung them from hooks in the ceiling. The lamps threw an eerie, yellowish sheen on the group of anxious faces, almost a deathly glow.

"Well, we have plenty of food," Bessie Mae said, sitting among stacks of canned goods and burlap bags of produce. She could cook up a meal, if necessary, in the back kitchen. "At least we won't starve."

BACK at his service station, Lawrence Will was doing a land-office business. Lines of cars waited impatiently to fill up their tanks, check their radiators, pump air into the tires, and top off their oil. Most would park their cars near their homes, ready to flee at a minute's notice. Others, loaded with families and many of their most precious possessions, were on their way out of Belle Glade. They were the last of the cars to leave, and all of them knew it was late, but hopefully not too late. No one wanted to be stuck out in the middle of the Everglades on one of two lonely roads leading from Belle Glade in a storm, out of gas, or with a flat tire. The last car stopped in front of the pump. Will immediately recognized the Model A of Arthur Wells, one of the largest farmers in Bean City.

"Starting out kind of late, Mr. Wells," Will said, nearly shouting through the wind gusts.

"Got stuck on the South Bay Road," Arthur Wells said. "Gonna ride it out up in Pahokee."

As he checked the tires, Will saw his children and wife behind the drawn window curtains, huddled in the back seat. Wells scribbled out a check for forty dollars, handed it to Lawrence, got in the car, and drove off.

Will put the check in his pocket and watched as the Model A made its way across the canal bridge and disappeared in a curtain of gray rain. How are they going to make it? he wondered. Cold and wet, he secured his pumps, brought in the last of the tools, and closed the service station door behind him. The wind was now gale force. It was getting dark, nearly dusk, and Will knew he was in for a long night.

Lights fed from the hotel generator still shone along the street, inside buildings and houses. The wind was blowing constantly, and strong gusts tossed loose objects down the street. The rain had changed angle, slicing down at forty-five degrees and slapping hard against the siding and windows. One of the windows rattled, and Will reminded himself to add more caulking.

Upstairs, his unfinished roof was already straining against the wind, groaning as it rose like an accordion with each gust. With the wind howling through his garage, Will worried that he might lose his entire building and all his investment. He realized that this same storm was striking the east coast of Florida and Fort Lauderdale where his family was living. He wondered how they were coping, wishing he was there with them. He and the carpenter nailed a few more securing planks and went downstairs. There was nothing more to do except wait out the storm.

BY six o'clock, dark angry waves were already breaking over the dike. The storm had dropped six inches of rain directly on the lake, while the flooded Kissimmee River poured in more. Lake Okeechobee had risen three feet in twenty-four hours. By 6:30, water was streaming over the lower points of the dike. Lake water quickly filled the canals and then overflowed their banks. The flat-lying fields flooded quickly. The water moved, inextricably joining large pools of rain water until a shallow lake was formed, leaving only trees, bushes, dikes, and houses standing out of the water like foreign objects. Then the lakes began to join together, forming one large body of water—a sea, really. The Everglades was reverting back to its primordial condition.

At 6:45 the storm-darkened sky threw a gloomy twilight over the Everglades, while a group of mostly men crowded around the radio at the Glades Hotel. The AM frequency crackled sharply with each lightning strike—a sure sign of a storm—but through the constant static, a voice announcing the news was loudly audible. The voice stated calmly that the people along the Palm Beach coast could rest assured because there was no danger from the approaching hurricane. Abruptly, the voice stopped, then it excitedly blared out that at that very moment, a monstrous hurricane was battering West Palm Beach.

Shock ran through the crowd. Relief was instantly replaced with anxiety. They were caught in a trap. Memories of Moore Haven and hundreds of dead ran through their minds; their recently planted crops, their homes, their families were all in danger. Some ran through the rain back to their houses; others stayed where they were. They had no other place to go.

Even as the residents of the mainland huddled against the punishing winds and cold torrential rains, Lake Okeechobee was battered into deadly submission. The wind that had been blowing for twenty-four hours from the north began to change direction, first from the northwest, then due west, directly off the lake.

As the eye of the hurricane approached the lake, the winds curved around in a tighter circle, shoveling the water into its center, cupping it in its grip. Trapped, the water piled up on itself until it formed a dome twelve feet high, looming some eight feet above the muck dike, which was rapidly dissolving. The watery mound was an unnatural state. Water must seek its own level. It prodded and probed, searching for weakness, seeking some way to escape. Then the winds changed and it found a way out. The first to feel the effect of the storm surge were the lake island residents. The people of Belle Glade, Miami Locks and South Bay would have to wait their turn.

THE LAKE ISLANDS

For the first time that day, Cliff Councilman could relax. Concerned about the rising lake water and the increasing strong winds, immediately after lunch he and his family had packed a few blankets and some food and left their Torry Island home. Most of the other island residents had chosen to remain in their homes. They wanted to be near their houses and farms and care for their livestock.

In their fourteen-foot launch powered by a Johnson 5.5-horsepower outboard motor, the Councilman family had crossed the choppy waters strewn with thick clumps of windblown hyacinth and tree branches to the dock at Chosen. After securing the launch, they crossed over to Isaac West's store, which most people considered to be the sturdiest building in the area. Twenty people milled around the store; some helped serve coffee; the rest made themselves as comfortable as possible. The telephone rang. Everyone looked up. Telephones were still novelties. Isaac West answered the telephone, listened grimly, and then hung up. "It's a hurricane. And the edge has reached West Palm Beach," he said. "And, it's definitely headed here."

What about the others on the islands, Cliff wondered? Someone had to warn them. With his family secured, he decided to return and alert the other residents.

Untying the launch, he cast off and motored along the south side causeway canal, fighting against the rain-driven north wind. The causeway afforded him some protection from the breaking waves. The leeward north side of the causeway was heaped high with hundreds of acres worth of wind-blown weeds. Tying his boat up at John Aunapu's former storefront dock, he grabbed young Frede Aunapu, and together they ran on foot to alert the other residents. Within half an hour, nearly all the residents on Bird and Torry Islands except for the Lees started for the mainland. They got as far as the causeway. It was underwater and blocked by tons of wind-blown hyacinth. Wet and cold, they retreated to the only remaining safe place on the island, the Aunapus' big metal packinghouse.

Cliff Councilman had left the group and returned to the dock for his launch, hoping to make it back to his family, but the water-soaked motor refused to start. He, along with the rest, was trapped. With the water slopping over the dock, he ran to the packinghouse.

Inside were twenty-one people mixed in between a couple of trucks, tractors, plows, disks, crates, and tools. Wind and rain battered the metal walls. As the water rose, they stood on top of crates, trucks, and tractors. How long could they stand like that? How much longer could the metal structure hold? Frede reached into each car and truck and turned on the headlights. The bright lights flickered as water lapped up against the bulbs. Still, they burned, and the water inexorably crept higher. The men waded through the waist-high water, gathered up planks, logs, and boards, and placed them on the cross beams of the packinghouse roof. First helping the women and children, Frede climbed up on the rafters and waited. The walls of the packinghouse seemed to breathe with each gust.

Below, the water covered the roofs of the cars. His father's new Buick was now ruined, Frede thought. The headlights still burned. A ghostly light dancing in the water lit up their faces, but it grew dimmer as the dark water continued its insatiable rise.

SOON after Councilman left Isaac West's store, a series of strong gusts shook the walls with such force that there was fear it would collapse. John Elliot decided to return to Max Morris's small but sturdily built house. Within a few minutes, Bill and Lois Hunt and a North Carolinian named White who were fleeing their own homes, joined him. They tried to make themselves comfortable in the sparsely furnished house lit by one kerosene lamp.

Less than an hour later, water from the breaking dike swept around the small house in increasing torrents. Water forced its way into the house, rising quickly to hip level. Elliot and the others barely had time to think of what to do when the house was washed off its foundation. Elliot sloshed to the back of the house when another surge of water threw the house against the canal road embankment. The front reared up, driving the back of the house underwater. Without thinking, Elliot dove out through the screened window. The house plunged into the canal. He broke the surface with pieces of splintered wood near the roof. It was pitch black as he grappled for the roof, cutting his hands on the metal sheathing.

In the front, as the house reared up and pitched into the canal, Bill Hunt, his wife, and White had jumped through the windows. Grabbing onto the eaves, they made their way to the roof, where they rode the flood unknowingly a few feet from John Elliot. Forced by the surging lake waters, the house began to move down the canal, where it crashed against the Belle Glade bridge over a mile away and immediately broke up.

John Elliot was thrown violently off the house into the angry canal waters. Struggling to the surface, he swam desperately with his one good hand to the bridge. He grabbed onto the structure, held tight, gathered his strength, and then pulled himself up. Once on top, he stood up and ran against the crosswind to the Glades Hotel. He could not believe that he had survived. The Hunts and their friend, he thought, must have drowned.

Cupping his bleeding hands, he ran into the hotel lobby. There he found confused and hysterical people on the first floor of the hotel. Seeing he was injured, he was led upstairs to have his hand bandaged. When he recounted his tale, the hotel refugees laughed. A house floating from Chosen! Not likely. His assertion brought the only joking about the storm that night. Looking outside the people could see barely a foot of water in the street. Everyone knew a barge might be washed down from Chosen, but never a house.

Before the night was through, fifty houses would have made the same journey.

BIRD ISLAND

On Bird Island, the Aunapu party did their best to keep dry and out of the rising water. Wind bowed the metal walls of the packinghouse with each gust. Rain pelted the metal roof with such force that a deafening roar precluded any conversation. Wet and cold, the packinghouse party suffered their fate silently. Sitting on the crossbeams, Ralph and Mary Cherry and their three young children had joined the group as they had waded across the water-swept island. In one corner, old blind Captain Ed King held the other two small Cherry children firmly in his arms, trying to console them.

From the opposite side of Torry Island, the wind gathered a row of cut apple custard trees in a long chain of tangled trunks and branches and swept the hundred-yard mass rolling and tumbling toward Bird Island. With the trees acting as sails, the wind carried the mass like a schooner scurrying across the choppy lake waters. It slammed into the packinghouse with a heart-stopping thud. Wrapping around the metal building in a mortal embrace, it crashed against it again and again. The trees acted like a dam, pilling up water and more debris behind it. The metal building groaned and strained against the additional weight. Then it began to bend. In slow motion one side, then the other doubled over and folded upon itself before collapsing into the canal.

Trapped in the twisted metal, Frede was pulled down and then dragged under the water.

This is how it is to drown, he thought, as a strange sense of calm overpowered him.

With his strained lungs burning, he took a gulp of water, welcoming death, but his body's survival reflex kicked in just as the building settled. He was free.

He kicked up and broke to the surface. Coughing up lungs full of water, he gasped for air and grabbed onto a wooden beam. Gathering his senses, he glanced around. Where was Elizabeth? Something struck his leg. He reached down, felt a head of hair, grabbed it, and pulled. Green, one of the black hands, bobbed to the surface. Elizabeth was still down there! Quickly Frede took a deep breath and dove, groping blindly in the black water. He felt a dress tangled in the wreckage, tugging against the current. It was Elizabeth, but she was stuck. A button on her jacket had caught in the tin roofing. He pulled with all his might, then ripped the button from the jacket, and, with Elizabeth in his arm, shot to the surface. Elizabeth, half-conscious, bobbed in the water. Fred grabbed onto a beam of the roof and held on, trying to orient himself.

They were still inside the packing plant wreckage. It moved and groaned in the wind-driven torrent. They had to get out before it completely collapsed. Barely making out a hole in the roof, they swam out just as the roof sunk under the waves. They grasped at a floating tree and hung on. Frede's leg was caught in between the trees, and he was repeatedly forced underwater as the tree bobbed and rolled. Elizabeth disappeared in the darkness. Finally, he freed himself. He found Elizabeth grasping onto another branch barely four yards away. They floated onto a barge, which they grabbed, and pulled themselves up onto its rain-slicked deck. Lying flat, they held on for dear life.

JACOB PORTER

Jacob Porter stepped out of his shack and stared into wind-swept rain. The wind roared like a steam furnace. Water had risen over the small irrigation canal and had covered his yard. His wife, Jennie, bemoaned that her herbs and vegetables would drown. But Jacob was more worried about the dike. Water around the house was black. It was lake water. Except for lightning it was pitch black. He stared through the blackness but could not see where water was coming over the dike. Then the water began to rise faster. They had to run! Jacob yelled to Jennie to get the children.

Jennie grabbed the baby, and Jacob took his boy and girl under his arms and dashed out into the raging tempest. Other families joined them. Rain blinded him as he leaned into the wind. Jennie and the baby huddled behind him. He wanted to get to one of the sturdily built stores in Chosen. Trees were down, their roots in the air like grabbing multifingered hands. He was afraid he might step into an unseen canal. Then he was shoved from behind by a wave. He lost sight of Jennie and the baby as another wave pushed him under. It was the third wave, deeper than the rest, that flooded over him and kept him from the surface. He fought to the surface with the children gripped tightly in his arms as he lost consciousness.

IT was dark—not just dark, but black. Black clouds covered the sky, the ground was black muck, and the dike was a black wall; even the water was black. Outside the blackness was broken by a couple of windows lit up by the forlorn gleam of kerosene lamps, signs that someone was still there, still alive, still able to keep a light shining, a light of hope.

The intermittent rain had changed to a constant angled downpour; as the storm crept closer, the angle lessened until it blew in parallel streams. The wind roared a deafening relentless shriek. As the eye of the storm approached, the wind gained strength, then shifted slightly out of the north-northwest—wind tide direction. The gale-force wind had been forcing the water over the banks of the dike along the southern edge of the lake. With waves breaking over its rim, the dike had been breached in a few spots. With winds gusting of over 150 miles per hour, the storm now aimed all its fury at the funnel pointing directly at the heart of South Bay.

SITTING in a wooden chair on the first floor, Lawrence Will's eyes kept jumping to the ceiling. The wind howled like a freight train passing over their heads. The walls swayed, but it was the unfinished roof he was most worried about. It rose and fell with each gust and then began to flap until a monstrous gust of wind, raging like two trains passing each other, lifted the roof and carried it away. He heard water slapping against the second floor, and then torrents spilled through the floorboards. For a moment, Lawrence Will almost lost heart.

With his roof gone, Will and the carpenter, Whitehead Smith, and his young mechanic sat in the dark dodging cascades of water streaming through the ceiling. The water had drowned the kerosene lanterns hanging from the rafters. Will had put on a sweater and over that a raincoat to keep dry. The building creaked and moaned with each wind gust. Though they knew they had built the building well, each wondered whether it could possibly withstand such punishment.

SUDDENLY the building stopped shaking. The men glanced at each other. With flashlights in hand, they stepped out the front door. They swept the street with light beams and were met with an incredible scene. Main Street was littered with boards, downed telephone poles, and building debris. The new Ford garage across the street was a flat pile of rubble. The three men cautiously walked along the street. A frantic mother yelled at them that she'd lost her child and asked that they please help find her. They were still searching when the eye passed over them, and the wind began with renewed fury. Will was between the drugstore and the Glades Hotel when a blast of wind spun him around. He landed in front of the drugstore, which he was surprised to find empty. Just before dark there had been twenty people inside. He found the little girl huddling in the doorway and gave her back to her mother, who then sought refuge in the Glades Hotel.

The young mechanic wanted to check on the safety of the bridge tender's family. The three men headed toward the canal. At each gust they had to grab onto anything anchored and hold on or be blown away. The bridge and the bank along the canal were the highest points in Belle Glade. Though the wind was blowing fiercely, the water was still only about a foot deep, and it never occurred to any of them that the water would rise much higher.

They made the canal as the back eye wall of the storm threw its strongest winds at them. The canal was clogged with debris: part of a houseboat, a barge on its side, walls and roofs of dozens of houses, and tangled messes of uprooted apple custard trees. Crammed up against the steel bridge was one of the Halloway brothers' barges. Hiding under the barge's roof from the storm's fury were Bill and Lois Hunt and White, who had made the harrowing rooftop journey from Chosen. Yet the water in Belle Glade had only risen another foot.

They tried to return to the hotel but were forced back by repeated vicious wind gusts. Finally, they gave up and retreated back to the canal and leaped onto the barge. With their flashlights, they examined the dank hold. The barge had a jagged hole just above the waterline. Rainwater streamed in through the floorboards. The barge was in danger of sinking.

Knee-deep in the rancid, oily bilge water, the men took turns pumping. The small pump moved some water, excruciatingly little water, but the strenuous work helped keep the men warm. They could ride out the storm in relative safety if the cable held. Trapped on the barge in the middle of the canal, they could only listen impotently to the occasional desperate cries for help drowned out in the dark, shrieking wind.

NANCY Martin paused and ran to the window. The wind had suddenly died, almost stopping. By the light of a kerosene lamp, Nancy Martin looked outside at the knee-deep water covering the entire yard and fields around their house. The only spot not underwater was the road bank.

"If we don't want to get stuck here until tomorrow, I think we should leave," she said.

The others agreed. They got into the two cars and began to drive to West Palm Beach. Near the Experimental Station, the back winds of the eye wall caught them. Vicious cross winds cutting across the road threatened to blow their automobiles into the canal. Afraid to continue, they parked their cars in front of the main building to wait out the storm. Savage wind gusts so viciously rocked the cars that Nancy was sure the next gust of wind would flip her car on its side. All she could do was hold on to life and pray.

COLD rain fell in wavelike sheets flapping in the wind. The waterlogged muck could absorb no more water. The drainage pumps had stopped working, but even if they had continued to pump, there was no place to dump the water. Lake Okeechobee was full. Gusting winds sent waves splashing over the lower sections of the dike. Dozens of little rivulets snaked their way down the dike's banks. They widened, carrying muck with them. Slowly at first, the water washed some mud here, cut a little gully there; the dike was losing form, opening spaces for water to escape from the lake.

Just after dusk, the water-saturated dike began to melt. Rain converted soil into a liquid black slush. Waves churned up by the 150-mile-per-hour winds crashed onto and then over the dike, spilling more black water down its liquefying banks.

TWO blocks away from the Pioneer Service Building, Mayor Walter Greer's small gabled wooden house began to shake so violently that he feared the walls could give way. The group that had gathered there had to leave the house. He ordered everyone to pair off, one man and one woman, and not to become separated. Then he and his wife grabbed what they could and fought their way to Tedder's Glades Hotel. In the confusion, his daughter and her friend Bonnie Parker, who somehow were paired up, were separated from the rest of the family. The girls were not missed until the Greers made it to the Glades Hotel. Someone said that the drugstore roof next door had just blown off into the street and that the girls were trapped underneath. Walter Greer rushed out into the street. Around the corner of the hotel, a gust blew him on his face, scuffing his elbows and knees. The big man lifted himself up and struggled to the overturned roof. Looking underneath he saw that the girls were not there. He retreated back to the hotel when again he was blown off his feet. Half-crawling on all fours like a wet bear, he made it back to the hotel where he told his wife that the girls were not under the roof.

Frantic, Mrs. Greer insisted she had to know whether they were safe or not. The newly elected mayor fought his way through the rain and wind across the street to the Belle Glade Hotel. The water reached up to his knees. He knew the black, murky water was from the lake. He burst into the hotel and found Georgia and Bonnie safe. Knowing his wife would not rest easy until she knew that the girls were safe, he once again fought his way across the street to the hotel and informed his wife that the girls were safe. Exhausted, he crawled up to the second floor and collapsed on the floor. He remained there asleep until the next morning.

WHILE Walter Greer slept upstairs in the Glades Hotel, Walter Peterson with his family in tow fought his way out of colored town. Blinded by biting wind-driven rain, he struggled through the rubble-strewn streets across 4th Street and up Avenue B. They had stayed in their house until one of the walls began to tear away, threatening to carry the entire structure with it. There were only two places he knew might be safe: two two-story hotels in the center of town.

Following his father, nine-year-old Ardie watched "tin roofs fly through the air like newspaper." In the confusion the family was split up. Ardie and his father battled their way into the Glades Hotel. His sisters and their husbands were forced to seek refuge across the street at the Belle Glade Hotel. It was the first time any of the Petersons had ever set foot in the "whites only" hotel. It was crowded; black and white families milled about nervously. Anxious faces glanced out the front. The dank air was heavy with the stench of fear.

When the water started to rise above the porch, all the children were ordered to the second floor. Ardie ran up the stairs and sat down on the hallway floor.

"Couldn't lean up against the wall because it was moving in and out," he said.

To prevent any adult from going upstairs, a guard armed with a pistol was posted at the bottom of the stairs. When the water started to rise, one woman stormed past the guard saying, "Go and shoot me but I'm going up."

The rest pressed up the stairs. The lobby flooded so fast that the last two people almost drowned in the stairwell. The water rose until it finally stopped within a few inches of the ceiling. The wind howled outside. The crowd of people watched in silence as the building shook and the walls oscillated, threatening at any time to come apart. Death, it seemed, was determined to carry them away. Yet against all odds, Tedder's Glades Hotel would hold out against all that the storm could give.

Across the street at the Belle Glade Hotel, nearly 150 people crammed into the dining room, sitting rooms, and hallways. Suddenly, during a powerful blow, the purr of the hotel generator stopped and the lights went out. Kerosene lamps were lit, placed on tables, and hung from rafters. The water was up to the first step of the hotel.

No one could see anything outside. The rain obscured the view; the wind roared with unrelenting fierceness. No one knew whether the water in the streets was rainwater or whether the dike had given away and it was lake water. The uncertainty raised everyone's anxiety level. Charlie Riedel arrived with his family. After securing the family in one of the upstairs rooms, Charlie walked around reassuring the terrified townspeople.

The eye passed directly over Belle Glade. For the first time in two hours, many of the people allowed themselves to hope that the worst was over. But those who knew better mentally braced for what they knew was to come—the back end of the storm, the roaring back end, the storm's second act, the finale in which it would try to deliver the knockout punch. They had only to wait twenty minutes.

Craving a couple of cigarettes away from the crowd, young Charlie Tryon and Tom Jackson went up the back stairs to the second floor to sneak a smoke when a vicious gust of wind slammed into the hotel. With a mighty groan and then a tremendous crash, the hotel shook and the roof flew off and sailed like a kite into the blackness. A downpour of water soaked the two boys. In total darkness, they carefully retreated back downstairs.

"It was as if God was punishing us for wanting a smoke," Charlie said.

On the first floor, alarm set in as black water began to rise up the front steps of the hotel. It covered the porch floor and then leaked inside through the front doors. Main Street was a raging river. Swiftly, it covered the entire floor in crazed eddies. Women screamed; people ran about. Charlie Riedel stepped up and took command. He quickly got the women and children upstairs, followed by the men. Behind the fleeing crowd, the water crept up the stairs an inch a minute. Exposed to the furious wind, they cringed in corners against the relentless downpour. The women, with sweaters and blankets wrapped over their heads, huddled over their children, trying vainly to protect them from the cold, cutting rain. The lakeside wall threatened to collapse; Riedel got the men to brace themselves against it. The men gritted against the pelting hail-like rain and leaned with all their strength, trying to keep the wall from collapsing onto their loved ones. Only a miracle would prevent the hotel from buckling into the water rampaging through the streets of Belle Glade. The building shook and, at times, seemed to rise up only to settle back down. Once again the entire building rose up off its foundation and then squatted down hard on its cement pilings, which ripped through the floorboards like a pin cushion, anchoring the building.

HENRY listened to the wind raking the side of the store. It scraped and scratched at the roof. He thought he heard a piece of siding slapping in the wind. Then the wind softened and died down. The air was ghostly still; the eye had passed over the store.

"The worst of the storm has passed," Henry said, trying to reassure the rest. "The store will hold."

With a flashlight in hand Henry walked to the front of the store. Without opening the front door, he looked outside into the night. He could see the canal had flooded its banks. Dark lake water careened down Canal Street carrying wood, tree branches, and pails. He watched as it rose slowly up the steps and then began to seep under the doors into the store. Suddenly the wind began again. It screamed across the roof, sending blasts through every crack. He felt a chill. The water continued to rise, covering the floor. Henry ran back and helped Bessie Mae Martin put the children on top of the counter. He then grabbed Bessie Mae by her waist with his big hands and hoisted her onto the counter. She reached out and took baby Robert in her arms. Henry sloshed around in ankle-deep water to the front of the store, checking on the damage to his goods and trying to think of how to keep more water from coming in. Water was rising up the door, pouring in around the jamb's sides. The Hillsboro Canal had been transformed into a three-mile-wide raging river. There was no way he could stop the water. Black lake water lapped against the front windows. Holding Bessie Mae's hand, he stood in knee-deep water.

Standing on the counter, Thelma watched the water rise with growing anxiety. A poor swimmer, she was afraid of the water. Memories of the hurricane in 1926, Mrs. Register's screams, and the water flooding the house came back. She was afraid, as afraid as she had ever been in her life.

Henry, seeing that the water was rising fast, put a table on the counter top and opened up the trap door into the attic. Into the black hole in the ceiling he hefted Bessie Mae. Then he handed her each of the children, followed by Tempie, before he pulled himself up out of the water. The store went dark; the water had snuffed out the kerosene lights.

It was pitch black. The flashlight had gone out. By touch Bessie Mae gathered the children around her as she cradled Robert in her arms. Ernestine was frightened. Like Thelma she was afraid of the water and couldn't swim.

Though alarmed, the children had the stoicism of pioneers and kept silent.

Henry could hear floating boxes and wooden barrels thumping against the ceiling like a herd of angry trapped animals. Everything was ruined. The water sloshed at his feet.

"Hey, Kid. The water is up over my shoes," Henry said matter-of-factly to Bessie Mae as he lifted his feet from the trap door. In the darkness, Henry crawled over to his wife and wrapped his long arms around her and three of the children.

Thelma's fears were partially soothed by the deep, resonant, reassuring voice of her father. She held tighter onto Annie Mae's arm.

Suddenly, the wind picked up and shook the entire store. The store swayed in the wind; water pounded its sides, then it groaned, slowly lifted up, and then floated off its foundation.

"Oh, God, we're moving," someone cried out.

Like a toy dollhouse, the surging waters carried the hapless store away from the lake. Two hundred yards away, the large Methodist church loomed like a white granite sentinel. The water pushed the house toward the church and then struck it with a deafening crunch. The impact forced the two-story church off its foundation. The two buildings shuddered; then, the smaller store caught a corner of the church and rose up at an obtuse angle. Water rushed under the store and turned it up on its side, then over on its roof.

"Mommy! Mommy!" one of the girls cried out in the dark.

The Martins were trapped under the store. Everyone was thrown up and over into the water. They were trapped inside a lightless coffin. Then the store broke apart. Pieces of roof and wall crashed in on the family, forcing them underwater, and then it bobbed to the surface.

Ernestine slid down the ceiling onto the roof. She was thrown and dragged along by the current underwater with broken pieces of the store. The onrush bounced her like a beach ball down Canal Street. She finally broke the surface, gasped for air, and then suddenly stopped. She felt cold water rushing at her face and rain pelting her like rocks. Forcing her head above the waves, she spit out water. She did not know where she was but knew she was not alone. Slowly turning her head she saw Thelma. The two girls were lodged on an overturned root stump of a massive rubber tree on the northern bank of the Hillsboro Canal. Like fingers of the hand of God, Ernestine later thought, the roots had reached and grabbed them out of the torrent and held them tight.

WHEN the store broke up against the church, twelve-year-old Thelma Martin was crouched beside Ernestine. The impact threw her headfirst deep into the water. Gasping for air she felt something hold her under the water. She thought, "I can't swim good and I'm going to drown," and lost consciousness. The current ripped her away from the house and tossed her up and over the canal, throwing her against the uprooted rubber tree.

Thelma struggled, but her leg was caught in between the roots and she couldn't move higher up the roots. Water splashed around her neck, and she fought to keep her head above the black water. She felt something on her free leg and reached down to brush it away. She felt cloth, then she felt skin, and she pulled it up out of the water over her head. It was her baby brother, Robert.

Two of Tempie's children, Hattie and Carl, were caught in the same tree. Like twining fingers, the roots grabbed the five children and held them against the onslaught of the wind and the boiling black water. Ernestine scratched her way higher up the root stand as the waves broke over her. The wind slapped her face and she could see nothing; she was blind.

Thelma, holding baby Robert in one hand, crawled against the wind and water as high up the roots as she could. She held Robert above her head as waves splashed over her head. With an iron grip on the baby and an iron will to survive, she held on, refusing to give in to her aching arms or the force of nature. Her foot, still caught on one of the roots, stopped her moving any higher. She was afraid that if the water rose any further, she would drown. But she refused to release her baby brother. She held him with her arms straight up over her head, out of the way of the breaking waves. A board with protruding spikes was lodged in her thigh just above the knee. Pain shot through her leg, but with a supernatural stubbornness, twelve-year-old Thelma refused to give in to either the pain or the freezing water.

The two Martin girls hung on. When Thelma's arms tired, she passed the baby to Ernestine and then took him back again. Back and forth they passed two-year-old Robert. Beside them Hattie struggled to hold onto her own brother until a large wave carried the boy screaming off into the night.

With Robert weighing heavy in her hands, Thelma turned to Hattie and asked her to help hold the baby.

"You hold him yourself," she yelled. Her own grip on the root was precarious, and she was scared. She felt her grip slipping and began to grab at anything, first at the slippery roots and then desperately at Thelma holding Robert above her head. Thelma pushed her away, afraid she would grab onto Robert and drown him.

Another wave surged up and over them, and then Hattie was not there.

As the last of the peanuts were eaten, Charles Thomas looked out through the kitchen window across the back yard. It was getting dark, though dusk was not due for another two hours. Outside in the backyard the fluid puddles joined each other, uniting into ponds. As more rain fell, the water spread until it covered the yards and fields, forming a vast lake. In the fading light, Charles saw waves breaking over the dike. He knew then that yesterday's assurances given to him in West Palm Beach were wrong. The hurricane was not drifting out to sea. It was here, right outside his window.

Without alarming the rest of the family, Charles told his wife that maybe they had better move to Victor Thirsk's house. They had discussed contingency plans with the Boots and the other white families. Thirst's house was the largest and best-built structure and could hold everyone in Sebring Farms. And, in case of emergency, it was better to be with other people who could help. After the peanut feast, the Thomas family got ready to leave.

BILL Boots watched the waters rise up to the fields, flow down the neatly hoed rows, then cover the stalks of the beans. With a farmer's innate fatalism, he accepted the whims of nature. It was simply bad luck. His crops would be a total loss if the water were not drained quickly in the next few days. But he was a farmer, and he could replant. The farm animals would survive even if they had to stand in a foot, or two, of water for a few days. The chickens would roost in trees and on roofs. This was a storm, a large storm, yes, but still a storm, and they had weathered many storms. He was most concerned about the dike. Located so ominously close, he began to doubt it would hold up to the vicious winds and rain. He knew that the black water covering the fields was not all rainwater. Some was coming from the lake.

By seven o'clock, Bill and Mattie Mae Boots had to make a decision. Outside, the ground was flooded two feet deep. Waves were breaking over the dike. The storm gave no indication of abating, and if the water kept on rising there was a good chance their house would float away. Yesterday, they had been safely aboard Bill Rawle's tug at South Bay. They had lost their chance. Now it was too late

Gathering up the boys and a flashlight, Bill and Mattie Mae made a dash to the Thirsk house. Outside, it was pitch black. Water reached their knees, and wind gusts blew them sideways. It took them fifteen minutes fighting the wind and stinging rain to make the hundred yards. Finally, they reached the Thirsk house. Three of the four steps of the cement stoop leading up into the house were underwater.

Inside the Thirsk house two gas lanterns burned brightly, casting a yellow pallor through the gloom. When the Bootses arrived, nearly everyone left in Sebring Farms milled about the Thirsk house. In the front room, most of the black families huddled around the few chairs and sat on the floor. In the kitchen and back rooms, the white families had bunched up—a total of sixty-three people.

Mrs. Thirsk handed Mattie Mae a damp towel to dry off as best she could. She wiped off Willie then handed it to Vernie. That was when Vernie realized how cold he was. Looking around the room, he saw familiar and strange faces in the ghostly shadows of the gaslight. He could smell the fear, the wet bodies, and the soaking muck—the same muck that his mother would chide the children for tracking into the house. He listened to the nervous talk and muffled whimpering.

"The weight will help keep the house from floating away," Thirsk said, referring to all the people inside.

Needing some hope, they all agreed that was true.

"I built this house myself. It'll hold any storm," Bill Boots said, even as the house shook, buffeted by a gust of wind.

Charles Thomas gathered his family around him. The entire family had made it to the Thirsk house except for Uncle Minor, who elected to stay at the "inside out house."

Most of the people huddling in the Thirsk house had experienced the 1926 hurricane. Thirsk and his wife and eleven neighbors had weathered the Moore Haven storm in the house. It had been bad. The house shook just like now. The wind howled just like now. But this wind was different. It had a different tone, more guttural, more monstrous. In 1926, they had not experienced the center of the storm; the force of an eye wall never passed over them.

Then there was the dike. The dike was on everyone's mind. Would the dike hold?

Some of the men had brought tools. Hammers were in hand to board up windows. Near the stove was an axe to cut firewood.

One look outside showed the water rising, and rising fast. Waves slapped at the door. Anxious eyes glanced at the door as if a wolf were outside, wailing to get in. But it wasn't a wolf. It was water. First it filtered silently in under the door. Dark muddy water eased itself into the house. Spreading steadily like a malevolent amoeba, it crept across the kitchen floor until stopped by the far sidewall. Then it inched its way up. The children were lifted from the floor and placed on top of tables and beds.

It was 8:10. The water level outside had reached four feet. It made no sound that could be heard over the howling wind. The top of the dike was awash in water. The storm surge rose up and at the dike. Overwhelmed, dit gave away, and like a drowned black rat snake, the dike disappeared under the waves.

A wall of water cascaded over the dike, sending a chain of ever-larger waves crashing through South Bay, Miami Lakes, and Belle Glade. Water rushed through Sebring Farms. Quickly it rose to ankle-deep, then it splashed at calves and then knees. It was rising a foot a minute.

"We got to get up into the attic," one of the men yelled.

The men went into the bedroom, moved the double bed aside, and placed a large wooden trunk that held all of Mrs. Thirsk's valuables and heirloom clothes under the trapdoor to the attic. Charles Thomas pulled himself up and then reached down to help the women and children up into the attic. Vernie Boots was, at fourteen, a man and one of the last to go up. As they were handing people up through the attic, a gust of wind hit the house and it shook, breaking a window. Wind and water stormed in. Vernie lost his balance, slipped, and fell on top of the broken glass, gashing his right hand to the bone near his fingers. Blood spurted out, and he wrapped a piece of shirt around it to stem the flow. The water was slapping at his chest and rising. He could taste the muddy water. It tasted like death.

The ceilings were eight feet high. He hoisted himself through the trapdoor. Trying to get more comfortable in the cramped attic, Vernie dangled his legs over the side, and his feet touched the water. He started to say something when he felt the reassuring hand of his father on his shoulder. Vernie had conducted himself like a man, and there was a sign of acknowledgment in that last touch from his father. Vernie lifted his feet out as the swirling water rose further.

Crouched beside Vernie, Mutt Thomas saw that the water had reached the top of the windows—twelve feet above the ground. It looked as if it might come up into the attic. He moved closer to his father.

In the front room, a second opening had been made in the ceiling through which most of the black, and some of the white, families had escaped into the attic.

The white families were one on side, and they huddled together quietly listening to the freight train roar of the wind and the rain whipping at the roof. During lulls, the cries and lamenting wails of the black families were heard as they prayed out loud and bemoaned their plight.

It was dark. Sixty-three people were trapped in a coffinlike air pocket in the cramped attic, one on top of the other. A flashlight would come on then quickly be turned off to conserve the batteries. Except for two vents at each end of the attic, there was no other opening but the trap door down to the raging waters. The house trembled as the water tried to lift it off its foundation. They had to make ready to escape. There was only one way out—through the roof.

Taking the axe he had grabbed from the kitchen, Charles Thomas began to hack at the roof. Thomas swung up with all his might. Wood splinters sprayed on everyone. He swung again. It was straining work. Then he hit with a crunch the thick metal roof, which had been nailed tightly over the wood. Swinging the heavy axe upward, pieces of thick wooden plank and metal sheeting grudgingly gave way. Desperately, he swung again and again until the axe finally broke through. Thomas had managed to cut open a small hole. Wet, cold wind blasted through the opening. The wind howled in like a screaming banshee with low moans and ghostly whistles. A guitar string sound stuck in low E reverberated through a hole into the cramped attic.

Thomas kept hacking at the roof until the hole was large enough to allow a man to squeeze through. Cautiously, he stuck his head through the jagged hole. He yelled back that he thought he could get out.

He squeezed through the hole. Sleetlike wind and rain slapped his face, stinging his eyes and his cheeks, forcing him to turn away from the wind. He squeezed through the opening, grabbed the metal ribs of the roof, and held on. A gust of wind caught him and flung his legs out from under him. He fell, slamming onto the rain-slicked metal roof. He held on and began to peel back the metal roofing. The hole was bigger. Thirsk shoved himself up through. Charles Thomas tried to move out of the way when the now floating house violently hit the new Clewiston Road bank. The entire house shuddered. Jarred, Thomas lost his grip just as a gust caught him, and he tumbled backward. Thirsk watched helplessly as the wind flung him off the roof into the black whirling waters.

Thirsk squeezed through the hole, gained a hold on the roof, and then pulled his wife up after him. Grasping at whatever piece of roof she could get a hold on, Mrs. Thirsk crawled to the peak of the roof where she could get a better grip.

The house crushed a second time against the road grade and sent a violent shudder through the structure that nearly shook Thirsk off the roof. He reached down through the hole and grabbed a boy. In his strong right hand, he pulled Mutt Thomas out through the hole. Thirsk pushed him up toward the top of the roof where his wife was. He reached down for another person when the house lifted up and crashed onto the roadbed one last time, then collapsed. The three people on the roof were thrown off into the night.

The house shifted again and slammed against the raised roadbed and shuddered, then settled. Again every beam and two by four of hard Florida pine moaned as it strained against the force of the water and the wind. Once more the house shifted and smashed against the roadbed. People screamed inside. The house turned and tilted, and one last time a wave lifted it up and it came down on the raised roadbed and broke apart. The sides buckled as the studs and slats broke like toothpicks with a series of sickening snaps; the roof collapsed, trapping the sixty people left inside, dragging them down into a water-filled mass coffin. Desperately, they scrambled for the openings, holding their breaths, grabbing their children and loved ones. The roof strained and then separated from the house. Vernie Boots shot a glance at his mother. Flashlights went on. The precious batteries were needed to show the way out—any way out.

"Whatever happens, stay together," he heard his mother cry out in the dark.

It was the last thing he ever heard her say.

With a blood-chilling groan, the roof broke up. Vernie, fighting the drowning waters, instinctively grabbed at anything to keep from being pulled under. His hand reached a piece of the ceiling that bobbed up under him, and he wrapped his arms around it and held on for dear life. He felt the water rush over him, pulling him down. But the buoyant wood broke the surface, and he gasped at rain-soaked air. Below, he could see the eerie glow of flashlights briefly lighting up the escape hole of the roof six feet underwater and sinking. There were people still inside. Then the lights went out.

It was black. No lights. No moon. No stars. Just black. The rain was black; the water was black; the waves were black; the air was black. He might as well have been blind as well as dead. But he hung on. Vernie Boots grasped that precious piece of wood and nails as he hung on to his life.

He cried out for his mother, his father, his brothers, and was answered only by the howling wind. It screamed in his face—the howls of the dead, the dead that he might soon be joining. He fought to keep afloat, fought to keep his head into the wind. He fought with all his might to keep from turning over into the black pitiless waters. Soaked, cold, and pelted by wind-driven rain, Vernie Boots hung onto his precarious life raft, not knowing whether he was the last person alive on the face of the Earth.

BLOWN off the Thirsk house roof, Charles Thomas came up bobbing. With all his strength, he struggled to swim toward the house. But with each stroke the current carried him farther away from the house. In the flashes of lighting, he saw the house, saw it stopped and saw it shudder. A wave broke over him, plunging him underwater, and he lost sight of the house. Caught in the current, he was dragged under. Desperately he grabbed at floating pieces of wood and trees but could not get a grip. He struggled to keep his head above water. In front of him he saw a white wave, then a fountain of dirty white water. There were the top crossbars of a telephone pole, and he lunged at the arm and pulled himself up. He hung there all night, wondering whether he could go on living with knowing that he had lost his entire family.

HOLDING his head down against the stinging cold rain, Mutt Thomas held onto the peak of the roof. In front of him was Mrs. Thirsk, her dress blowing like a storm flag. Mutt looked back at where he had just crawled up. He saw Mr. Thirsk reaching into the hole. Who would come out next? His mother? One of his sisters? He glanced back at Mrs. Thirsk. Sheer terror danced on her face as she opened her mouth in a scream muffled by the roaring wind. He looked back down when the house jerked suddenly, shuddered, and then tilted up on its side for one long agonizing second before breaking apart. He tumbled from his perch and fell into the raging black waters. Almost immediately a corner post shot out of the water like a missile and splashed down near him. With a couple of hard strokes, he made it to the post and wrapped both arms around it. He was not sure where the water was carrying him. For a while he thought he was out in the middle of the lake since the waves were so high and kept breaking over him one after another. All he could wonder now was if he would ever stop.

MIAMI LOCKS

The Hughes family huddled in their houseboat. The wind viciously buffeted the houseboat, and it began to sway like a rocking horse, first side to side and then from stern to bow. Edna was frightened. Though she had taught hundreds of young children to read and write, no one had taught her how to swim. She was afraid of water; she was afraid of drowning.

The rising water in the canal pulled at the mooring lines, and the boat strained. One of the mooring lines broke, and the boat was violently flipped around and then jerked hard. The boat listed on its side and began to sink. John grabbed Edna and Paul and fought his way to the deck. The boat heaved up; he grabbed his wife in his right arm and Paul in his left just as a wave of black water threw them overboard into the raging canal waters. They bobbed up to the surface, John desperately holding his family.

Edna Hughes threw her arms around John's shoulder, grasping him tightly while trying to help him hold their son. A wave broke over their heads. She spit out mud-flavored water and gasped. Her hands were raw and tired, and she felt them numbing in the cold water. Brush and boards, flung by the water, knocked her hands back until she could no longer hold on.

The three people were thrown over and under the water. John held his family tightly against him until they were caught on some debris. The suction of the undertow ripped his wife and son from his arms.

Edna felt her husband grab at her and then felt the strength of his massive hands wane, and she gagged on another wave and slipped away. Trying to grab the two, he felt them break from his grasp, and then he was alone. He wanted to scream, but no sound came out of his mouth. His throat was clogged with water, mud, and agony.

PAHOKEE

Suddenly, at 9:45, the wind's mournful groan stopped. A deafening silence filled the Padgett house as the family members looked at each other, wondering. The silence, after such a constant wind roar, was eerie. They listened for sounds. The eye was passing directly over Pahokee. They were in the center, the core, the very heart of the storm.

"Suddenly we all felt funny. We had to grasp for air. We couldn't breathe," Lillian said.

As the eye passed over, the pressure dropped so low that the Padgetts experienced oxygen deprivation and nearly fainted. The barometric pressure had fallen dramatically.

Outside, two of the black farm hands sauntered up to the house to report the storm damage. Calvin told them to return quickly to their homes as this was the eye and that the worst winds were coming right behind it. The two men left the Padgett house in a slow walk, obviously not believing that the storm was not over. They were never seen again.

The lull lasted one hour and fifteen minutes. The hurricane's eye looked directly down on Pahokee, examined its handiwork and then, unsatisfied, it gathered up more strength. Taking one last breath it aimed its total fury at Pahokee. The storm had saved its worst for Pahokee.

Behind the Padgett house, the water rose in rapid increments, carrying trees and pieces of houses and barns and fences. Flashes of lightning gave a strobe-light glance through the driving rain to anyone staring out of the house. The Pelican River had returned to its own. Surging waters angrily reclaimed its old banks and triumphantly sallied over them. The town of Pahokee perched on its sand ridge and became an island, a frail refuge in an angry sea of black lake water.

The folks inside heard a sharp snapping sound coming from the roof over the roar of the wind. The eastern cupola of the house came crashing down. Rainwater flooded the top floors, and water oozed through the ceilings. Another soaking wet family who had lost their home stumbled into the Padgett house. Even the houses on the sand ridge, thought to be floodproof, were being swept away. Water was lapping at the backdoor steps. Lillian wondered at that moment whether the house would hold. Calvin Shive gathered the families together and they prayed, as a long-lost people prayed thousands of years before, for the ancient Indian Calusa god of evil, Huracan, seemed determined to destroy them all.

AT Canal Point, just two miles north of the Shive house, B. A. Bourne, a botanist for the Bureau of Plant Industry sugarcane breeding station, was in charge of reading barometric and wind data. The *Monthly Weather Review* states that he reported, "at 7:48 p.m., the barometer was 28.54 inches and the wind 60 m.p.h. from the northwest; and at 8:18 p.m. the anemometer cups blew away after the velocity reached 75 m.p.h. from the northwest, the barometer at this time reading 28.25 inches. By 9:00 p.m. the barometer had fallen to 27.87 inches with an estimated wind velocity of 150 m.p.h. from the northwest. There was a dead calm between 9:30 and 10:00 p.m. when the center passed over the station, the lowest barometer reading being 27.82 inches at 9:45 p.m."

CHAPTER 11
SUNDAY NIGHT

The cloud parted around us, there was a sudden blinding brilliance of
sunlight.... As my sight grew accustomed to the glare, I began slowly
to realize the astonishing vastness and beauty of the place we had entered.... The eyewall was an enormous bank of whiteness sloping
steeply upward to 50,000 feet or higher.... It seemed to be built of
roll upon roll, coil upon coil of bundled clouds like a massive pile of
folded towels. It soared up to a clearly delimited rim, and within that
lay a blazing, spotless hole of sunlit blue sky. Below patches of seas
boiled in a seething mayhem of broken water. It was a perfect eye....
But it was God's stadium.

—Pete Davis, "Inside the Hurricane"

WEST PALM BEACH

Battered by 150-mile-per-hour winds, the pregnant sea rose up to its
full eighteen-foot height and then heaved its swollen belly across
the Straits of Florida. The long, flat unprotected coast of Palm
Beach lay like a prostrate baby waiting to absorb the full fury of its pent-
up wrath. The dome of water, the storm surge, broke over Palm Beach,
drowning the island's mansions and ten thousand coconut palm trees.
Waves lashed at the tops of two-story mansions. Thirty-foot royal palm
trees bowed, bent, and then broke. Fabled Palm Beach all but disappeared
under a fifteen-foot wall of water.

Palm Beach took the brunt of the storm surge's fury. The barrier
island slowed but did not stop the storm surge. The sea slashed across
Lake Worth and crashed into West Palm Beach. Waves sloshed up
Clematis, Banyan, and Datura Streets, washing up mounds of sand and
sea debris that reached Olive Avenue. The storm huffed and puffed
and blew down wooden structures, heaping them into piles of pick-up
sticks. Only the few reinforced concrete buildings withstood the gale
force. And they stood, battered and bruised, like a prizefighter after the
nine count.

Sandwiched between the tracks of the Florida East Coast Railroad and the Seaboard Airline Railroad, the black community rested on the Atlantic Ridge, the highest point of land in Palm Beach County. Thanks to the railroads and local prejudices, colored town never flooded. But the houses, many built from discarded materials, could not withstand the hurricane's 150-mile-per-hour winds. One by one, first the roofs, then the walls, the houses along 22nd Street blew away until only two remained intact. Walls and cars cartwheeled down the street. Huddled inside the Tillman house, thirty people listened anxiously to the wind.

Mr. Tillman was proud of his house. He had deliberately constructed it with strong materials. But even a well-built house could not stand up to these winds. He knew the roof would not last long. A savage gust shook the house, the roof groaned, and a beam snapped. Dark sky peered into the kitchen. They had to abandon the house. Shouting over the wind, he organized people into pairs. The wind cooperated. Taking advantage of a lull, they hurriedly filed out of the house holding hands. Following a path through a field, the soaking wet group of refugees fought their way to the most secure structure in colored town—the reinforced concrete municipal trash incinerator on 23rd Street. There, along with another hundred refugees, they waited out the storm.

THE MARTIN STORE

When the Martin store slammed into the Methodist Church, Henry Martin was thrown onto his back. The shock spun the store around and upturned it onto its roof. For a moment it stopped in that unnatural position, as if contemplating what to do. From behind, the water piled up and pushed the store around the corner of the church, ripping away the sides. Freed, the submerged roof shot to the surface. It caught Henry Martin from below, lifted him out of the water, and threw him to one side. He bobbed in a cauldron of boiling water and broken lumber. He immediately grabbed onto part of the roof with one hand, and with the other groped in the water for Bessie Mae. She was not there. He took a deep breath to dive for her, but a wave broke over his head, pelting him with pieces of water-tossed broken lumber. A beam hit his head above his eye, almost knocking him unconscious. He breathed deeply and regained his senses. He felt something struggling around his legs. It was Sonny, and he grabbed him, lifted him up and onto the piece of broken roof. Suddenly Raymond bobbed to the surface beside Henry and Sonny.

"Daddy, I'm here, too," Raymond said, grabbing onto the roof.

"Hold on, Son," Henry yelled at Raymond. He instinctively tightened his grip on Sonny as their makeshift raft began to spin.

His eyes desperately tried to see through the night and into the angry black waves. He yelled out for Bessie Mae but was answered only by the screeching wind. It was pitch black. Bolts of lighting flashed. Strobelike light gave microsecond glimpses of a scene from the blackest reaches of hell. What had been a quiet street in a small country town was now a raging torrent of black-water vomit.

The makeshift raft was tossed up and over the breaking waves. Lumber shot like missiles over their heads. The water was filled with nail-studded, jagged wood, and one board hit Sonny in the chest, implanting a nail close to his heart. Henry jerked the board away and wrapped his arm completely around Sonny.

The floodwaters carried them swiftly over the Hillsboro Canal. Five-foot waves broke over their raft. The spinning raft narrowly missed smashing into another house. Overweighted with three people on one side, it kept tipping on one end, threatening to flip over.

"I'll get on the other side so it won't sink," Raymond shouted at Henry, and before he could respond, his son swam to the other side of the roof. At that moment a massive wave broke over them, flipping the roof up and over. In a flash of lighting, Henry saw Raymond struggling to hold on as a board violently struck his son's head. Then nothing. Henry bobbed to the surface with Sonny still in his grip and grabbed onto another floating object, and as that was ripped from his grasp he desperately grabbed onto another. It seemed like hours that he and Sonny floated. The constant fight against the waves and current and flotsam had weakened Henry. He knew Raymond had been killed, and he was afraid he'd let Sonny slip away.

"Oh, Lord, please save my only son," Henry murmured as he felt his strength give way. Then something hit his back and they stopped moving.

"Daddy, I've got hold of a telephone pole," Sonny cried out.

Henry let go of the post and grabbed onto the top of the uprights of a telephone pole. The water was fifteen feet deep.

Exhausted, Henry wrapped his arms around Sonny and locked his legs in the cross bars and held on for the rest of the night.

SOUTH BAY

South Bay was the most vulnerable spot in the Everglades. The North New River Canal terminus sat at the extreme southern axis of the muck dike. During storms or high winds, the south and eastern sides of the dike acted as a funnel, forcing wind-driven water directly at the Everglades town. High water was a common occurrence in South Bay. Whereas most of the houses in South Bay were built along the canal or the lakeshore, its residents had only to look out their windows to see firsthand the rising lake.

Though the wind had blown the lake water close to the edge of the dike, most South Bay residents believed the reports that the storm was tracking off to the north. Yesterday's radio reports had the hurricane coming ashore that afternoon. Scores of frightened people had packed up and left to seek shelter in Pahokee or Clewiston, only to return a bit embarrassed when it became apparent that the reports were false alarms. After Saturday's scare, they felt the rains and wind—if they were part of the hurricane—were the tail end of the storm blowing itself out to sea.

Throughout Sunday afternoon, Captain Edwin Forbes listened intently to the radio trying to cull bits of news regarding the storm. When it came to weather, he, like all sailors, never had enough information. Through the static, voices on the radio insisted the storm was blowing out to sea; Forbes was not convinced. There was something about those clouds. Captain Forbes owned one of the few radios in South Bay, and in his office, hanging on the wall, was the town's only telephone. A single line connected it to Belle Glade. While the radio announcer repeated reports that the storm was veering out to sea, the phone rang. The staticky, distorted voice on the other end reconfirmed his worst fears. The hurricane had struck Palm Beach and was to pass directly over Belle Glade and South Bay.

Grabbing his rain gear, Captain Forbes raced to the canal docks where his two tugs, the *Fox* and the *Arlene G*, were moored. His daughter, Louise, and son-in-law, Bill Rawle, were on board the *Fox*.

"Keep the engine running and the bilge pump going, or she might sink," Forbes yelled across the gunwale to his son-in-law.

Rawle had already secured the Fox in anticipation of the storm, but there had not been enough time to send another warning to his mother and her family, and now it was too late. Still he glanced every few minutes up the canal bank, hoping to see Mattie Mae.

The wind had raised whitecaps in the canal. The five boats tied up below the spillway at the South Bay dock rocked at their moorings. In front of the two Forbes tugs were two barges operated by the Huffman Construction Company. The largest had been converted into living quarters for the road workers. Above, trapped inside the lock itself, was a small vacation houseboat that bobbed, lost in a cage of concrete.

Forbes, with his two sons, Jack and Charles, raced through South Bay, banging on doors, urging everyone to take refuge on the Huffman barge. Many immediately headed for the quarter boat but others, with yesterday's false alarm still fresh in their minds, chose to stay in their homes. Braving drenching downpours and wind blasts, the townspeople streamed to the canal where the barge's crew helped them board. Buffeted by the gale force wind and the choppy waters, the large boat bounced hard against the dock. Each person had to step gingerly over the gunwale—careful not to slip between the boat and the dock where their foot or leg would be crushed. One of the last on board was the South Bay Methodist minister grasping a rain-soaked Bible and the belief that the end of the world was at hand.

Within forty-five minutes, two hundred people, half of the population of South Bay, were on board. The burden of so many people weighed heavy, and the barge rode low in the water. Charlie Forbes, concerned that the barge was riding deeper in the water than even the additional weight justified, dropped into the seven-foot-deep hold. The acrid smell of spilt diesel and rank bilge water permeated the air within the hold. He landed in water up to his waist. Rainwater pouring off the deck had filled half the barge's hold, threatening to sink it. From out of the galley Harvey Mitchell grabbed a ten-gallon cooking kettle, jumped down with Charlie, and the two men began to fill it and pass it over their heads to people above. Alternating when they tired, most of the men and women began to bail for their lives.

On deck was a notoriously fickle bilge pump. Ivan Van Horn, the barge operator, started the pump, and by constantly oiling it to keep it dry, he kept the pump working. Laboring against the wind and rain, he, like the tenacious Dutch boy of lore, kept at his station throughout the storm.

Wet and cold, the townspeople huddled together in the cramped living quarters and prayed. Every piece of loose debris that smashed against the steel hull of the boat echoed through the hold. The steel barge cables tied to the lock docks strained and groaned against the force of the wind and water. Captain Edwin Forbes knew that the barge was on the verge of sinking. Verses of "Amazing Grace" and "Nearer My God to Thee" rose from the bunkhouse. Led by the minister, some of the passengers prepared for the end with funeral songs and prayers. Finally, near midnight, the bailing and the bilge pump had lowered the water level enough to give the bailers a break.

AT first believing they could ride out the storm in their house, Lee and Maribell Rawls ignored Captain Forbes's evacuation warnings. Maribell was eight months pregnant with their first child and did not want to move. She instinctively covered her swollen stomach; positive it was a boy because it kicked so hard, she had named him William.

Near dark, they abandoned their house to ride out the storm at L. M. Grimes's sturdy house. With their three-year-old German shepherd named Kazan tagging faithfully behind, they fought their way along the half-mile to Grimes's home, where they found that John McAllister, with his wife and son, had also taken refuge.

Soon after dark, water began to seep into the house, and it became apparent that they could not stay where they were. Wrapping a shawl around Maribell's shoulders, Lee led them out of the house, hoping to reach the barge. Fighting the driving rain and 130-mile-per-hour winds, they finally reached the dock, but the barge had drifted out into the middle of the canal. The lock was closed, and water from the lake poured over the gates. The houseboat, which had sat at the bottom of the emptied lock, was now floating to where they could step onto its roof. Inside they found six other people—South Bay schoolteacher Larry Hardy, his wife, and two other couples.

Turning to his dog, Lee called out, "Come on, Kazan."

"You can't bring the dog here. There's no room!" someone yelled.

Lee glanced at Kazan, soaking wet, waiting for his master. He'll never make it, he thought.

"Go, boy," he shouted. "Go home." Lee gave a little good-bye wave and then turned. Steadying himself, he pulled open the door and disappeared inside.

The wind and the water flooding over the lock spillway tossed the houseboat about. Feeling nauseous, Maribell ran outside to vomit. As she leaned over the gunwale, she saw that the lines securing the boat to the lock were about to break. If the boat broke its moorings, it would be swept over the lock gates into the turbulent black waters of the canal. Forced to abandon the boat, the group slowly crawled along the lock wall, fighting wind gusts that threatened to fling them into the violent wash turning like a boiling cauldron a foot below them. With her stomach inflated by her unborn baby, Maribell had to carry herself higher than the others, exposing her body to the furious wind. She crept along until she could go no farther.

Lee turned to her and said, "Get on my back."

Carefully, lifting one hand at a time, she wrapped her arms around his neck as sheets of cold hard rain cut at her face. Lee desperately grabbed onto the lock wall, digging his fingers between the slippery wet planks. Slowly he pulled the two of them along. Finally, they reached the edge of the lock where they were able to leap, one by one, onto the pitching quarter boat barge, which had drifted back close to the wall.

Soaked and cold, they ducked inside the crowded cabin where the two hundred residents of South Bay, half the population, were huddled. Exhausted, Maribell wrapped her arms around her stomach, felt her baby kick, and then broke down and cried. While crawling along the lock wall, she heard in the dark the screams of townspeople being swept away in the current—cries that would haunt her for her entire life.

THE tugboat, the *Fox*, strained against its moorings. Glancing out of the pilothouse window, Bill Rawle felt a gnawing aching in his stomach. In his three decades on the lake, he had never seen a storm as bad as this. Images of his mother raced through his mind. Why hadn't the Bootses stayed yesterday?

In front of him, through the driving rain, he could just see the large Huffman barge bang and pull against the dock. The spillway was a raging waterfall. Uprooted trees, broken houses, and splintered furniture shot down the canal. Debris crashed into the *Fox*'s steel hull. Above the spillway, the houseboat lodged in the lock appeared and disappeared in the black rain. The lights from the quarter boat were the only sign that people were out there fighting against the storm. The only sign that people were still alive.

He could see that the quarter boat rode dangerously low in the water. Between pauses in the driving rain he saw people on deck hunched over the stern. Should he help? But how? If he left the *Fox*, it might sink. As long as there was light shining from the quarter boat, Bill Rawle decided he'd stay with the *Fox*. He was afraid to leave—afraid to leave his wife, afraid that if he left, his mother and her family would show up. But he knew in his heart that no one could survive out there. Not in this storm. Over the howling wind he heard people screaming in the darkness as they were swept away. He cringed, not able to keep away the thought that one of those crying for help was his mother.

PAHOKEE

The eye of the storm centered itself directly over the lake. Along the eastern shore, the wind direction changed from north-northeast to the south as the back of the hurricane eye wall passed over Pahokee. The dome of water that the 150-mile-per-hour winds had kept corralled was now pushed northward toward Pelican Bay and at the dike across Pelican River. The surge easily smashed through the silt muck barrier and then rushed up the low land of the former riverbed. Everything in its path was washed away. The sand ridge at Pahokee became an instant island as water surged up along both sides. The wind drove in more lake water, up and over the ridge, moving low-lying houses off their foundations and uprooting trees.

At Padgett's Island, twelve of the Padgett family's black farmhands took refuge in the sturdy two-story Padgett farmhouse. Another thirty-four field hands left heir flimsy shacks for the large barn, where they settled in between the tractor and other farm equipment. The storm surge careened up the Pelican River, over Padgett's Island, and smacked directly into the barn. They were afraid of being trapped. Climbing up to the rafters, they tried to escape the rising water through a hole in the roof. All but two, an old man and his granddaughter, managed to escape before the building was turned on edge and collapsed onto itself. Caught between two massive struts, the old man and his granddaughter managed to avoid the collapsing beams. With one arm he grabbed the granddaughter, and with the other he held onto a post and rode the surge through the back swamps and fields of the old Pelican riverbed. They survived. The other thirty-two who had escaped were washed away and never found. Without a pause, the storm surge carried away the Padgetts' farmhouse and all twelve its occupants. Neither the farmhouse nor any of the field hands were ever found.

OVER the roaring wind scouring the Padgett's Pahokee house, Calvin Shive heard a vague pounding noise coming from behind the kitchen.

"Listen," he said. They heard it again.

With Dan Carpenter, Calvin got up, went into the kitchen, and looked out the window into the black night.

"Look out back. There's a house floating by!" Dan called out.

In the glow of lighting flashes and flashlight beams, Calvin and Dan watched in horrific fascination as a one-story house with two desperate people holding onto the roof slowly floated by the back yard. Suddenly it turned and lodged up on their backyard, settling at an obtuse angle. The two men ran out and helped the couple off the roof and brought them into the house.

Lillian, in the bedroom with Duncan, was not aware of the new arrivals. Duncan had trouble breathing, and she was trying to comfort him when she noticed the wall breathing. It moved in and then out. She yelled for her father. The bedroom wall had begun to tear away from the house.

Outside Calvin and Dan gathered up some long planks, nailed them to the wall, and secured it to the floor. As a carpenter, it was all Calvin could do, but as an ordained minister, he could pray. And pray he did. For now they were all in the hands of God.

ADRIFT in the blackness, Vernie Boots fought to keep his head above water. Five-foot black waves crashed down on him as he desperately tried to keep his little raft from flipping over. It spun back and forth, threatening at any moment to dump him into the water. He tried to keep the raft facing into the wind. With his feet dragging in the water like a rudder, he managed to keep a windward heading, but the effort was sapping his strength.

Feeling his strength ebb away, Vernie wanted to cry out for his mother, but he knew she was probably dead. That thought haunted him through the night as he fought for his life. He held onto that piece of ceiling as the waves pounded over him. As he drifted in the storm, he imagined that his mother, father, and brothers were all dead. How could they be alive? How could anyone have survived? How could he survive? He felt lonely, abandoned, and scared. But he was not about to give up. He would survive. He had to. If there was any chance he might find his parents or brothers, he had to live. Alone on his tiny raft, that one burning thought kept Vernie Boots alive.

CHAPTER 12
DEATH IN THE AFTERNOON

Monday, September 17

In Flanders fields the poppies blow
Between the crosses, row on row.
—Lt. Col. John McCrae, "In Flanders Field"

A cross the eastern horizon, an unbroken pale line stretched low and gray. Nothing was silhouetted against it, because there was nothing there: no trees, no houses, no levies, no sawgrass. The wind had died down to a few gusts, and the black waves had flattened out to an agitated chop. From horizon to horizon there was nothing save for Vernie Boots and his broken piece of ceiling. Alone in the dark, he was cold, wet, and hungry. He had swallowed a lot of water, and the gritty taste of muck filled his mouth. Still holding on tightly to his makeshift life raft, he wondered whether he was the last person alive.

The hell-hound roar of the storm had stopped. The wind sounded like a sad forlorn whimper. No, it was a moan. Then he heard it again—another moan. Daring for the first time to raise his head above the piece of ceiling, Vernie glanced around his life raft. Off to his right he saw that a larger part of the ceiling he had been clinging onto all night was connected to his piece. The joists had twisted around. He heard the moan again, and in the ghostly glow of dawn's light he saw his brother, Willie.

"Willie!"

"My hand—I can't move my hand," Willie cried out.

Throughout the night Willie had ridden less than ten feet away from Vernie on the same piece of ceiling, and neither brother had seen the other. Willie cried out again. Clambering over splintered boards and protruding nails, Vernie reached his younger brother. An iron spike from the split ceiling had completely pierced through Willie's hand, in essence nailing him to the ceiling, saving his life. Vernie pulled his brother's hand from the nail. Willie never made a sound. It barely bled; the cold water had cauterized the wound.

"Where's Mama?" Willie asked.

Vernie just shook his head.

As the light shone dimly on the two brothers, Vernie realized they were in the Everglades and not the lake. A couple of uprooted custard apple trees on their sides stood out of the water. It can't be too deep, Vernie thought. He slid slowly off his life raft. His feet touched bottom. Soft mucky bottom, but it was land, the first land he had touched in nine hours. The water reached up to his navel. Water three feet deep spread out in all directions—to the eastern horizon, to the west, to the north, and to the south it was all water, one vast ocean of black water.

"We gotta go, Willie," Vernie said.

Willie nodded. Wrapping his hand in a piece of his shirt, Willie started off behind Vernie. The two brothers began to trek to the north to the edge of the lake and, Vernie hoped, home. Before they had gone far, they heard a distant shout.

"Over here." It sounded like it came out of the sky.

They stopped and saw a figure sloshing through the water a half mile behind them. He shouted again, and then they saw that it was their brother Roy. When Roy caught up, they started off again, blindly at first until they spotted the tops of the four royal palm trees of Bolles Hotel in Miami Locks. Now they had a target.

"Hey, wait!" They heard someone yelling off to their left. Behind them, about a half mile farther out into the sawgrass, they saw someone splashing though the water. The three Boots boys slowed their march.

"It's Virgil!" Roy exclaimed.

The splashing figure got bigger and bigger until they finally recognized Mutt Thomas. Grasping the corner post all night, he had been carried nearly a mile farther out into the Everglades where the water was only a foot deep. As he trudged toward the lake, the water deepened up to his waist and then his midriff. Thinking he was going in the wrong direction, he had stopped until he spotted the three Boots boys. There was no place to rest and wait for Mutt, so the Boots boys kept on wading slowly until Mutt caught up to them. The four stunned boys waded in waist-high water all morning.

"Are we the only ones alive?" Mutt asked.

No one spoke. The answer was too much for any of them to think about. Vernie, though, believed his parents were dead.

Near noon they arrived at Sebring Farms. There was nothing—no houses, no barns, only a couple of piles of rubble, rows of custard apple trees, tangled rubbish, and broken lumber. The dike was gone. Nothing stood in the distance except the four tall royal palm trees, their fronds bent and bowed low. The boys spotted the steel tower of the turn bridge at Miami Locks and began to make their way there. They saw the keeper's house and the Bolles hotel and beyond, barges tied up at the docks and boats cruising the canals. Boats meant people.

Just outside Sebring Farms they found the Lees' house lodged on a canal bank. The floods had swept it off its foundation and carried it a quarter of a mile with the Lee family inside, all of whom survived. The Lees gave the boys pieces of sugar cane to chew on. A welcomed treat.

The boys waded on until they came to a canal where people were being ferried across by boat. While waiting their turn, Mutt heard someone yelling out his name.

"Mutt! My God, Mutt. Over here!" Mutt glanced across the flooded canal, and there was his father.

"Daddy, Daddy!" Mutt cried out. Jumping into the canal, he swam across to his father.

Embracing, father and son broke into tears. Charles Thomas had searched all morning and believed he had lost his entire family. He thought it was a miracle that his son had been saved.

Finally, after ferrying across the canal, the Boots brothers were led to the Bolles Hotel—the only structure still standing in Miami Locks. People too tired and still in shock rested anywhere they found a dry spot. The former luxury hotel in the swamp, the come-on for thousands of Everglades land buyers, had sustained damage, but it was still standing. When the first survivors arrived to seek refuge at the hotel, the caretaker had refused to let anyone inside. An angry crowd gathered in front of the hotel, threatening the caretaker. He was led away and was never seen in the area again.

At the hotel, dazed people were milling about; others had gone inside to rest or be treated as best they could without medical aid. Any news of survivors or dead was eagerly awaited. People desperately asked each person they encountered whether they had seen relatives or friends. Most of the survivors had lost everything they had in the world; many had lost their entire families.

Vernie, Roy, and Willie Boots sat on the east bank of the Miami Canal, too exhausted to cross over. They watched boats slowly moving through the canal, some people searching, others carrying refugees. Their only thought was "What now?"

As the water receded, Henry and Sonny climbed down from their precarious telephone pole perch. The water was three-feet deep in all directions. When Henry hit the ground, he almost doubled over. His foot was badly sprained. He felt his face and the gash above his eye. Sonny was naked. The water had completely stripped him of his clothes. He had two nail punctures in his chest, one just above the heart and another below it. His chin had a severe gash but was no longer bleeding. He stared at his son, who stoically stared back without a whimper. Henry reached down and hugged Sonny, something he rarely did.

The only land above water was the eroded top of a broken dike. It was the remains of the dike road between Belle Glade and Pahokee. Keeping on top of the dike road, father and son started off toward Belle Glade. Henry figured they were about three miles from town. Soon the shock wore off and the cold returned. Sonny was shivering, and Henry tried to warm him. Shortly they met two black men trying to open a trunk washed up on the dike. Henry took a board and broke open the lock. Inside were clothes. He took a shirt and draped it around Sonny, and they continued on toward Belle Glade.

Along the dike they witnessed a sampling of the scope of the disaster. Entangled trees and fence had formed long, twisted windrows along the dike. Tangled up in the wire and branches were hundreds of drowned cattle, horses—and people. Hundreds of corpses had been carried by the storm surge from Belle Glade, Chosen, and the Islands. In the pale morning light, white bodies glowed like macabre tree ornaments along with black bodies. There were too many to even count. So many dead, Henry thought, trying to divert Sonny's gaze from the horrific scene. Henry held his son's head to his chest while he forced himself to stare into each face. One might be Bessie Mae or any of the children. Near Dead Man's curve he saw a body that he was sure was Raymond's. He tried to cross over the tangle of trees and wire, but he was too weak and tired. A few steps beyond he saw Minnie Lucy. She was standing ghostlike, and then she disappeared. He knew exhaustion and grief were affecting his mind. He lowered his head and walked in a straight line to Belle Glade.

SOUTH BAY

Ivan Van Horn stepped off the still-pitching deck of the quarter boat onto the dock. Tired and worn out, his legs barely held under him as he stood on solid ground. Looking around at what was left of South

Bay, he wondered how many more had survived. He gazed at the three-quarter-inch steel cable securing the boat to the dock. It had cut halfway through the pilings on the dock. Another hour of the storm, and all the bailing would have been in vain. If the quarter boat had broken from its mooring, there was little doubt in Van Horn's mind it would have sunk.

Slowly the survivors stepped off the quarter boat. Some stumbled as they stepped onto the steady dock, trying to get their land legs. Others got down on their knees and began to thank God for their deliverance. A few managed to thank Van Horn.

South Bay had been completely destroyed. Nearly every building not broken up had floated away or washed off its foundation. The pocket inlet of Lake Okeechobee that had given South Bay its name and prosperity had received the brunt of the hurricane's fury and the storm surge.

With his legs wobbling under him, Mark Challancin followed his father off the barge. Less than a few yards from the North New River Bridge, Mark saw the body of his best friend's father. His head was crushed. Was Oliver dead? The young Wilder was found dazed but alive in a guava tree a half mile away.

Carefully, Lee Rawls helped Maribell off the deck of the barge onto the dock. She sat down on the dock and embraced her inflated stomach. She felt a kick, looked up, and gave Lee a reassuring smile. With only a few bruises and scrapes, she and their baby had made it.

Lee glanced around at the total wreckage. The canal was clogged with boats and barges resting at all angles. Broken lumber littered the streets, and houses rested on canal banks. There were few people in the streets. Most of the people who had stayed in South Bay had been washed away. How could anyone have lived through that storm? he wondered.

Then he heard a bark.

It was Kazan! He called out, and Kazan ran to his master and licked his hand. Lee stooped down and hugged Kazan. The faithful dog had survived. His family had survived.

SOON after Lee and Maribell Rawls fled the Grimes' house, the Grimeses and the McAllisters, believing the house was ready to collapse, left for their car. The surge drowned everyone except Mrs. McAllister and Grimes. Out of the fourteen people who remained in the house, eight drowned. Grimes, though he survived, later died of his injuries. Half of the South Bay dead were never recovered.

THE exhausted survivors, many injured and hungry, needed food and medicine. Transportation was paralyzed. The roads and canal embankments used as secondary roads were washed out and impassable. Most of the canals were clogged with debris and broken boats. The boats and barges lodged in the canals had sunk and were damaged or immobilized by wreckage. Splintered wood, crumpled custard apple trees, and twisted metal roofing piled high at the bridges, and the locks dammed the out-flowing water. From the lakeshore, a three-mile inland sea covered the entire area. The only form of transportation was small, shallow draft boats that could maneuver across the watery wasteland with impunity. The fishermen whose boats had survived the storm siphoned the water from the gas, dried the carburetors of their outboard motors, and got them to run.

The boats, their outboard motors rudely disturbing the quiet after the storm, went first to family farms to search for relatives and friends. They passed near the lake dike banks covered with dead fish and birds. At pros-perous farms there were no houses, no animals grazing in fields—only dead cows with their legs stiffly in the air, headless horses, and denuded chickens. A few found family and friends; the rest were corpses floating in black water. Stunned and confused survivors were taken aboard and transported back to the relative havens of South Bay and Miami Locks.

The tops of some dikes were the only land above water. Along the bro-ken dikes survivors picked their way through the muck and over rubble. The injured waited on soggy banks nursing their wounds, too numb to move. There was no food or fresh water. A boat was sent to Clewiston in the hope that there might be food or water there.

ONCE the wind died down, Bill Rawle took his little motor skiff off the *Fox* tug and slipped it into the canal above the lock. Slowly he made his way out through the rubble-strewn canals around the lake to Miami Locks. When he reached Miami Locks, his heart fell. The village was in ruins. Bodies of dead animals lined the banks of canal dikes. Others floated in the distance. Shocked survivors sat on the banks staring glassy-eyed as he motored past. Desperately he searched for Mattie Mae, Bill, and the rest of his boys. There was nobody. Had he lost his whole family?

CLEWISTON had not escaped unscathed. Its streets were flooded. The rail-road track, ripped from its bed, was a twisted ribbon of steel. Houses were blown off their foundations. But the storm's center had been farther north and the hurricane's winds offshore. The storm surge that swept through Belle Glade and South Bay, then back at Pahokee, had this time spared Clewiston and Moore Haven.

Though Clewiston was dealing with its own recovery, upon news of the scope of the tragedy in South Bay and Miami Locks, the townspeople re-acted quickly. A flotilla of small boats set out from Clewiston, some bringing much-needed food. Most carried back survivors. Others returned with a grim cargo of the drowned.

AT Miami Locks, Vernie and his brothers desperately looked around for familiar faces: neighbors' faces, friends' faces, family faces. More boats puttered in from the lake. Some were from Clewiston, bringing in food and supplies and taking out refugees. Others were local boats that had survived the storm and had been pressed into service, searching for survivors and collecting the dead. Moving slowly up the canal, Vernie heard and then saw a familiar boat. In the small fourteen-foot motor skiff was his half-brother Bill Rawle. The three brothers were too exhausted to realize that they had been saved.

IN Belle Glade, Lawrence Will crept out of the barge's hold. The Hillsboro Canal looked like a construction dump, completely jammed with broken houses and sunken boats and trees. Crawling over the head-high rubble that clogged Main Street, he made his way to his building. The roof had blown off and there was extensive rain damage, but the Pioneer Building was one of the few structures in Belle Glade that remained standing. The once-prosperous little town was now a shambles. Ten-foot piles of rubble, twisted metal, and broken wood blockaded the streets. There were telephone poles, house beams, and dead pets. There were automobiles crushed under intact roofs. Ragged ripped clothes fluttered in the trash. Main Street was covered with soaked flotsam. Though a few scurrying clouds dumped an occasional shower, the air was crystal-clear, as if Mother Nature were taunting the survivors with a sharp view of the hell she had left them.

Stepping over and around piles of splintered wood and twisted rubble, Will sloshed his way in knee-deep water back toward the canal. There he found the contorted body of Raymond Martin. Nearby, dumped like a broken doll, was the corpse of his little sister Lucy, who, because of her short-cropped red hair, was assumed to be a young boy. The two bodies were gently taken to the pool hall in Tedder's hotel and laid on the pool table. He thought about his own family and what might have happened to them. He had to get to Fort Lauderdale.

DURING the height of the storm, Dr. Buck spent the night in a small back bedroom in Tedder's hotel. With him were Willie Emma Wells, her infant son Edward, and the town druggist. Taking out a couple of a dresser drawers and stacking them, he rested his feet straight out in front of him, as casually as if he had not a worry in the world. He gave the people around him a sense of ease even as they were forced to shout at each other to be heard above the roar of the wind.

Even before the winds had died down and gray dawn crept across the horizon, Dr. Buck left Willie Wells and her son and made his way down the black corridors to the front of the hotel. In the lobby a dozen injured people had filtered in during the night. By the light of an oil lamp, he examined a boy and his mother who had superficial cuts on their faces and arms from flying debris. They were the first refugees from Chosen. He knew more would be coming soon. He needed medical supplies. The water on the first floor had fallen a few feet and then retreated out the front door. He hoped the worst was over.

He stepped outside. Belle Glade was painted in a gray twilight. Strong wind gusts out of the southwest battered him. From the porch of the hotel, Dr. William Buck glanced up and down Main Street. Immediately it brought back memories of battlefield towns destroyed in the Great War. Towns along the Le Marne, in Ypres and Flanders. A week-long bombardment from Axis artillery cannon could not have done as much damage as lay before his eyes. A few buildings stood, damaged, windowless, with roofs missing. Between them were piles of jumbled rubble, jigsaw puzzles of crushed homes and buildings dumped haphazardly in the streets. The survivors began to emerge from beneath the wreckage. They moved like shell-shocked troops, eyes glassed over, unbelieving or afraid to believe the scene that lay before them. Dazed, unorganized, people wandered with no purpose. Most had lost their homes; their loved ones were missing. Everyone was thirsty and hungry. There was little food and no drinking water. Like the ancient mariner, they were surrounded by water everywhere, but it was lake water, blackish water, and it smelled of death.

Dr. Buck had seen masses of troops who had lost their officers become a danger to themselves. With no leaders, undisciplined, they had searched for someone to tell them what they should do. There were helpless people out there who needed to be rescued, and injured to attend to. The dead had to be brought in and buried before disease broke out. The people had to be given something to do, to feel useful and to take their minds off their own personal tragedies. He wanted to prevent looting. Idle and desperate men were dangerous. Authority had to be restored.

"Get the boys together," he said to Henry White.

White, the local American Legion adjutant, did not have to ask, "which boys?" Dr. Buck meant the men from the local American Legion Post.

Dr. Buck, dressed in a white shirt, had his trademark black bag with him, but other than that he had no medicine. He sent one of the men with the pharmacist to the drugstore next door to look for any useful drugs. He especially wanted alcohol to disinfect wounds. Hopefully there would be some drugs to fight infections.

While the water had receded, the entire first floor of the hotel remained soaked and there was the omnipresent stench of muck. Any injured would have to be treated upstairs. He organized the women in the
hotel as nurses.

Dr. Buck knew this was to be the battle of his life.

White returned with seven men, half of them carrying pistols jammed
into their belts.

"Couldn't find anymore," White said.

To get from one side of the street to the other, people were crawling over
the debris. Dr. Buck ordered the men to get more people to help. He wanted
half of them to clear a path through the rubble in front of the hotel. He
knew that shortly casualties would be coming in. The rest he organized into
search parties that started through the town, section by section.

"Anyone who you need to work, you get them to work," he told
the men.

AFTER depositing the bodies of Raymond and Lucy in the makeshift
morgue in the poolroom at the hotel, Lawrence Will returned to the
canal. Across the debris-clogged canal, he saw a huge uprooted rubber
tree lying on its side. At its base the roots fanned out, and he saw movement. Rushing over, he found Thelma Martin still holding baby Robert
above her head. Beside her Ernestine lay limply in the roots, too
exhausted to move. Thelma's foot was still solidly lodged in the roots. She
had a nail in her knee. Will took the children back to the hotel. The
baby, limp and discolored, seemed dead, and the two young girls were cold
and in shock.

At the hotel, Dr. Buck quickly examined Robert and declared, "He's
alive." He asked Lois Hunt and Fay Greer to take him upstairs, dry him
off, and rub whiskey over his body.

"Every half hour give him a few drops of whiskey," Dr. Buck instructed.

The women took the children. In one of the upstairs makeshift nursing
rooms, they took turns and doted over Robert, and thanks to their care
he survived.

Thelma and Ernestine were dried and wrapped in blankets. Overnight little Thelma Martin became a celebrity. Her exploits were recounted in a
hastily printed booklet with pictures and accounts of the storm, published
three weeks later. The image of a little girl saving her baby brother made exceptionally good press. The media and the Red Cross recognized that people needed a hero. The outside world needed someone they could identify
with, and that would help collect funds, clothes, and food for the victims.

By midmorning, more wide-eyed survivors from Chosen and South Bay
filtered in with horrifying stories of hundreds of dead. Little by little the

breadth of the disaster became obvious. Belle Glade was the center of a world-class catastrophe.

At first, the dead were laid out face up for easy identification in the first floor of the hotel. But soon more room was needed. Burying the dead was out of the question. There was no place to dig a grave. Dr. Buck knew that with the heat and humidity a corpse would rot in a couple of days. They had to be buried, and that meant taking the bodies to West Palm Beach, Clewiston, or north to the high ground around Port Mayaca.

Sewage from the town's cesspools overflowed into backyards and side alleys, and gasoline from underground tanks oozed out, leaving a multi-colored rainbow blotch that rippled eerily over the black water. There were no dry clothes and few places dry enough to even rest, and in a land of abundance there was no food. Knee-deep water covered the entire town. What little produce and meat remained had been contaminated by lake water. In a brisk walk through the clutter on Main Street, Dr. Buck saw that with no fresh water, little food, and hundreds if not thousands of decaying corpses floating in stagnant water, Belle Glade was ripe for an epidemic.

Lacing up campaign boots left over from his army service, he made his rounds, stopping to take care of an injured person or comforting the dying. A few people needed to have broken arms or legs set. He operated under horrific conditions—like in a battlefield—with no anesthesia or drugs, and little antiseptic except for bootleg whiskey. He felt he and his patients could hold on until help arrived. What he did not know was that no one outside Lake Okeechobee knew what had happened in Belle Glade. There were no telephones—the lines and the poles were down. No one had a ham radio. The roads were flooded, the bridges were out, and the canals were clogged with debris and sunken vessels. Their closest help, West Palm Beach, was undergoing its own recovery from the damage the hurricane had left and gave little thought to what might have happened in the distant Everglades. Dr. Buck's assumed rescue was not on its way.

BEWILDERED people filtered in from Chosen with stories of entire families lost. At first people talked of dozens dead, then hundreds. The rural roadbeds and dikes were littered with bodies—mostly black migrant farmhands. Of all the Everglades towns and hamlets, Chosen had been chosen to suffer the most.

Once the wind had died down and the water retreated, Frede Aunapu and Elizabeth BeaDer slipped off their barge and headed for Chosen. Most of the town's houses had been swept away, leaving a few stilts jutting through the surface like late afternoon beard stubble. Already people were stacking the dead along the road in improvised body dumps. Elizabeth was shocked that most of the bodies were black. She wondered, "Couldn't they swim?" Later she was told that most, but not all of them, were actually black victims. Many drowned people turn black from oxygen starvation.

Walking along what was the Belle Glade–Chosen Road, they reached the Hector Supply House, one of the few buildings still standing between Chosen and Belle Glade. West's store loomed over the canal, and Stein's two-story house stood alone in a forsaken landscape of black muck. They were the only other structures in sight.

WEST PALM BEACH

Monday morning's dawn lit a ravaged West Palm Beach. There wasn't a building or house that had not been damaged. Windows had been blown out; roofs had collapsed. At the height of the storm, the entire downtown area was under water. Dunes of beach sand covered the main streets. Clematis Street was a shell of its former self. Piles of lumber and rubble cluttered the streets. Lots that once held large wooden buildings were now a jumble of broken lumber—like a giant pick-up sticks game, beams and posts were piled head-high. Few of the flimsy wooden houses and buildings built during the real estate boom had survived.

There was no electricity, no transportation, and little unspoiled food left. Except for a few ham radio operators there was no communication with the rest of the world. For all practical purposes, Florida's third largest city had simply vanished. There was even less information from the Everglades. Eastern Palm Beach County was absorbed in its own recovery, and few gave any thought about the Everglades. There had not been a word of news from the western part of the county. For most people in West Palm Beach, no news was good news. However, by noon, people, especially those who had family in the Everglades, did begin to worry. Vivid visions of 1926 Miami and Moore Haven haunted them.

LILLIAN Padgett's uncle, Con Shive, could only stare out of the shattered front room window. The street was littered with broken wood and downed trees. Across the street at the Woodlawn Cemetery, the few trees that stood had been stripped of their leaves and most of their branches. The elder Shive's house had survived with broken windows and some water damage. He considered himself lucky. He had built the sturdy little house with his own hands. Other neighborhood houses had been reduced to piles of jumbled rubble. Ominously, there had been no news from

Pahokee or Belle Glade. The roads were probably flooded, he thought, but by nightfall, when he had not heard from Pahokee, his concern changed to worry.

THE first news out of the Everglades arrived from Pahokee. Dr. John Hall, bringing in injured from Pahokee, informed the officials that there were "ten confirmed white dead and probably fifty to seventy-five Negroes killed." He also said they needed assistance around the lake.

AFTER clearing a path in front of his funeral home, West Palm Beach undertaker Harold Ferguson carefully backed his hearse out onto a littered street. The hearse had a double function. As a hearse, the long, black converted truck had taken its share of dead to be buried, but it also served as an ambulance. He started out toward Belle Glade along the Palm Beach Road, driving around rubble and downed trees. Once past Military Trail, the road still had about a foot of water but was relatively clear. There were reports of dozens of injured in need of care in Pahokee and Belle Glade. With luck, he might be able to fit most of the seriously injured in the back of the ambulance.

NO news had arrived from the east coast. Lawrence Will worried about the safety of his family. Had Fort Lauderdale suffered as much as Belle Glade? His house was well built, but, as he looked around at the damage in Belle Glade, he wondered whether any building, no matter how strong, could have stood up to this hurricane. When he heard that someone was needed to go to the coast, he volunteered to go to Fort Lauderdale. On foot, through knee-deep water, he walked to the Experimental Station. From there he hitched a ride on a truck to Fort Lauderdale.

A tornado spawned by the storm caused the only real damage the city had suffered. Once assured his family in Fort Lauderdale was safe, he reported the conditions in Belle Glade to the Red Cross and the Coast Guard. Though he knew the situation was bad, Will was not aware of the complete status in South Bay and Chosen. The local Coast Guard Station quickly prepared a rescue fleet. Will told them that they would need small boats. At the Fort Lauderdale Canal Dock, Hamp Holloway gathered together half a dozen boatmen and a fleet of small boats, which he tied to the bow of a cabin cruiser. Stocking up on groceries and medicine, they set off up the New River Canal in his cabin cruiser with the smaller boats in tow. A young doctor volunteered to accompany them to Belle Glade.

The canal was flooded and a swift current from the water emptying out of the Everglades fought against them. The sixty-one-mile journey took sixteen hours. Once the group reached South Bay, Holloway could not get his fleet of boats past the locks. Half a dozen boats and barges were sunk in the middle of the canal, and the lock was clogged with piles of debris. Shocked at the scale of the death and destruction, the doctor changed his mind and caught the first truck back to Fort Lauderdale.

BELOW Miami Locks, a lone two-story house stood like a solitary sentinel near the roadway. Even before the storm, the old house had had a dilapidated look. Its owner was an elderly, partly deaf man named Callahan. Alone and without any information, the old man rode out the storm. That morning, as he did every morning, he dressed, had breakfast, and set out on foot for the South Bay Post Office. He saw people searching through the water but couldn't hear them when they talked to him. Finally curiosity got the better of him and he stopped, cupped his hand around his ear, and asked, "What the hell is going on?"

"We had a hurricane. Where are you going?" one of the men shouted.

"I'm going down to the post office to see if I got some mail."

"There ain't no post office—it's gone!"

"Gone! Gone where?"

The post office, run by Maude Wingfield out of her store, had been built out into the lake on pilings. The storm surge had carried it off without a trace.

CLUTTER on the road from Pahokee began to change from trees and branches to wood and twisted metal roofing. Henry Martin knew they were near town. He had only one objective: he had to get Sonny to Dr. Buck. The boy was injured and shivering in his wet shirt, and Henry was afraid he, too, might die. He was sure that, except for Sonny, he had lost his entire family. If Sonny died, too, he would lose the will to live.

They crossed over the Hillsboro Canal Bridge and saw that Tommy Wells's house was gone. Were Tommy and Willie Emma also dead? he wondered. On Main Street people walked around in a daze—some nodding recognition, while others moved along silently, like zombies.

"Where's Dr. Buck?" he asked.

"At the Glades Hotel. That's where they're taking everybody."

He reached the hotel and helped Sonny up the stairs. Dr. Buck was in the lobby attending to a patient.

"Do everything you can for him. He's the only one I have left." Henry said.

"Henry, I have three of your children upstairs in bed, and they are going to be all right."

A disbelieving Henry Martin stared silently at the doctor.

"I even have your baby up there."

One of the women took Sonny and Henry upstairs, where Henry found Thelma, Ernestine, and baby Robert. He hugged his three children as he fought back tears.

"I'm sorry, Henry. Your oldest son is in the pool hall with the rest of the dead," Dr. Buck said.

Downstairs as Henry passed along the rows of bodies, he saw Minnie Lucy's head.

"That's my youngest girl," Henry said.

"No, that's a boy," Dr. Buck said.

Henry just shook his head. He knew it was his girl. She had been infested with redbugs in the summer and had her hair cut short like a boy's.

He reached down and held her head in his hands. On the next table over was Raymond; his head gash was visible. But Henry had no time to mourn. He had to find Bessie Mae and the other children.

IN Belle Glade, no one was allowed to remain idle. Men widened the paths that snaked through the rubble, while others searched buildings and under rubble for survivors, for food, for clothes, while still others searched for drugs or potable water—anything salvageable because there was so little left. By noon, hundreds of refugees had arrived from Chosen, South Bay, and the outlying areas. Greetings were now "Have you seen . . . ? Do you know what happened to . . . ?" Desperate people moved about searching for relatives. Space to sit and rest became a premium in Belle Glade. There were too many people. Dr. Buck pictured thousands of hungry and hurt refugees coming to Belle Glade. The steps of the Glades and Belle Glade Hotels were obstructed with storm-shocked people. Able-bodied men consoled their loved ones. Children cried out for their dead mothers. "Have you seen . . . ?"

WALTER and Ardie Peterson left the Glades Hotel and walked back to their neighborhood. There they found that "one half ruined shack was all that remained of colored town." Not a trace of their house remained. They had lost everything. They had no place to live, no food, and only the clothes on their backs. What were they to do?

By the time they returned to the hotel, Sheriff Everett was rounding up men to help search for the living and the dead. Ardie was separated from his father and grouped with the other children and women. The women and children were a distraction to the men who were needed for reconstruction. They consumed what little precious food and drinkable water there was, and they were subject to disease. Little medicine or medical supplies survived the storm. There was no water except for some boiled black lake water. Then there was the recovery of the dead—a gruesome task no man wanted his women or children to witness. In West Palm Beach, there were hospitals, food, and shelter. In Palm Beach, there would be help.

The life-and-death decisions that an army field doctor must make steel a person. A dangling appendage here—cut it off; a chest ripped opened by shrapnel—stuff the hole with rags to stop the bleeding; eyes scarred from mustard gas attack—wrap them up in oil-drenched towels. He could afford no second thoughts. Dr. Buck gave the most difficult order in his life: he ordered the evacuation of the women and the children to West Palm Beach forty miles away.

Women who hadn't slept or eaten in two days, who had survived near drowning, and who had lost family members were sent on a forced march to West Palm Beach. Many carried infants in their arms, most had just the clothes on their back. There were no cars or trucks to carry them. They had to walk, and the roads were under water.

To discourage anyone from staying, a rumor was spread that the hurricane was turning around and coming back. Amid much anguished crying and protesting, the two hundred women and children who could walk began the trek to West Palm Beach.

The exodus of pitifully ragged refugees trudged through knee-deep water along what they hoped was the road to West Palm Beach. Nothing was as it seemed. There were no familiar places. Their town, the fields, the road—everything had changed. Outside Belle Glade a vast primordial black water lake spread out before them. Those in the lead probed the ground with sticks searching for the roadbed. They were afraid of falling into one of the canals overflowing onto the road. The ragged tops of side canal dikes and a few standing telephone poles were their only guides. The only places to rest were the few muddy banks poking their crowns out of the water.

Ardie Peterson, his mother, and his sisters walked a respectful distance behind the other women and children. Off to one side of the road, Ardie spotted a pale object floating on top of a clump of lilies. He waded toward it and stopped. A small white baby, pale amid tangled stalks, bobbed with its eyes opened, staring out blankly at premature death—a troubling sight that would recur in Ardie's dreams again and again for the next seventy years.

The forsaken column lumbered into the Experimental Station, where the water was only two feet deep. A few of the women who were too exhausted to continue remained there. All the houses and outbuildings were used to house the women and children, but it was clear that there was no food and little water. Their best chance was to continue on to Six-Mile Bend and wait for rescue, which must surely be on its way.

AT dawn, as the wind died down, Nancy Martin and her party left the Experimental Station. A caravan of cars made its way down the Palm Beach Road, clearing trees and debris from the road. They finally reached West Palm Beach, the first to do so from Belle Glade, but they were unaware of the destruction in Belle Glade. Not until they reached West Palm Beach and saw the damage did Nancy insist on going back.

Josh Carter reluctantly drove Nancy back. At Six-Mile Bend, the women who had marched out stopped them. They were not allowed to pass on to Belle Glade. Nancy got out of the car determined to walk to Belle Glade if necessary, but the crowd stopped her. The women begged Josh to return to West Palm Beach and make sure help was on its way because they could go no farther.

HAROLD Ferguson stopped his ambulance at the Twenty-Mile Bend Bridge. Black water emptying from Lake Okeechobee poured in an angry torrent under, and over, the bridge. He tested the depth of the water with a stick and then gingerly drove his ambulance across. At Six-Mile Bend, on the opposite bank of the canal, he found nearly one hundred women and children huddled at the small house of bridge tender Register.

Ferguson loaded up his ambulance with the weakest of the women and children and immediately returned to West Palm Beach, without going on to Belle Glade. By the time he reached West Palm Beach, it was dark. The entire trip had taken eight hours. Relying on survivors' reports, Ferguson informed the Palm Beach Post that he believed there were forty whites dead and perhaps as many as eighty Negroes—far more than were reported in the press that day. No one, not even the survivors, understood the extent of the storm deaths. Officially, by Monday night only four people were reported dead in Belle Glade. That was the four bodies counted by a county official.

Near evening, under the auspicious orders of the Red Cross, a caravan of trucks was dispatched to Belle Glade. Finding the women and children at Six-Mile Bend, the rescuers loaded them into trucks and took them to refugee camps set up in churches and public buildings in West Palm Beach.

After Nancy Martin's group left, George Tedder grabbed a Kodak Brownie camera and drove in the opposite direction. Pulling into Belle Glade, he was stopped by rubble in the road. He got out and walked to the center, taking photographs as he went. In the course of three hours, he took over two hundred photographs—the only photographs shot immediately after the storm. Shot after shot showed destroyed and crumbling buildings, houses floating miles from their original locations, piles of rubble, and unburied dead. Lime-covered bodies floated eerily before the camera's lens.

NAPOLEON Broward's big canals were raging rapids of water gushing toward the Atlantic and Gulf of Mexico. The normally stately, slow-moving river of grass rippled with water, spilling toward Florida Bay. While Lake Okeechobee drained, the rain-swollen Kissimmee restocked the lost water. The storm had passed directly over the Kissimmee River Basin, dumping a foot of rain on already-waterlogged land. Millions of gallons of water were discharged each hour into the lake. A sheet of water stretching from two miles north of Lake Okeechobee to the Florida Bay formed a massive inland sea. Clewiston, Belle Glade, Moore Haven, South Bay, and Okeechobee were under water. Eighty percent of South Florida was flooded and would remain so for the next ten days. The Everglades had reverted back to a Pleistocene sea and was reluctant to give up.

NEAR noon, Charles Thomas, with his thirteen-year-old son Mutt, returned to Sebring Farms. They found Uncle Minor Thomas searching for lost family members. He had stayed in the "wrong side out" house, which, like the Thirst house, had floated off its foundation and been crushed against the Route 27 roadbed. He managed to ride the top of the roof until the storm abated. Victor Thirsk searched among the rubble for his wife. No one, either alive or dead, was found at the farms. Thirsk, the three Boots boys, along with Charles and Mutt Thomas, were the only Sebring Farms survivors. Everything they owned—every piece of furniture, every family memento, all memories of the dead—were gone. It was as if they had never existed. Only their bodies would be final proof that they had lived and died.

BILL Rawle took his three half-brothers in the skiff back to South Bay. Onboard the tugboat *Fox*, his wife dried the boys and dressed them in warm clothes. Once the boys were safe and secure, Bill set out in the skiff for Sebring Farms. His mother was out there, maybe hurt, needing help, and he was determined to find her.

It was just after noon when Bill Rawle arrived at Sebring Farms. He had first motored to Miami Locks, inching his way past sunken boats, trees, and rubble floating in the canal up to the swimming hole. He found the Thomases, Lees, and Victor Thirsk searching for survivors and dead.

"Have you found anybody else?" Rawle asked.

"Your dad's over there," Charles Thomas said, pointing to a row of corpses lying out on a canal bank, their faces respectfully covered with cloths.

"And my mom?"

Charles Thomas just shook his head.

"Maybe out there," Minor Thomas said, pointing to the other side of the road bank. "We haven't gotten that far yet."

For the rest of the afternoon, until dusk, the survivors of Sebring Farms searched for their loved ones. Cries into the air returned silence. Along canal banks, under piles of brush, in culverts, and at pump stations they searched. No one else was found alive.

After searching for five hours, darkness had begun to settle in on the Everglades. They found seven bodies floating in the water and on the canal banks. With his anchor rope, Rawle tied the corpses behind his skiff and then slowly hauled his sorrowful cargo back to South Bay.

DISHEARTENED, Charles and Mutt Thomas waded back to the Bolles Hotel. Canned food from the construction company's boats was brought in, and a kitchen was set up in the hotel to feed the people. Exhausted and mentally drained, Charles and Mutt searched for any cramped space on the floor where they could sleep. When they found a corner on the first floor, they lay down, and Charles Thomas fell into a deep, disturbed sleep.

WEST PALM BEACH

Clematis, Datura, and Banyan Streets were littered shoulder-high with broken lumber and metal roofs. Cars were buried under mounds of debris. Blown-out windows stared out of crippled structures. Only a few reinforced concrete buildings stood as a reminder that a once-vibrant city stood there.

Through the rubble, a few souls slowly picked their way across the streets. No one was sure what had happened. No one wanted to believe what he or she saw. Blank stares met blank stares. Disbelief faced confusion. A numbed populace picked their way to their homes. Most found piles of broken wood. The lucky ones had a house, even if it had no roof or was washed off its foundation. Some found boats on their front yards. The stately palm trees that had stood along the streets and had given the town its most enduring character were twisted or doubled over. West Palm Beach wondered how any town could recover from this much destruction.

LILLIAN PADGETT

It was still raining in spurts as Lillian drove with her husband and father down Main Street to Bacom Point. The storm had deposited a house squarely in the middle of the street. They had to negotiate around large downed trees and had to physically move debris. The lakeside of the Pahokee ridge was swept clean. Where there had been rows of neat one-story wood-frame houses, now there was nothing. They had little hope that their house would still be there.

It was hard to recognize Bacom Point. Landmark trees had been blown away. Their neighbors' houses were gone, but their home—though washed off its foundation—was intact. It had lodged against the large cypress tree in their front yard that shaded them in the summer. Calvin proclaimed it a miracle. Inside the house, Lillian found that the water had risen only three feet and had not damaged her linens or the beds. At least they would have some place to sleep. It was still structurally strong.

"Don't worry—the house can be moved back on its foundation," Calvin told her.

Still they could not stay there, there was little room in her in-laws' house, and there was also the problem of feeding everyone on limited supplies. Lillian and Ruth decided to try to make the drive to West Palm Beach where an uncle had a house that they could stay in—if that house was not badly damaged.

Barely making five miles an hour, they drove along Connors Highway. The highway, the canals, and the fields—the entire Everglades—were one large lake. The road was completely under water. Only the occasional canal berm poked above the water. The men took turns walking in front of the cars with long poles tapping the ground for hidden obstacles. The usual one-hour ride took eleven. By the time they reached West Palm Beach, the house was full of people who had lost their homes. They continued on to another uncle's house west of Military Trail in Greenacres. Using the car jack handle, Duncan broke into the boarded-up house. The musty two-bedroom house was their home for the next two months.

WILLIE Emma Wells cradled Edward tightly to her breast. The silence from outside was as eerie as the howling winds of last night. From her window she saw people moving slowly through the rubble. There was debris everywhere. Where had all that trash come from? she wondered. Belle Glade had become one continuous trash dump.

Tommy left to check on the house and to see about Bessie Mae and the kids.

Toward noon Willie Emma heard familiar long strides resonate down the hotel corridor.

Henry Martin, his eyes glazed with fatigue, stood in the doorway and rested his hand on the frame. He took a deep breath. Henry had just returned from Chosen looking for Annie Mae.

"Where's Tommy?" he asked.

"What about Bessie and the kids?" she asked.

"They picked up Raymond and Lucy but couldn't find Bessie or Annie Mae," he said in a dead voice. "The girls and Sonny are downstairs."

For a moment he stood in the doorway, a monument of defeat. Then he turned and disappeared into the hallway.

An hour later, Tommy returned.

"Have you seen Henry?"

"Yes, he was just here," Willie answered.

"How did he say Bessie and the children were?"

For the first time in her life, Willie hesitated. She knew how much her husband loved his sister and was afraid to tell him the truth.

"He told me they were all right," she lied.

"I haven't seen Bessie Mae, but Raymond and Lucy were brought in dead downstairs," he said, then turned and left.

Tears welled up in Willie's eyes. She hugged Edward closer to her bosom. She had lied to her husband and he knew that she had lied—a lie that was to trouble her for the rest of her life.

CHAPTER 13
THE AFTERMATH

September 17–20

The corpses were heaped in huge piles, nearly all stark naked, spread-eagled like great ginger cookies, eyes, tongues, and entrails protruding, the skin of their hands sloughed off and hanging from the wrists like opera gloves. After the first few days colored and white were indistinguishable. All had lost their skin.

—*Lawrence E. Will,* Okeechobee Hurricane and the Hoover Dike

MONDAY, SEPTEMBER 17

By midmorning, the walls and the front counter of the Glades Hotel lobby were covered by scores of handwritten notes. Most were hastily scribbled ripped pieces of paper left by survivors looking for lost family members. Others simply informed anyone that they were alive. A few were death notices. The hotel had become the central gathering point for refugees dribbling in from Chosen and South Bay. With no place to go, men and women waited at the hotel for relatives to appear. At times they witnessed tearful happy reunions, but mostly they waited in vain.

Leaving the hotel, Henry Martin headed to the store. With his bad ankle he walked as briskly as he could down Main Street. On each side men trying to clear paths were moving broken lumber and trees from the streets. At Canal Street he stopped. The canal was clogged with boats and debris. From the corner west there was no building standing except the Methodist church, which sat at an angle, partially resting on its foundation. This was what they had hit when the store began to drift. Wood was piled up around the church, but after a quick glance Henry saw that there was nothing of the store, or Bessie Mae, or Annie Mae.

Half a block west where his store had once stood, there was nothing but a vacant waterlogged lot littered with twisted rubble. A few feet away the Hillsboro Canal raged with water emptying from Lake Okeechobee. He searched for the two-ton safe he was sure could not have traveled far. He never found it. He asked every person he passed whether they had seen Bessie Mae. No, they had not seen her. They, too, were searching for missing family or friends.

Finding nothing, Henry returned to the Glades Hotel. As he strode up the steps to the lobby, a Chosen survivor stopped him. She told him she had heard that Annie Mae's body had been found a mile beyond Isaac West's store. Henry turned and left without a word. He trudged the three miles to the Chosen body dump.

Once out of town, an eerie silence surrounded Henry. The clatter and songs of birds that normally filled the air was gone. There were no birds. The grinding chirp of insects was missing. No frogs croaked along the canal banks. Even the dogs were silent. Nothing moved except for a gentle breeze blowing from the south that was heavy with the stench of fresh muck and death.

At every stop where the dead had been gathered, Henry walked the rows of corpses, forcing himself to stare into each vacant face and at every broken body—one might be Annie or Bessie Mae. They were the faces of the drowned, some grimaced in agony, others posed in serene tranquility. There were battered bodies with freshly scarred limbs; others lay peacefully as if they had just fallen off to sleep. There were white bodies and black bodies dumped together, all sharing in death the equality that had so eluded them in life. At first Henry could not believe that all these people were from Chosen and Belle Glade. Did the storm blow in bodies from across the lake? There were so many dead, but Annie Mae wasn't one of them. Instead of Annie Mae, he found another girl's corpse. She was Annie Mae's size and had her coloring, but her eyes—still staring out in awe at an unexpected death—were dark. Exhausted and suffering from the effects of hypothermia and his injuries, a dejected Henry Martin walked back to the Glades Hotel.

TUESDAY, SEPTEMBER 18

Annie Mae was not in Chosen. When the Martin store had broken against the church, she grabbed at the floorboards in a panic. She watched the vent window in the gable go past as the store flipped over. It collapsed, and she was thrown into the water and dragged under. Desperately kicking with her dress tangled in the rubble, she struggled to reach the surface. After what seemed like eternal minutes, she finally broke through. A piece of the store rolled over her, breaking her left shoulder blade. She fought to remain conscious. With her good arm she grabbed onto a part of the house and held on for the next four hours until the water stopped moving. It was pitch black, and she had no idea where she was. Gingerly she stepped off her piece of wood onto a canal bank and collapsed. Nearby a houseboat with its keel up had been thrown up on the bank, and she crawled under it to get out of the cold, stinging rain. Cold and disoriented, with twenty-nine puncture wounds and badly bruised, she huddled, doubled over in pain. Her broken shoulder throbbed as she waited for rescue, or morning, or death.

Annie Mae lay there for two days in a pained fog, wondering whether she had the strength to live. She huddled under the houseboat unable even to stand. All her clothes except for her slip had been ripped off. Downpours of cold rain pelted her. Night came and went as she drifted in and out of consciousness. Tuesday morning two black men found her shivering. One took off his sweater and covered her before walking her to Belle Glade. For the entire two-mile walk Annie Mae said nothing. Shock was setting in.

The trio reached the bridge over the Hillsboro Canal, and Annie Mae remembered, "I was walking across the Pahokee Bridge and I saw a man coming towards me. I thought, 'He looks familiar,' but I didn't recognize him. Then he spoke to me, called me by name, and I realized it was my daddy."

Henry Martin put his arm around his daughter and hugged her.

IN West Palm Beach, once the winds had died down and light dawned, the Tillman family left the incinerator. Their house, lacking a roof, was soaked inside but still standing. They found the roof two blocks away and with the help of neighbors dragged it back and raised and secured it to the standing wall studs. They had a home again—one of the few on 23rd Street that had remained relatively intact.

Throughout colored town, neighbors helped neighbors. Houses and churches became homes to hundreds of families. As in most tragedies that strike the black community, the residents did not expect any help from the white-controlled city, or Palm Beach County. Years of neglect and Jim Crow postures had made them self-sufficient. They would take care of their own themselves.

IN the city, no looting was immediately reported. Martial law was never declared, although as a precaution the militia was activated to augment the police. Company C of the 124th Infantry National Guard was called

out to patrol the streets. Troops roped off Clematis Street. Men cleared the
rubble and searched for any dead. All able-bodied men over sixteen were
pressed to work. General chairman of the Relief Committee George Carr
pleaded for volunteers. Even those under sixteen were utilized. Fourteen-
year-old Willie Rawls was put to work shoveling sand off Ocean Boulevard. The call went out, "All Boy Scouts will please report to headquarters
for service."

Initial reports there were encouraging—few bodies had been found. As-
tonishingly, though there was talk of dozens of dead, only two confirmed
deaths had been reported that afternoon—so few that the local papers felt
obliged to list the injured. As if to put the tragedy into perspective, the
Tuesday *Palm Beach Post* published a list of the babies born during the
storm. West Palm Beach might have been destroyed, but the "tourist and
investor scaring death tolls" were low. Within twenty-four hours, that
would dramatically change.

Outside help was slow in coming, some believed because Palm Beach
was synonymous with wealth and the rich didn't need money. Actually,
no one outside Florida had any idea of the scope of the tragedy. Poor communications rather than indifference delayed help.

At Sebring Farms, when the order came to send the women and children
to West Palm Beach, Charles Thomas could not give up his only living
child. He kept Mutt close by him, in sight at all times. The whole afternoon
they waded, stumbled, and tripped over debris searching for their family until dusk and exhaustion finally forced them back to the hotel to sleep. At
dawn the next morning, the Thomases resumed their heartbreaking task.
Probing outward in concentric circles from the farm, they found Mutt's
mother partially covered with house rubble. Later one of his sisters was
found farther out in a tangle of custard apple brush and wood. Her sister was
spotted floating on her back beyond the others. At a neighbor's farm they
found Aunt Berta and Uncle Mays, who had first come to the Everglades
in 1910 to help dig Napoleon Broward's canals. One by one they found the
rest of the Thomas clan until only two cousins were unaccounted for.

Charles's wife and children were brought back to the Bolles Hotel and
placed in the boathouse by the lakeshore. The next day they were
wrapped in sheets and put in hastily constructed pine boxes sent in from
Clewiston. The first of the dead were identified and placed in coffins with
their names chalked on the end, and the coffins were nailed shut and
then placed on a large seine boat tied behind a tugboat. As the sun set,
Charles Thomas and the rest of the mourners boarded the funeral tugboat. During the night, the towboat broke loose and slowly drifted with
its sad, macabre load onto a rocky reef just out of Clewiston. It was dark

and the tug had to continue on to Clewiston with its passengers. The dead would have to wait.

The next morning the funeral barge was pulled off the rocks and taken to Clewiston. Charles Thomas had to bury his family. With a determination that was to haunt him for the rest of his life, he insisted that his family be buried as soon as possible.

"The pine coffins were then taken from Clewiston by trucks to Ortona Locks, on the other side of Moore Haven. We buried the dead that night at twelve o'clock. Later on my daddy went back and had cypress wood crosses erected. The name of each person was painted on with white paint. Daddy always kept the place clean and the markers up," recalled Mutt Thomas.

BY Tuesday afternoon, the first of the Coast Guard boats reached South Bay. The confiscated rumrunner christened the *Black Maria* nudged its bow through the broken boats, trees, and lumber damming the North New River Canal. Many times the Coast Guardsmen had to get out and cut away branches blocking their progress and to retrieve corpses. Slowly they forced their way to South Bay but were finally stopped by sunken barges below the locks. They not only brought the first supplies and medicine to South Bay but were also a sign that the outside world had finally sent help.

FOR two days Henry Martin and Tommy Wells searched for the woman they both loved. Henry treaded over the waste of what had been Belle Glade, looking under each plank, behind every pile. By the steel bridge, Tommy Wells searched along the canal bank for any trace of his house— his medals from World War I, Willie Emma's linens, her china, or anything else. All he found was an empty canal littered with the remains of broken dreams. Near where the north side of the house had stood he spotted a glimpse of metal. Cleaning the muck off he saw it was his toolbox. The heavy metal box had fallen through the floorboards and anchored itself in the muck canal bank. He dug it out of the muck. Not far from his toolbox, Tommy found the body of a young black man tangled in wire fencing. Using a board, he dug a hole in the soft canal bank muck and buried him. He threw the board over the grave, then picked up his tool box and carried it back to the hotel. It was all he ever found of any of their possessions.

The next day when he returned, he found that the bloated body had popped up out of the soft ground. He buried it again. When he returned the following day, the bloated corpse had again surfaced. He was forced to do something he never wanted to do or to see done again—burn a body. With the coal oil that the relief agencies were distributing to burn bodies, he doused the corpse and set it on fire.

While Willie Emma agonized over the loss of everything, she was glad that all three of her family had survived. But she was worried about Tommy. Each morning he left the hotel to search the scarred landscape for his sister. Day after day he trudged along the canals searching through each pile of rubble, watching as the boats passed with their sad cargo in tow, for any signs of his sister. By the fourth day, he knew she must be dead. He tried to keep his anguish to himself. But when Bessie Mae died, Tommy Wells had lost another mother, and there was nothing the stoic soldier could do to hide his grief.

With Thelma, Ernestine, Annie Mae, and Robert in the hotel hospital and Sonny resting upstairs, Henry again set out to search for Bessie Mae. Recurring pictures of Bessie Mae's last minutes haunted him. She had never been a good swimmer, so he held out little hope that she was alive. The least he wanted to do was to bury her. The thought of her body lost in the Everglades, ravaged by scavengers, burned in his mind.

Early the next morning, Henry and Tommy borrowed a flat-bottomed boat and motored to the farms to search for survivors. At Loney Martin's farm there was nothing, not a trace of his house or barn. Only a large rubber tree had survived upright. Loney, his wife, and their four children were never found.

In the old rubber tree behind where Loney's house once stood, Henry found water-carried debris in its upper branches.

"The flood was twenty-seven feet high," he said later, shaking his head.

Given a storm surge of twelve feet topped by five- to seven-foot waves, flotsam lifted to over twenty feet was to be expected. Few structures in Belle Glade were over twenty feet high.

At the Martin farm Henry found nothing—no house, no barn. The fences were gone, the freshly planted fields under water. There was no trace of a family who had fought for eight hard years against isolation, adversity, and diseases; against rain, floods, and drought; against scorching heat and crop-killing freezes. There was no trace that a family had lived, loved, and suffered the joys and travails of life. It was as if a God-sized eraser had excised an affront to its divine supremacy. So completely had the storm erased every trace of human endeavor in the sawgrass lands that later people wondered whether anyone had ever lived there.

All the black farmhands were gone. None had survived.

Henry slogged around in the two feet of water that covered the entire Everglades, searching until his battered body could take no more. By the time he returned to Belle Glade, he was suffering from hypothermia and had contracted a lung infection. He did something he had never done in his life—he gave up. Henry Martin was a man defeated. Bessie Mae Martin was never found.

WEDNESDAY, SEPTEMBER 19

Forty miles separated Belle Glade from West Palm Beach. Forty miles of uninhabited sawgrass, swampland, and sloughs now under a sea of muck water two to three feet deep. For two days, those forty miles were an almost insurmountable obstacle, sealing the Everglades from the outside.

Information slowly dribbled out of the Everglades. The first survivors to reach the coast had no idea as to the extent of the damage or loss of life. Even the women of the Belle Glade march witnessed only a few dozen dead. First reports told of fifty, or maybe as many as a hundred, people killed—as many as in Moore Haven. A higher count than that was unthinkable. People in West Palm Beach were concerned, but city authorities were overwhelmed with their own recovery and rescue efforts.

Even from West Palm Beach, the transfer of information to the outside world was slow. The radios were gone; any batteries had been drained. Two ham-radio operators managed to get a couple of messages out. But the notice that Palm Beach County had suffered a major calamity was so slowly disseminated to the outside that Florida governor John Martin was not advised until Wednesday morning. Once informed, he set out immediately to survey the situation.

"In six miles between Pahokee and Belle Glade, I counted twenty-seven corpses in the water or on the roadside but not taken from the water. Total dead on the roadside and not buried and counted but not in plank coffins was one hundred and twenty-six," the governor said.

Later that day he was to see many more bodies burning and being trucked away.

A solemn Wednesday *Palm Beach Post* listed the known dead. Thousands of people read and reread the columns searching for news of loved ones. By then, there was no denying that a world-class disaster had struck Palm Beach County, and no amount of name nit-picking would change that fact. The word *hurricane* was now freely used.

A glance across the sawgrass plains outside Belle Glade revealed what looked like a field of white daisies blowing gently in the wind. They were white flags attached to four-foot sticks stuck in the muck, each one beside a body waited to be recovered. The bloated bodies filled their clothes, bursting at their seams, like grotesque Mardi Gras balloons. Their skin disintegrated at the touch, sending off a putrid, suffocating stench. Corpses that had been buried in the muck swelled and then bobbed to the surface before their gas-filled organs burst and they deflated into slimy bags of bones. Decay was everywhere—fish lay along the banks, farm animals lay

in the fields. It was a sight that turned the stomachs of even hardened veterans of World War I.

The "cemetery detail," or body gathering, was strictly a man's job.
Women were not allowed to see the body gathering since it was considered too gruesome for a woman. Even for the men, however, the recovery
of these decomposed bodies was so repulsive that each was given a stiff
drink of Prohibition whiskey donated by local rumrunner Jack Mansley,
who became an unlikely hero.

All the shallow draft boats were pressed into service to search the
flooded farms and hamlets for survivors and to recover the dead. Young
men and old were sent out with an outboard motor and a bale of rope to
different farms. The ones who knew the people were sent to look for
friends and relatives. When they found bodies, they would tie the rope
around their ankles. After gathering up half a dozen or more, they returned with their dismal cargo floating behind them. Lawrence said,
"They looked like bunched grapes tugged along behind the boats."

Dead floated in flooded fields; dead were caught up in tangles of brush
and barbed wire fences; dead were sucked into culverts; dead were trapped
in collapsed houses, entangled in rubble.

The first were brought to Belle Glade and identified. Carpenters
worked full-time to construct crude coffins. The names of the deceased
were then scratched in chalk on the outside and the coffins piled up beside the canals. There was no way to move them on land since the roads
were still impassable, blocked with debris. While boatmen gathered up
the bodies, other men worked at clearing roads for rescue vehicles.

Men, mostly blacks, were rounded up into work gangs. Pairs of white
"man hunters," some armed with rifles, searched for "single" unattached
black men who might be slackers. Large gangs of up to two hundred men
were then forced to clear roads and canals. George Tedder took a photograph of one gang of 175 men marching across the Hillsboro Canal bridge
to clear the road to Pahokee. Others, again mostly black men, were used
to handle the bodies in the recovery and cemetery details.

When identification was impossible, the bodies were taken to body dumps
in the middle of the fields and doused with coal oil. Black plumes of heavy
smoke scarred the Everglades sky as piles of bodies were burned. Clouds of
black vultures circling overhead now led searchers to rotting corpses.

"Those buzzards were like bird dogs," said Luke Mason, one of the
youngest members of the search teams. "Led us right to the bodies.
Though sometimes I wish they hadn't."

CECIL Warner searched the wreckage for his friend Arlin Martin. He
found Henry Martin's cousin under a pile of broken wood two hundred

yards north of the Hillsboro Canal. He turned over the body and reached down around his bloated stomach and removed an alligator money belt. Inside was the $1,140 he had made while working in the automobile factories. Just two days before the storm, Cecil had helped him count the money—his farm money. Across the street, a Red Cross official spotted him removing the money belt. All the authorities had orders to prevent looting of corpses. Wedding rings and bracelets were targets of opportunity. The Red Cross official demanded the belt. Cecil explained that the corpse was Aaron Martin, Henry Martin's cousin, and that the belt and money should go to the family.

The Red Cross man insisted it be given to him. "I'll see that they get it," he said.

Not wanting to be accused of looting, Cecil handed over the money belt.

"You can retrieve this at the Red Cross," he said and left.

That was the last the Martins heard of the money.

As Thelma rested in the upper rooms of the Glades Hotel, the story of her dramatic rescue of her baby brother caught the people's imagination. A $1 sensationalist booklet with photographs was rushed to publication a few weeks after the hurricane proclaiming the little twelve-year-old Belle Glade girl a genuine heroine. Thelma, however, was too injured and shocked to appreciate it, and the shock never wore off. After her wounds healed, Thelma Martin refused to discuss the night of the storm, preferring to keep the traumatic night buried deep in her subconscious.

Henry knew they could not stay in Belle Glade. There was no place for them to live. He was suffering from a lung ailment. Sonny, Thelma, and Annie Mae had lesions, and Robert had pneumonia. After the canals and roads were cleared of debris, the Martins were loaded onto a boat and sent to a hospital in Miami. Within a few days, they had recovered enough to be released from the hospital and sent to a crowded refugee house ten miles north in Hollywood.

THURSDAY, SEPTEMBER 20

On Thursday, as the Martin family recuperated in the Miami hospital, the hurricane storm, now much reduced in intensity, passed into Ontario, Canada, where it merged with another disturbance and officially ceased to exist. It had suffered in its northern jaunt. Contrary winds and a strong jet stream had forced it inland, starving it of water. Still carrying an enormous amount of water, it had soaked Georgia, the Carolinas, and Virginia, causing massive flooding. When the storm

did find water again, it was cold and heavy. With the life-giving warm water gone, the storm rapidly degraded and died without being mourned, but
it was never forgotten.

FOR Nancy Martin, the news coming out of the Everglades could not
have been worse. Stories of hundreds, and then thousands of dead circu-
lated in the press. Streams of refugees clogged the roads; hospitals were
full. Churches, town halls, schools, and other buildings that had survived
the storm were converted into refugee centers. Nancy and her husband
visited every center, stopped and asked each group of new refugees for any
news of their family. She did not know whether they were still alive and
needed help or whether they were dead and waiting to be identified.
They might be some of the unlucky to be buried, unnamed and unknown,
like the hundreds of dead being trucked back to West Palm Beach.

Nancy and Josh searched for two weeks until finally they found Henry
and the children in the Hollywood refugee camp. In the tearful reunion,
Henry Martin thought only of returning to the Everglades. He had a family to support. He had to feed them; he had to build a house. It was September and there was still time to plant, still time to find Bessie Mae.

IN the West Palm Beach dark, the trucks began to appear. Quietly, they
stole in under the cover of night with their boxed cargo covered from prying eyes. A few at first, they parked and unloaded that cargo: dozens of
chalk-marked coffins, then scores, then hundreds. After a few days of
steady traffic, it seemed there were too many dead for anyone to care. The
trucks carrying the Everglades dead came day and night with unidentified
bodies stacked like cordwood in the back. By the fifth day, the trucks were
recognized from far away by their smell and the long trail of opaque body
fluids dripping from the back. There were no coffins, no name tags, only
a tarpaulin unceremoniously thrown over them.

A pair of National Guardsmen were posted at the Woodlawn Cemetery
entrance to restrict access. More guardsmen patrolled the cemetery
perimeter to keep sightseers and those who wished to gawk away. At the
west end of the cemetery beside the railroad tracks, a steam shovel dug a
long trench parallel to the railroad track. The coffins were slipped in side
by side, some on top of others, and quickly covered.

SHUT out from the only cemetery in West Palm Beach, trucks with dead
blacks were directed to a lot beside the city incinerator near Tamarind
Street. For years this area had served as a clandestine burial ground. Poor
blacks who could not afford a burial plot or even a coffin buried their
dead at night. To the east of the city incinerator another trench was dug,

bodies dumped in, and then covered over, and followed by another hole. There was no time for coffins, tombstones, or mourning. Six hundred seventy-four unidentified black corpses were buried without procedure.

The black survivors were treated little better. Many were rounded up for the worst of the cemetery detail work, loading and unloading the stinking, rotting bodies. White National Guardsmen watched over them as they worked. Many were single men with few ties to the area and little incentive to help. Whether through religious or superstitious beliefs, many blacks had a special reverence for the dead and were handed the additional insult of being forced to manhandle corpses.

The victims were interred in many cemeteries. The largest concentration, sixteen hundred people were buried north of Pahokee in Port Mayaca. Outside Moore Haven, the Thomas and Boots and Hughes family dead were buried in Ortona Cemetery, where scores of victims of the 1926 hurricane rested.

But not all burial grounds accepted the Everglades dead. One truckload of bodies was taken to be buried in Miami but was turned away because of the advanced state of decomposition. The truck returned to Belle Glade, where the corpses were burned.

JUANITA

By midweek, news reports of the storm's destruction had reached Miami. The Red Cross pleaded for volunteers. Anybody. For once skin color made no difference. Juanita Wilson, frustrated at not being allowed to travel to Puerto Rico to help her countrymen, refused to remain idle. She organized a group of black Miami volunteers to help the victims in the Everglades They formed a caravan of Model T's and drove all day toward West Palm Beach. Route 1, Florida's main road up the east coast, had been partially destroyed in places. The Wilsons' old Model T faithfully chugged along, but its tires were old and worn, the inner tubes heavily patched. Driving over debris-strewn roads, they had frequent flat tires.

As the afternoon dragged on, their progress was slow. Night was approaching as they drove toward Lake Worth, and their anxieties increased. Lake Worth was strictly a Jim Crow town. No black person could be found within its city limits after dark. Like many Jim Crow towns, there were signs posted saying, "Nigger, don't let the sun set on you."

Exhausted after their nerve-tiring trip, they finally pulled into West Palm Beach. The next morning they reported to the Red Cross and were assigned to a group traveling to the Everglades. The early-morning sky was clear as Juanita Wilson and the Miami volunteers were ferried across the canal from West Palm Beach to Twenty-Mile Bend. The bridge was out. Another truck met the volunteers on the west bank and drove them to Belle Glade.

The sawgrass plains had been wiped clean as if a giant straight-edged razor had slashed the lands.

"There wasn't a blade of grass anywhere. It was a pure black sea of muck. Quite beautiful," Juanita remembered with a nod of her head.

The initial beauty of the devastated landscape was quickly replaced by the human horror that greeted her in Belle Glade. Two weeks had passed since the storm. They were among the first black volunteers to arrive. She was assigned to the black section and immediately set up to get people their basic necessities.

"By the time we got there, people were on their feet," she said.

Juanita Wilson and the black Miami volunteers found a changed Belle Glade. No longer was Belle Glade a quiet farming town. No longer was the lake seen as a benign source of fresh fish and scenic beauty. No longer was Belle Glade the most desired place to live in southern Florida. No longer did Belle Glade have jobs for those that wanted them or food for the taking. There were no jobs, there were no crops, and there was no food and little drinking water. For many, Belle Glade had become the last place on Earth they wanted to be.

There had been progress, though. The streets had been cleared and the rubble piled up in vacant lots or along the sides of the roads. The water had finally receded, though mud and muck covered everyone's clothes. People were living in a few tents supplied by the Red Cross. Housing, even donated tents, was still scarce. So each afternoon the Miami volunteers were trucked out of the Everglades and brought back to sleep in West Palm Beach.

The American Red Cross ended up donating hundreds of tents for people who stayed or returned before their houses were rebuilt. It distributed money to help the homeless rebuild their houses. At times funds were slow in reaching the victims. The Red Cross must have been worried about hurricane disaster donations. Don Morris, in his "The 1928 Hurricane in Florida," the same pamphlet that told of Thelma Martin's heroics, stated that

```
    this book is being published, sufficiently soon after
    the storm that it may be useful in the work of the Amer-
    ican National Red Cross in raising money for relief and
    rehabilitation.
        A. L. Schafer, in charge of the relief work here for
    the American National Red Cross, has said that money is
    not being contributed as fast as it should be, probably
```

because of the fact that this territory is associated so
closely with Palm Beach, the millionaires' playground.

Lawrence Will notes that Dr. A. L. Schaefer was a "colored physician."

SOUTH BAY

Slowly the Everglades was evacuated. Bill Rawle sent Vernie and his brothers to an uncle's house in West Palm Beach. After burying their family, Charles and Mutt Thomas left for Fort Lauderdale. Some people thought the Everglades would never be a safe place to live. There was talk of forbidding people to return to the Everglades, of building a barrier to keep them out. Yet the draw of the rich Everglades soil overcame personal fear. Within two months, people who swore they'd never come back returned to Belle Glade. There was "too much muck in their shoes" to keep them away.

THE storm did not kill equitably. More than three-quarters of the people killed in the 1928 storm were black. Living in flimsy shanties, many built of tarpaper and scrap wood in the least desirable areas—near canals or up against the dike—they were the first to feel the water's wrath. An elevation of a few feet would have saved lives. In Pahokee, only a few whites were killed. Most farm owners had houses in town on the ridge or near it. The migrant farmhands had no place to retreat to when the reverse surge broke over the Pelican River dike, sending a wall of water up the old Pelican River and killing hundreds.

Not one of the blacks that took refuge in the Thirst house attic at Sebring Farms survived. There was no one to miss them, no one to look for them, and no one who cared whether they were found or not. The ones not burned were shipped to West Palm Beach, where most were buried in the mass grave site at Tamarind Avenue. The grave site was covered and forgotten except in local neighborhood oral accounts. The site was so completely lost administratively that the city paved 25th Street over part of the grave site and sold the remainder for development. The lot was later officially recognized as a mass grave. In 1991, a formal funeral service was conducted for the 674 black storm victims of 1928. Local African American leaders lobbied to build a permanent memorial, yet the site remained a forlorn weed-covered lot until the city of West Palm Beach repurchased the lot and erected an historical plaque commemorating the 674 dead. A simple but elegant memorial will be erected over the remaining grave sites. Robert Hazzard of The Storm of 28 Memorial

Coalition hopes to build a museum dedicated to the 1928 hurricane near the memorial.

A disproportionate number of young mothers, especially those burdened with infants, like Bessie Mae Martin, had died. Women survivors told of their dresses snagging on submerged objects and dragging them under. Many did not know how to swim, and most refused even in the face of a horrible death to give up their babies.

WHEN finally allowed by the authorities, the Martin family moved back to Belle Glade, living first in a tent near Chosen before moving into a newly built house. Henry Martin never recovered financially. The storm and the loss of Bessie Mae, the store, and the farm had sapped the entrepreneurial spirit from him. He began to farm again, but the dream of being the largest landowner in the Everglades and having a chain of stores throughout South Florida drowned in the black waters of Lake Okeechobee on September 16, 1928.

Henry Martin never remarried. As he'd drive by the old store site along Canal Street. or across the sawgrass plains, he'd stare out as if still looking for Bessie Mae.

THE search for the dead continued for six weeks. Sixteen hundred bodies were trucked to Port Mayaca north of Pahokee and buried in high ground. A month after the storm, nearly ninety bodies had been recovered in the Belle Glade area. Another twenty-eight bodies had been found during the last two weeks of October. The search for the dead was halted November 1, 1928—not because there were no more bodies to find but because there was no more money. The official body count was approaching two thousand. The high figure made many local civic leaders feel uncomfortable.

In November, the Red Cross gave its assessment of the number of dead that seemed absolute in its exactness. An early figure of 2,300 dead was published but was quickly retracted as inaccurate and unscientific. By the time the counting had stopped, officials could point to a figure lower than 2,000: 1,836 sounded better than 2,000.

The officials worked very hard to keep the death count as low as possible. Some were still determined not to scare away the tourists, and old habits died hard. Local powers, developers, and boosters wanted to quickly forget the storms and return to normal, to the boom years when everyone was making money. The *Everglades News* lamented, "The stacks of coffins on the dock at Canal Point is [sic] hurting the real estate market."

The undercounting of the victims has been debated for seventy years. At the time, many officials admitted there were many more deaths than the official count. A simple summation of the reported number of people buried—Woodlawn Cemetery 69; Tamarind mass grave 674; Port Mayaca 1,600; Ortona two score; a trench dug along the road bed near Miami Locks another 40 bodies—totals more than 2,400. Around the Everglades dozens of unreported grave sites dotted any high ground. Dead were carried away and buried as far away as the town as Sebring. How many were buried and never noted in the official records? Was the man Tom Wells buried on the north bank of the Hillsboro Canal counted? How many hundreds of unidentified bloated corpses were burned in the sawgrass fields surrounding Belle Glade and South Bay? And, of course, how many people were never found, lost in the Everglades, buried in the muck until their bones were plowed up decades later? While the exact number will never be known, the true figure is more likely close to three thousand, or nearly 50 percent of the population. Everyone lost someone.

The state, county, and ad agencies wanted finality. Money was needed for the living, not the dead. People wanted to get on with their lives. Water still covered the Everglades, and fields remained flooded. Parts of South Bay and Belle Glade still had standing water. It wasn't until November that the Water District got its pumps repaired and back on line, pumping. By December, a semblance of normalcy had returned to the Everglades. Fields were plowed and planted with vegetables, some houses had been repaired, families began moving back, and the water had gone. Most people lived in two tent cities, one located on the south side of the Hillsboro Canal for the whites, the other to the west for the blacks. Later that month the state and federal governments announced plans for a massive new dike to replace the muck dike destroyed in the storm. The new dike was to tame and punish Lake Okeechobee.

As if echoing the sentiments of the day, the hurricane of 1928 is still referred to locally as the '28 storm. For Everglades farmers and their families, it was the defining date—everything happened either before the storm or after it.

STARK reminders of the storm would surface for years as farmers plowed their fields. It was not unusual to hear a farmer say, "I plowed up someone's bones today."

"We would find human skulls and play with them," Bob Martin said. "We were just kids and didn't know any better."

WHILE a high body count easily dramatizes the scope of the disaster, number crunching the dead belittles the real tragedy of the 1928 hurricane, its effects on the survivors. The hurricane had changed not only the Everglades landscape but the lives of hundreds of families. It had a strong psychological effect on the survivors. They had gone through the equivalent of war. They were shell-shocked, their senses numbed in the face of their experience and staggering loses. Though they lived in a time when emotions were hidden and stoicism was a virtue, there was no denying that their lives and mental state were inexorably changed. Each survivor dealt with his or her suffering differently.

Charles Thomas was continually haunted by that September night. Except for his son Mutt, he had lost his entire family. He kept his sorrow hidden, trying to bury his grief in hard physical labor.

"My dad had always worked hard, but after the '28 storm he worked harder," Mutt Thomas related. "In the field where he worked, black laborers would ask him what they should do next. His mind would be somewhere else, and he wouldn't answer them. He wouldn't even know they were standing there."

Charles Thomas worked himself into becoming one of the largest landowners in the Everglades.

MANY survivors found it too painful to remember. Ernestine and Thelma Martin had never spoken about their long terrifying night on the tree stump, not even between themselves, until the author interviewed them seventy years later.

Nancy Martin developed a hurricane phobia. At the very mention that a hurricane might strike Florida, she demanded someone drive her to West Palm Beach or Frostproof, out of harm's way.

SOME found solace in God. Agonizing over the loss of his sister, Tommy Wells went through a spiritual conversion. The wild boy and war hero from northern Florida became a preacher. Eventually he moved his family to Everglades City on the Gulf Coast, where he started his own church near the Everglades thousand islands, Florida's last frontier.

VERNIE Boots studied in Fort Lauderdale, leaving high school just before acquiring his diploma. With his intuitive mind and active imagination, he developed a number of grassroots inventions, but memories of the storm never left him.

"I think about it every day," he said.

DUNCAN Padgett recovered from his attack of heartworm. The same humor that had carried him through life, had won the heart of Lillian Shive, and had helped him overcome his illness now also helped him become mayor of Pahokee.

Ruth Carpenter gave birth to a son, Milton, who carried on Calvin Shive's love of the earth. He eventually became president of the American Orchid Society.

MARIBELL Rawls had her healthy baby boy. For the next twelve years, William Rawls was watched over faithfully by the family dog, Kazan.

Frede Aunapu married his sweetheart Elizabeth BeaDer.

LAWRENCE Will, the gregarious service station owner, stayed in Belle Glade, becoming one of its leading citizens. Self-styled "cracker historian," he recorded the oral histories of many of the Everglades's early settlers and went on to write six history books about the 1928 hurricane and early life in the Everglades. The Lawrence Will Museum, located on Main Street in Belle Glade, is dedicated to preserving Glades history.

JUANITA Wilson settled in Belle Glade. With her enthusiasm and tireless energy, she became a driving force to educate black children and was a champion fighting for racial integration. Thousands of black migrant farm children were offered a better life through the education opportunities Juanita managed to win through her tireless fights with the Palm Beach County School Board.

TODAY many survivors would be diagnosed as suffering from survivor's syndrome and posttraumatic stress, except in 1928 there were no such things. People suffered in painful stoic silence.

THE great Florida hurricanes of 1926 and 1928 started a disastrous downward economic spiral. After the Miami hurricane of 1926, Florida's real estate boom went bust. The national press that had fueled the real estate boom with stories of instant profits now harped on its demise. Banks in Chicago and Ohio that had lent against land in Florida lost millions of dollars, and some collapsed. Consumer confidence fell. People who had never even set foot in Florida found themselves impoverished by the land bust.

With the 1928 storm followed by headlines of thousands of dead, the rest of the country wanted nothing to do with Florida land deals. For all they cared, the state could be given back to the Seminoles, and it almost was. Large tracts of land were abandoned; tax forfeitures nearly bankrupted the state.

Though the stock market did not crash until October 21, 1929, the economic effects of the hurricanes of 1926 and 1928 were felt like a ripple across the nation. A cumulative effect slowly snowballed as bank after bank closed. Economic red flags waved in the afterbreezes, and Americans took a second look at get-rich schemes, fraud, and overpriced stocks—but not enough, it seems. Between the end of 1928 and September 1929, the stock market soared another 81 points. The Dow Jones Industrial Index hit the giddy high of 381 before critical mass was reached.

THE storm forever changed not only the lives of the survivors but the Everglades themselves. Today Lake Okeechobee is completely surrounded by the massive forty-foot-high Hoover Dike. Constantly monitored by the United States Corps of Engineers, the levee has served its purpose. It has never broken. It has protected the farmers and fertile Everglades farmlands from a repeat of 1926 and 1928. However, gone are the dead rivers. Gone are the massive sweeps of grass beds—the lake's fish hatcheries. Gone are steamship lines. Boats still ply the lake, and the intercoastal waterway's Okeechobee Canal, one of Disston's dreams, cuts through central Florida to the lake, connecting the Atlantic Ocean with the Gulf of Mexico.

The Everglades farm area has expanded over fivefold since the hurricane. It continues to be the American winter breadbasket. After years of trying to make a profit planting and refining sugar, the Southern Sugar Company went into receivership. United States Sugar Corporation bought the remains of Southern Sugar, and through better management and science finally was able to produce profitable sugar in the Everglades. Today miles upon miles of dark green sugarcane grow to the horizon, strangely reminiscent of the old sawgrass plains. But to see the old sawgrass plains as they once were, a casual tourist only has to cross Route 75, Alligator Alley, as it crosses the Everglades from Fort Lauderdale to Naples. Secure in their cars, tourists can conjure up images of the sights that greeted the first Calusa Indians in their search for wild game.

Like before the '28 storm, the lake is still a political yo-yo for special interests. Droughts and deluges unevenly alternate between seasons and years. Farmers, fishermen, developers, environmentalists, and Seminole Indians are at constant odds over the lake level and its water use. The Corps of Engineers, caught in the middle, can never satisfy one side or the other. Water politics is as important as ever in the Everglades.

IN 2001, Florida went through the fourth year of the worst drought in its history. Vast wildfires burned Polk County, closing Route 4 between Tampa and Orlando, the home to Disney World and the Universal Studios theme park. Thousands of acres of forest and mucklands smoldered for months near the old Martin family homestead.

The drought dropped the water level of the much-abused Lake Okeechobee to new lows. Bass fishing, a major source of recreation and employment in the area, collapsed, and the scores of marine creatures that dotted Okeechobee were left high and dry as the lake shore retreated. Agricultural and surface runoff, with no place to go, accumulated in the lake. The levels of phosphate and other pollutants increased. Pahokee's public water system's water was declared unfit to drink, reducing people to buy their drinking water.

On the other side of the levee, clouds of black muck dust rose in the air behind large tractors with laser guidance systems for vertical control of land surface. As they prepared the fields for planting new sugarcane seed pieces, one tractor unearthed in its black wake a scattering of white bones. Human bones. The last of the 1928 hurricane victims? One more of the uncounted dead? With each unearthing there is not a survivor or their children who do not wonder whose bones they might be.

MEANWHILE, a generation of Everglades farming families would carry the psychological scars of the 1928 hurricane for the rest of their lives. And, for better or for worse, the Everglades was forever changed.

BIBLIOGRAPHY

BOOKS AND ARTICLES

Barnes, Jay. *Florida's Hurricane History*. Chapel Hill: University of North Carolina Press, 1998.

Belle Glade Chamber of Commerce. *1928 Hurricane*. Belle Glade, Fla.: Belle Glade Chamber of Congress, 1928.

Brown, Canter, Jr. *Florida's Peace River Frontier*. Orlando: Univesity of Central Florida, 1991.

———. *Fort Meade 1849–1900*. Tuscaloosa: University of Alabama Press, 1995.

Buker, George E. *Sun, Sand and Water: A History of the Jacksonville District, U.S. Army Corps of Engineers, 1821–1975*. Jacksonville, Fla.: Jacksonville District U.S. Army Corps of Engineers, 1981.

Burnett, Gene M. *Florida's Past: People and Events That Shaped the State*, volumes 1 and 2. Sarasota, Fla.: Pineapple Press, 1988.

Carpenter, Milton. *The Ruth Carpenter Story*. Unpublished.

Douglas, Marjory Stoneman. *The Everglades River of Grass*. Sarasota, Fla.: Pineapple Press, 1988.

Dovel, Junius Elmore. "A History of the Everglades of Florida." Ph.D. dissertation. Chapel Hill: University of North Carolina, 1947.

Florida History Antiques Index Web page. www.apex_ephemera.com/Florida/History.

Herring, Bennie, II. '28 Storm. West Palm Beach, Fla.: Palm Beach Post, 2002.

History of Jupiter Web page. www.history.jupiter.fl.us.

Hurricane Center Miami Web page. www.aoml.noaa.gov.hrd.

Larson, Erik. Isaac's Storm. New York: Crown, 1999.

McGoun, William E. Southeast Florida Pioneers: The Palm and Treasure Coasts. Sarasota, Fla.: Pineapple Press, 1998.

McIver, Stuart B. Dreamers, Schemers and Scalawags: The Florida Chronicles. Volume 1. Sarasota, Fla.: Pineapple Press, 1994.

Monthly Weather Review, Weather Bureau, Washington, 1928.

Morris, Don. The 1928 Hurricane in Florida. Photographic pamphlet, 1928.

Palm Beach Post. Articles from September 8 through September 23, 1928. West Palm Beach, Fla. 1928

Reardon, Leo Francis. The Florida Hurricane and Disaster. Miami: Miami Publishing, 1926.

Smith, Joseph Burkholder. The Plot to Steal Florida. New York: Arbor House, 1983.

Suplee, Curt. "El Niño/La Niña." National Geographic (March 1999): 72–95.

Tannehill, Ivan Ray. Hurricanes: Their Nature and History. Princeton, N.J.: Princeton University Press, 1959.

Tuckwood, Jan, and Eliot Kleinberg. Pioneers in Paradise: West Palm Beach, the First 100 Years. Palm Beach: Palm Beach Post, 1994.

UNISYS Web Page. weather.unisys.com/hurricane/atlantic.

Will, Lawrence E. A Cracker History of Okeechobee. Belle Glade, Fla.: Glades Historical Society, 1977.

———. Okeechobee Catfishing. Belle Glade, Fla.: Glades Historical Society, 1990.

———. Okeechobee Hurricane Killer Storms in the Everglades. Belle Glade, Fla.: Glades Historical Society, 1990.

———. Swamp to Sugar Bowl. Belle Glade, Fla.: Glades Historical Society, 1984.

INTERVIEWS

By Robert Mykle

Vernie Boots
Nancy Boots
Lillian Padgett
Thelma Martin
Ernestine Martin
Robert Martin
Juanita Wilson
Harvey Poole
Mark Challancin
Elizabeth Aunapu

Albert Aunapu
Clarence Pate
Willie Emma Wells
Ann Taylor
William Rawls
Marvin Urwin
Preston Tillman
Robert Hazard
Vernon Dexter
Ardie Peterson

By Ruth Irwin

Charles "Mutt" Thomas
Vernie Boots
Nancy Martin
Sonny Martin
Floyd Oliver Wilder

By Debbie Wells

Annie Mae Martin

INDEX

OTHER COOPER SQUARE PRESS
TITLES OF INTEREST

AFRICA EXPLORED
Europeans on the Dark Continent,
1769–1889
Christopher Hibbert
344 pp., 54 b/w illustrations, 16 maps
0-8154-1193-6
$18.95

AFRICAN GAME TRAILS
An Account of the African Wanderings of
an American Hunter-Naturalist
Theodore Roosevelt
New introduction by H. W. Brands
600 pp., 210 b/w illustrations
0-8154-1132-4
$22.95

ANTARCTICA
Firsthand Accounts of Exploration and
Endurance
Edited by Charles Neider
468 pp.
0-8154-1023-9
$18.95

ARCTIC EXPERIENCES
Aboard the Doomed Polaris *Expedition*
and Six Months Adrift on an Ice-Floe
Captain George E. Tyson
New introduction by Edward E. Leslie
504 pp., 78 b/w illustrations
0-8154-1189-8
$19.95 cloth

CARRYING THE FIRE
An Astronaut's Journeys
Michael Collins
Foreword by Charles Lindbergh
512 pp., 32 pp. of b/w photos
0-8154-1028-6
$19.95

THE DESERT AND THE SOWN
The Syrian Adventures of the Female
Lawrence of Arabia
Gertrude Bell
New introduction by Rosemary O'Brien
368 pp., 162 b/w photos
0-8154-1135-9
$19.95

EDGE OF THE JUNGLE
William Beebe
New introduction by Robert Finch
320 pp., 1 b/w photo
0-8154-1160-X
$17.95

EDGE OF THE WORLD:
ROSS ISLAND, ANTARCTICA
A Personal and Historical Narrative of
Exploration, Adventure, Tragedy, and
Survival
Charles Neider
New introduction
536 pp., 45 b/w photos, 15 maps
0-8154-1154-5
$19.95

THE FABULOUS INSECTS
Essays by the Foremost Nature Writers
Edited by Charles Neider
288 pp.
0-8154-1100-6
$17.95

GREAT SHIPWRECKS AND CASTAWAYS
Firsthand Accounts of Disasters at Sea
Edited by Charles Neider
256 pp.
0-8154-1094-8
$16.95

THE GREAT WHITE SOUTH
Traveling with Robert F. Scott's Doomed South Pole Expedition
Herbert G. Ponting
New introduction by Roland Huntford
440 pp., 175 b/w illustrations, 3 b/w maps & diagrams
0-8154-1161-8
$18.95

IN SEARCH OF ROBINSON CRUSOE
Daisuke Takahashi
256 pp., 23 b/w photos
0-8154-1200-2
$25.95 cloth

THE *KARLUK'S* LAST VOYAGE
An Epic of Death and Survival in the Arctic, 1913–1916
Captain Robert A. Bartlett
New introduction by Edward E. Leslie
378 pp., 23 b/w photos, 3 maps
0-8154-1124-3
$18.95

THE LIFE AND AFRICAN EXPLORATIONS OF LIVINGSTONE
Dr. David Livingstone
656 pp., 52 b/w line drawings and maps
0-8154-1208-8
$22.95

MAN AGAINST NATURE
Firsthand Accounts of Adventure and Exploration
Edited by Charles Neider
512 pp.
0-8154-1040-9
$18.95

MY ARCTIC JOURNAL
A Year among Ice-Fields and Eskimos
Josephine Peary
Foreword by Robert E. Peary
New introduction by Robert M. Bryce
280 pp., 67 b/w illustrations, maps, & diagrams
0-8154-1198-7
$18.95

MY ATTAINMENT OF THE POLE
Frederick A. Cook
New introduction by Robert M. Bryce
680 pp., 45 b/w illustrations
0-8154-1137-5
$22.95

A NEGRO EXPLORER AT THE NORTH POLE
Matthew A. Henson
Preface by Booker T. Washington
Foreword by Robert E. Peary, Rear Admiral, U.S.N.
New introduction by Robert M. Bryce
232 pp., 6 b/w photos
0-8154-1125-1
$15.95